Anonymous

The Iron Age Manufacturers Index

Relating to the Hardware, Iron, Steel, Machinery and Metal Trades

Anonymous

The Iron Age Manufacturers Index
Relating to the Hardware, Iron, Steel, Machinery and Metal Trades

ISBN/EAN: 9783337182021

Printed in Europe, USA, Canada, Australia, Japan

Cover: Foto ©ninafisch / pixelio.de

More available books at **www.hansebooks.com**

.... Supplement to THE IRON AGE, July 1, 1897

The Iron Age Manufacturers Index....

RELATING TO THE

Hardware,
Iron, Steel,
Machinery
and Metal Trades

Revised to June 10, 1897

FOR the convenience of the trade the following Index has been compiled giving the names of manufacturers and their products in the Hardware, Iron, Metal and Machinery Trades. It has been prepared in response to the demand for a reliable Index of the lines of business to which it relates, and it is hoped that it will be of service to buyers both in this country and abroad, covering as it does a wide range and representing in detail a great variety of products.

The addresses of the manufacturers and further information in regard to their goods may be obtained in the advertising columns of THE IRON AGE.

THE IRON AGE INDEX

For the Addresses of Manufacturers reference may be made to the advertising columns of
THE IRON AGE.

Accumulators, *Hydraulic*—
Lloyd Booth Co.
Waterbury Farrel Foundry & Mch. Co.
Watson-Stillman Co.

Accumulators, *Steam*—
Watson-Stillman Co.
Henry R. Worthington.

Acid, *Sulphuric*—
Matthiessen & Hegeler Zinc Co.

Adjusters, *Blind*—
Millers Falls Co.
Russell & Erwin Mfg. Co.
VanWagoner & Williams Hardware Co.

Adjusters, *Casement*—
Reading Hardware Co.

Adjusters, *Hammock Rope and Hitching Strap*—
Covert's Saddlery Works.

Adjusters, *Shaft and Pole*—
Covert's Saddlery Works.

Adjusters, *Window Stop*—
Taplin Mfg. Co.

Adzes—
L. & I. J. White.

Adzes, *Ice*—See *Ice Harvesting Tools.*

Aerators and Coolers, Milk—See *Coolers, Milk, and Aerators.*

Agents, *Hardware Manufacturers'*—
C. M. Avery.
Hermann Boker & Co.
John Chatillon & Sons.
John H. Graham & Co.
Dodge, Haley & Co.
Hartley & Graham.
U. T. Hungerford.
W. H. Jacobus.
Schroetter Bros.
Tower & Lyon.

Agricultural Bolts, Shapes—See *Bolts, Shapes, Agricultural.*

Air Compressors, Hoists—See *Compressors, Hoists, Pneumatic.*

Air Lift Pumps—See *Pumps, Air Lift.*

Air Receivers, Tanks—See *Receivers, Tanks.*

Alarms, *Electric*—
W. R. Ostrander & Co.

Alarm Gauges—See *Gauges, Alarm.*

Aluminum—
American Metal Co.
Pittsburgh Reduction Co.
Scovill Mfg. Co.

Aluminum Bars, Castings, Cups, Sheets, Tubing, Ware, Wire—See *Bars, Castings, Cups, Sheets, Tubing, Ware, Wire.*

Ammonia Valves—See *Valves, Ammonia.*

Ampere Recording Meter—See *Meter, Ampere Recording.*

Analytical Chemists—See *Chemists, Analytical.*

Anchor Bolts—See *Bolts, Anchor.*

Anchors, *Building*—
Pleuger & Henger Mfg. Co.

Anchors, *Ship, Boat, &c.*—
W. & J. Tiebout.

Andirons—
Bradley & Hubbard Mfg. Co.
Peck, Stow & Wilcox Co.
Pleuger & Henger Mfg. Co.
R. W. Whitehurst & Co.

Anemometers—
B. F. Sturtevant Co.

Angles and Tees—
Ætna-Standard Iron & Steel Co.
Lockhart Iron & Steel Co.
Ogden & Wallace.
Passaic Rolling Mill Co.
Phœnix Iron Co.
Pierson & Co.

Angle Boring Bit Stock—See *Bit Stock, Angle Boring.*

Angle Knives—See *Knives, Angle.*

Animal Cages, Pokes, Tethers—See *Cages, Pokes, Tethers.*

Annealing—
I. S. Spencer's Sons.

Annealing Furnaces—See *Furnaces, Annealing.*

Annunciators—
W. R. Ostrander & Co.

Anti-Friction Metal—
Wm. Cramp & Sons Ship & Engine Building Co.
Theo. Hiertz & Son.

Anti-Rattlers—
New York Belting & Packing Co.

Antimony—
American Metal Co.
John Davol & Sons.
Wm. S. Fearing.
Hendricks Bros.

Anvils—
Eagle Anvil Works.
Lewis Tool Co.
Millers Falls Co.
Van Wagoner & Williams Hardware Co.

Anvil and Vise—
Eagle Anvil Works.
Fulton Iron & Engine Works.

Anvil, Drill and Vise—See *Vise, Drill and Anvil.*

Apple Corers and Parers—See *Parers, Apple.*

Arbors, Saw—
Simonds Mfg. Co.

Arches, Curved Corrugated—
Youngstown Iron & Steel Roofing Co.

Arc Lamps—See *Lamps, Arc.*

Armature Disc Notching Machines
—See *Notching Machines, Armature Disc.*

Armature Discs—See *Discs, Armature.*

Armor—
Bethlehem Iron Co.

Army and Navy Scales—See *Scales, Army and Navy.*

Arresters, Spark—
Fred. J. Meyers Mfg. Co.

Art Auger Bits—See *Bits, Art Auger.*

Art Goods, Metal—
Bradley & Hubbard Mfg. Co.

Artesian Well Pumps—See *Pumps, Artesian Well.*

Artesian Well Supplies and Tools
—See *Well Supplies and Tools.*

Artesian and Water Works Strainers — See *Strainers, Artesian and Water Works.*

Asbestos Plaster, Roofing, Sheathing—See *Plaster, Roofing, Sheathing.*

Ash Cans, Sieves, Sifters—See *Cans, Sieves, Sifters.*

Ash Traps, Grate—See *Grate Ash Traps.*

Assembling Machines, Bicycle Wheel—
Pratt & Whitney Co.

Attachments, Pipe Wrench — See *Wrench Attachments, Pipe.*

Attachments, Square—See *Square Attachments.*

Attorneys—See *Patent Attorneys.*

Auctioneers—
E. Bissell, Son & Co.

Augers and Bits—
Bridgeport Gun Implement Co.
Connecticut Valley Mfg Co.
Ford Bit Company.
Peck, Stow & Wilcox Co.
Snell Mfg. Co.

Auger Bits—See *Augers and Bits.*

Auger Handles—See *Handles, Auger.*

Augers, Ice—See *Ice Harvesting Tools.*

Augers, Dried Fruit and Sugar—
Enterprise Mfg. Co.

Augers, Expansion Fore—
E. C. Stearns & Co,

Augers, Hollow—
Millers Falls Co.
Silver Mfg. Co.
E. C. Stearns & Co.

Augers, Taper—
E. C. Stearns & Co.

Automatic Drills—See *Drills, Automatic.*

Awl Handles—See *Handles, Chisel, File, Awl, &c.*

Awls, Peg, Brad, &c.—
New England Specialty Co.
Stanley Rule & Level Co.

Awls, Scratch, Belt, &c.—
Bemis & Call Hardware & Tool Co.
Billings & Spencer Co.
Buck Bros.
C. E. Coe.
Knapp & Cowles Mfg. Co.
H. H. Mayhew Co.
Millers Falls Co.
Peck, Stow & Wilcox Co.
Tuck Mfg. Co.

Awnings, Iron—
American Steel Roofing Co.
Garry Iron Roofing Co.
Kansas Metal Roofing & Corrugating Co.
Stewart Iron Works.

Awning Hooks, Pulleys—See *Hooks, Pulleys.*

Axes, Chopping—
Mann Edge Tool Co.
L. & I. J. White Co.

Axes, Ice—
Peck, Stow & Wilcox Co.
L. & I. J. White Co.

Axe Brackets, Racks, Stones—See *Brackets, Racks, Stones, Axe.*

Axles, Car—
Cambria Iron Co.
Central Iron & Steel Co.
Frankfort Steel Co.
La Belle Steel Co.
Pierson & Co.
A. & P. Roberts Co.

Axles, Wagon and Carriage—
Singer, Nimick & Co.
F. W. Wurster & Co.

Axles and Wheels—
Thomas Carlin's Sons.
Lansing Wheelbarrow Co.

Axle Clips, Cutters, Grease—See *Clips, Cutters, Grease.*

Axle Iron—See *Iron, Axle.*

Axle Lathes—See *Lathes, Axle.*

Axle Washers—See *Washers, Axle.*

Babbitt Metal—
Bridgeport Deoxidized Bronze & Metal Co.
Theo. Hiertz & Son.
Paul S. Reeves.

Back Saws—See *Saws, Hand, Panel, Back, &c.*

Badges, Hat—
R. Woodman Mfg. & Supply Co.

Bags, Game—
Waterbury Brass Co.

Bag Fillers—See *Fillers, Bag.*

Baggage Checks—See *Checks, Baggage, Key, &c.*

Baking Pans—See *Pans, Baking and Roasting.*

Balances, Sash—
Caldwell Sash Balance Co.
Pullman Sash Balance Co.
E. C. Stearns & Co.

Balances, Spring—
Bridgeport Brass Co.
John Chatillon & Sons.
Peck, Stow & Wilcox Co.
Pelouze Scale & Mfg. Co.

Bale Ties—See *Ties, Bale.*

Baling Wire—See *Wire, Baling.*

Ballots, Society—
H. O. Canfield.

Ball Bearings—See *Bearings, Ball.*

Ball Floats, Copper—See *Floats, Copper Ball.*

Ball Joints—See *Joints, Ball.*

Balling Irons—See *Irons, Balling.*

Balls, Fuller Rubber—
H. O. Canfield.

Balls, Ox—
Peck, Stow & Wilcox Co.
Reading Hardware Co.
Russell & Erwin Mfg. Co.

Balls, Steel—
Ball Bearing Co.
Boston Gear Works.

Balls, Ten Pin—
Boston & Lockport Block Co.
John Sommer's Son.

Balls, Ten Pin—See *Ten Pins and Balls.*

Band Saws—See *Saws, Band.*

Bands, Gaff—
W. & J. Tiebout.

Bands, Hose—See *Hose Attachments.*

Bankers—
Brown Bros. & Co.

Banquet Lamps—See *Lamps, Table, Banquet, &c.*

Barb Wire—*Wire, Barb.*

Barb Wire Carriers—See *Carriers, Barb Wire.*

Barn Door Bolts—See *Bolts, Barn Door.*

Barrel Carts, Covers, Drainers—See *Carts, Covers, Drainers.*

Barrel Heaters, Swings, Trucks—See *Heaters, Swings, Trucks.*

Barrels, Tumbling—
Brown & Sharpe Mfg. Co.
Henderson Bros.
Waterbury Machine Co.
Whiting Foundry Equipment Co.

Barrows, Toy—See *Toy Barrows.*

Barrows, Wheel—
American Steel Scraper Co.
Boston & Lockport Block Co.
Buffalo Scale Co.
Dain Mfg. Co.
Iowa Farming Tool Co.
Kilbourne & Jacobs Mfg. Co.
Lansing Wheelbarrow Co.
Sidney Steel Scraper Co.
G. L. Stuebner.
Syracuse Chilled Plow Co.

Barrow Wheels—See *Wheels, Barrow.*

Bars, Aluminum—
Pittsburgh Reduction Co.

Bars, Bicycle Chain, Copper—See *Bicycle Chain, Copper.*

Bars, Commutator—
Forest City Electric Co.

Bars, Eye—
Passaic Rolling Mill Co.
Phœnix Iron Co.
A. & P. Roberts Co.

Bars, Ice—
L. & I. J. White Co.
Wm. T. Wood & Co.

THE IRON AGE INDEX.

Bars, Iron—
Ætna-Standard Iron & Steel Co.
Allentown Rolling Mills.
Alphonse Bouchet.
Burden Iron Co.
Central Iron & Steel Co.
Crescent Steel Works.
Dover Iron Co.
Milton Mfg. Co.
Old Dominion Iron & Nail Works Co.
Pennsylvania Bolt & Nut Co.
Phœnix Iron Co.
Pierson & Co.
Pottstown Iron & Steel Co.
Railway Supply Co.
Joseph T. Ryerson & Son.
J. H. Sternbergh & Co.
W. H. Thompson & Co.
A. R. Whitney & Co.
F. W. Wurster & Co.

Bars, Locomotive Cylinder Boring —See *Boring Bars, Locomotive Cylinder.*

Bars, Muck—
Bethlehem Iron Co.
Jerome Keeley & Co.
J. Tatnall Lea & Co.
J. J. Mohr.
Nicolls, Wheeler & Co.
Pottstown Iron Co.
Frank Samuel.
E. H. Wilson & Co.

Bars, Shutter—
Brass Goods Mfg Co.
Hobart B. Ives & Co.
Norwalk Lock Co.
Peck, Stow & Wilcox Co.
Reading Hardware Co.
Russell & Erwin Mfg. Co.
Stanley Works.

Bars, Steel—
Alphonse Bouchet.
Cambria Iron Co.
Justice Cox, Jr.
Denman & Davis.
J. W. Hoffman & Co.
Junction Iron & Steel Co.
Ogden & Wallace.

Phœnix Iron Co.
Pottsville Iron & Steel Co.
A. & P. Roberts Co.
J. T. Ryerson & Son.
W. H. Thompson & Co.
Tudor Iron Works.
W. H. Wallace & Co.
A. R. Whitney & Co.

Bars, Tin Plate—
Junction Iron & Steel Co.

Bases, Garment Stand—
Stowell Mfg. & Foundry Co.

Base Knobs—See *Knobs, Base, Floor.*

Basin Plugs—See *Plumbing Supplies.*

Basket Handles, Wire—See *Handles, Basket, Wire.*

Basket Trucks—See *Trucks, Basket.*

Baskets, Card—
Fred. J. Meyers Mfg. Co.

Baskets, Fish—
E. T. Barnum.
Fred. J. Meyers Mfg. Co.

Baskets, Hanging—
Fred. J. Meyers Mfg. Co.

Baskets, Sponge, &c.—
Columbus Wire & Iron Works.
Gilbert & Bennett Mfg. Co.
Fred J. Meyers Mfg. Co.

Baskets, Sponge, Wire—See *Household Articles, Wire.*

Baskets, Waste—
Columbus Wire & Iron Works.
Estey Wire Works Co.

Bathtubs—
Humphryes Mfg. Co.

Batteries—
W. R. Ostrander & Co.

Battery Plates, Rolled Zinc—
Matthiesen & Hegeler Zinc Co.

Battery Zincs—See *Zincs for Leclanche Batteries.*

THE IRON AGE INDEX.

Beam Hooks—See *Hooks, Beam.*

Beams and Channels—
Allentown Rolling Mills.
Cambria Iron Co.
Passaic Rolling Mill Co.
Phœnix Iron Co.
Pierson & Co.
Pottsville Iron & Steel Co.
A. & P. Roberts Co.
Wm. H. Wallace & Co.
A R. Whitney & Co.

Beams, Scale—See *Scale Beams.*

Bearings, Ball—
Ball Bearing Co.

Bearings, Lead Lined Car—
Paul S. Reeves.

Bearings, Oilless Shaft—
North American Metaline Co.

Bearings, Roller—
Ball Bearing Co,
Mossberg & Granville Mfg. Co.

Beaters, Egg—
Edward Darby & Sons.
Fred. J. Meyers Mfg. Co.
Turner & Seymour Mfg. Co.
Wire Goods Co.

Bed Casters, Fasteners, Keys, Links, Screws—See *Casters, Fasteners, Keys, Links, Screws.*

Bedstead Fasteners—See *Fasteners, Bedstead.*

Bedstead Fastener Setting Machines—See *Machines to Set Bedstead Fasteners.*

Bedsteads, Brass and Iron—
Ansonia Brass & Copper Co.
E T. Barnum.
Edward Darby & Sons.
Fred. J. Meyers Mfg. Co.

Beef Shavers—See *Shavers, Beef.*

Belaying Pins—See *Pins, Belaying.*

Bellows, Blacksmiths', Molders', &c.—
Osborn Mfg. Co.
Geo. M. Scott.

Bell Cord Couplings—See *Couplings, Bell Cord.*

Bell Cranks—See *Cranks, Bell.*

Bell Hangers' Bits—See *Bits, Bell Hangers'.*

Bell Levers, Pulls—See *Levers, Pulls.*

Bells, Bicycle—
Bevin Bros. Mfg. Co.
Bridgeport Brass Co.
Bridgeport Gun Implement Co.
Chapman Mfg. Co.
N. N. Hill Brass Co.
Edward Miller & Co.
Scovill Mfg. Co.

Bells, Car—
Bevin Bros. Mfg. Co.

Bells, Cow and Sheep—
Bevin Bros. Mfg. Co.

Bells, Door—
Arcade Mfg. Co.
Norwalk Lock Co.
Peck, Stow & Wilcox Co.
Reading Hardware Co.
Russell & Erwin Mfg. Co.

Bells, Dumb—
Logan & Strobridge Iron Co.
Pleuger & Henger Mfg. Co.
Reading Hardware Co.
John Sommer's Son.
A. C. Williams.

Bells, Electric—
W. R. Ostrander & Co.

Bells, Engine—
Bevin Bros. Mfg. Co.

Bells, Gong—
Bevin Bros. Mfg. Co.
Geo. Johnson.
Peck, Stow & Wilcox Co.
Pleuger & Henger Mfg. Co
Reading Hardware Co.
Russell & Erwin Mfg. Co.

Bells, Hand—
Bevin Bros. Mfg. Co.
N. N. Hill Brass Co.

Bells, House (on Carriage)—
Bevin Bros. Mfg. Co.
W. R. Ostrander & Co.
Peck, Stow & Wilcox Co.
Reading Hardware Co.
Russell & Erwin Mfg. Co.

Bells, Lever—
W. R. Ostrander & Co.

Bells, Pneumatic Call—
W. R. Ostrander & Co.

Bells, Sleigh—
Bevin Bros. Mfg. Co.
Chapman Mfg. Co.
N. N. Hill Brass Co.

Bells, Tea and Call—
Bevin Bros. Mfg. Co.
Bradley & Hubbard Mfg. Co.
Chapman Mfg. Co.
Peck, Stow & Wilcox Co.
Russell & Erwin Mfg. Co.

Bells, Telephone and Clock—
Bridgeport Brass Co.
N. N. Hill Brass Co.
Plume & Atwood Mfg. Co.

Bells, Toy—See *Toy Bells.*

Belt Awls, Buckles, Clamps, Couplings, Elevators, Fasteners, Hooks, Supports—See *Awls, Buckles, Clamps, Couplings, Elevators, Fasteners, Hooks, Supports.*

Belt Dressing—
Alexander Bros.
Jos. Dixon Crucible Co.

Belt Lacing, Leather—
Boston Belting Co.

Belt Lacing, Rawhide—
Shultz Belting Co.

Belt Lacing, Steel—See *Hooks, Belt.*

Belt Shifters—
Builders' Iron Foundry.

Belt Tighteners—
Geo. V. Cresson Co.
Dodge Mfg. Co.
Hoggson & Pettis Mfg. Co.

Belting Bement—See *Cement, Belting.*

Belting, Chain—
Jeffrey Mfg. Co.
Roberts Mfg. Co.
Stanley Works.

Belting, Leather—
Alexander Bros.
Boston Belting Co.

Belting, Link—
Link-Belt Engineering Co.

Belting, Rawhide—
Shultz Belting Co.

Belting, Rubber—
Boston Belting Co.
N. Y. Belting & Packing Co.

Belting, Woven Duck—
Main Belting Co.

Belts, Bicycle, Tennis, &c.—
Chapman Mfg. Co.

Belts, Polishing—See *Buffing and Polishing Machines.*

Benches, Draw—
Gould & Eberhardt.
Morgan Construction Co.
Mossberg & Granville Mfg. Co.
Waterbury Farrel Foundry & Machine Co.

Benches, Wash—
Hill Dryer Co.

Benches, Wire Draw—
Trenton Iron Co.
Turner, Vaughn & Taylor Co.
Waterbury Machine Co.

Bench Hooks, Drill Lathes, Scrapers, Screws—See *Hooks, Drills Lathes, Scrapers, Screws.*

Bender, Bicycle Spoke—See *Spoke Header and Bender, Bicycle.*

Benders, Rail—
Jos. F. McCoy Co.

Benders, Tire—
Butts & Ordway.
Champion Blower & Forge Co.
Fulton Iron & Engine Works.
Plenger & Henger Mfg. Co.
Wiley & Russell Mfg. Co.

Bending Machines—See *Forming and Bending Machines.*

Bending Rolls—See *Rolls, Bending.*

Bent Rifflers—See *Rifflers, Bent.*

Berry Washers—See *Kitchen Articles, Wire.*

Bessemer Converters—See *Converters, Bessemer.*

Bevels—
Athol Machine Co.
Henry Disston & Sons.
Stanley Rule & Level Co.
L. S Starrett Co.
J. Stevens Arms & Tool Co.

Beveling Shears—See *Shears, Beveling.*

Bicycle Bells, Belts, Lamps, Locks, Luggage Carriers, Oilers, Pumps, Scales, Stands, Vises, Wrenches—See *Bells, Belts, Lamps, Locks, Carriers, Oilers, Pumps, Scales, Stands, Vises, Wrenches.*

Bicycle Brakes, Chain, Forgings, Grips, Guards, Hubs, Nipples, Saddles, Spokes, Tires, Tubing—See *Brakes, Chain, Forgings, Grips, Guards, Hubs, Nipples, Saddles, Spokes, Tires, Tubing.*

Bicycle Chain Machinery, Drills, Hub Machines, Nippers, Rim Drilling Machines—See *Chain Machinery, Drills, Hub Machines, Nippers, Rim Drilling Machines.*

Bicycle Chain Bars—
Finished Steel Co.

Bicycle Lamps, Electric—See *Electric Lamps, Bicycle.*

Bicycle Lock and Coasters, Combined—
Weedsport Drill Co.

Bicycle Machinery—
E. W. Bliss Co.
Davis & Egan Machine Co.
Garvin Machine Co.
Pratt & Whitney Co.
Prentiss Tool & Supply Co.

Bicycle Parts—
Belden Machine Co.
Billings & Spencer Co.
Bridgeport Gun Implement Co.
Hartford Machine Screw Co.
Indian Orchard Screw Co.
New Britain Hdw. Mfg. Co.

Bicycle Spoke Wire—See *Wire, Bicycle Spoke.*

Bicycle Spoke Header—See *Spoke Header and Bender, Bicycle.*

Bicycle Spoke Threaders — See *Threaders, Bicycle Spoke.*

Bicycle Wheel Assembling Machines—See *Assembling Machines, Bicycle Wheel.*

Bicycles—
Ames Mfg. Co.
Canton Cycle Mfg. Co.
Cash Buyers' Union.
Crawford Mfg. Co.
Hampshire Cycle Mfg. Co.
Iver Johnson's Arms & Cycle Works.
John P. Lovell Arms & Tool Co.
Fred. J. Meyers Mfg. Co.
Monarch Cycle Mfg. Co.
Geo. N. Pierce Co.
Pope Mfg. Co.
Reading Standard Mfg. Co.
Remington Arms Co.
Speirs Mfg. Co.
E. C. Stearns & Co.
R. H. Wolff & Co.

Billets, *Open Hearth—*
  Bethlehem Iron Co.
  Cambria Iron Co.
  Passaic Rolling Mill Co.
  Phœnix Iron Co.
  Pottsville Iron & Steel Co.
  A. & P. Roberts Co.

Billets, *Steel—*
  Bethlehem Iron Co.
  Justice Cox, Jr.
  Junction Iron & Steel Co.
  Jerome Keeley & Co.
  J. Tatnall Lea & Co.
  A. Milne & Co.
  Pilling & Crane.
  Pottstown Iron Co.
  Riverside Iron Works.
  Frank Samuel.
  E. H. Wilson & Co.

Billiard Table Bolts and Cushions
  —See *Bolts and Cushions.*

Binding Chain and Posts—See *Chain and Posts.*

Binder, *Log—*
  Stowell Mfg. & Foundry Co.

Bird Cage Hooks and Springs—See *Hooks, Springs.*

Bird Cages—See *Cages, Bird and Animal.*

Bit Braces, Gauges, Gimlets, Stock Drills—See *Braces, Gauges, Gimlets, Stock Drills.*

Bit and Square Levels—See *Levels, Bit and Square.*

Bit Stock, *Angle Boring—*
  John S. Fray & Co.
  Millers Falls Co.

Bits, *Art Auger—*
  A. L. Adams.

Bits, *Bell Hangers'—*
  H. H. Mayhew Co.
  Snell Mfg. Co.

Bits, *Bridle—*
  Imperial Bit & Snap Co.
  Pope's Island Mfg. Corporation.

Bits, *Caster—*
  E. C. Stearns & Co.

Bits, *Countersink—*
  Knapp & Cowles Mfg. Co.
  Snell Mfg. Co.

Bits, *Expansive—*
  R. H. Brown & Co.
  Connecticut Valley Mfg Co.
  Tower & Lyon.

Bits, *Pod—*
  H. H. Mayhew Co.
  Snell Mfg. Co.

Bits, *Screw Driver—*
  Connecticut Valley Mfg. Co.
  Goodell Bros. Co.
  Knapp & Cowles Mfg. Co.
  H. H. Mayhew Co.
  Snell Mfg. Co.
  Standard Tool Co.
  Tuck Mfg. Co.

Blacking, *Shoe—*
  Palmer Hdw. Mfg. Co.

Black Plate for Tinning—See *Plate, Black, for Tinning.*

Blacksmiths' Bellows, Buffers, Buttresses, Creasers, Drills and Tongs—See *Bellows, Buffers, Buttresses, Creasers, Drills and Tongs.*

Blades, Hack, Scroll, Wood Saw—
  See *Saws, Hack, Scroll, Wood.*

Blades, *Metal Shear—*
  John Loyd.
  Pittsburgh Shear Knife & Machine Co.
  Samuel Trethewey & Co.
  L. & I. J. White Co.

Blades, *Saw, Blanks—*
  Pierson & Co.

Blanket Straps—See *Straps, Blanket.*

Blankets, *Printers' Rubber—*
  New York Belting & Packing Co.

***Blanking* and *Forming*, *Sheet Metal*—**
Harvey Hubbell.

***Blanks*, *Gear*—**
Frankfort Steel Co.

***Blanks*, *Key*, *Stove*—**See *Keys*, *Stoves*.

***Blanks*, *Snap Gauge*—**
Billings & Spencer Co.

***Blanks*, *Thumb Nut*—**
Billings & Spencer Co.
J. H. Williams & Co.

***Blanks*, *Thumb Screw*—**
J. H. Williams & Co.

***Blast Furnace Blocks*—**See *Blocks*, *Blast Furnace*.

***Blast Furnaces*—**See *Furnaces*, *Blast*.

***Blast Furnace Machinery*—**
Allentown Rolling Mills.
D. R. Lean Co.
Mackintosh, Hemphill & Co.
New Castle Engineering Works.
Philadelphia Engineering Co.
Pittsburgh Shear Knife & Machine Co.
W. B. Pollock & Co.

Blind Adjusters*, *Fasteners*, *Hinges
—See *Adjusters*, *Fasteners*, *Hinges*.

***Block Scrapers*, *Butchers'*—**See *Scrapers*, *Butchers' Block*.

***Blocks*, *Blast Furnace*—**
M. D. Valentine & Bro. Co.

***Blocks*, *Bucket*—**
Stowell Mfg. & Foundry Co.
G. L. Stuebner.

***Blocks*, *Deck and Snatch*—**
W. & J. Tiebout.

***Blocks*, *Differential Pulley*—**
Boston & Lockport Block Co.
Moore Mfg. Co.

***Blocks*, *Lead*—**
Stowell Mfg. & Foundry Co.

***Blocks*, *Leveling*—**
Wiley & Russell Mfg. Co.

***Blocks*, *Locomotive*—**
Ostrander Fire Brick Co.

***Blocks*, *Pillow*—**
Dodge Mfg. Co.

***Blocks*, *Scribing*—**
Hoggson & Pettis Mfg. Co.

***Blocks*, *Swage*—**
Pleuger & Henger Mfg. Co.
Wiley & Russell Mfg. Co.
Wells Bros. & Co.

***Blocks*, *Tackle*—**
Boston & Lockport Block Co.
Fulton Iron & Engine Works.
Lane Bros.
Jos. F. McCoy Co.
Rhode Island Tool Co.
Stowell Mfg. & Foundry Co.
W. & J. Tiebout.
Trenton Iron Co.
Union Hardware Co.

***Blocks*, *Top Prop*—**
New York Belting & Packing Co.

***Blooming Mills*—**
Mackintosh, Hemphill & Co.
William Tod & Co.
Totten & Hogg Iron & Steel Foundry Co.

***Blooms*, *Charcoal*—**
Nicolls, Wheeler & Co.

***Blowers*—**
American Blower Co.
Buffalo Forge Co.
Champion Blower & Forge Co.
Pennsylvania Machine Co.
B. F. Sturtevant Co.

***Blower Stands*—**See *Stands*, *Blower*.

***Blowing Engines*—**See *Engines*, *Blowing*.

***Boards*, *Ironing*, *Bread*, &c.—**
Hill Dryer Co.

***Boat Anchors*, *Hooks*—**See *Anchors*, *Hooks*.

THE IRON AGE INDEX.

Boats, Steam—See *Steam Boats.*

Bobs, Plumb—
Henry Disston & Sons.
Logan & Strobridge Iron Co.
Peck, Stow & Wilcox Co.
Reading Hardware Co.
Russell & Erwin Mfg. Co.
Stanley Rule & Level Co.
Tower & Lyon.
T. F. Welch Mfg. Co.

Bobbin Winding Machines—
Fairmount Machine Co.

Boiler Heads, Furnaces, Injectors, Inspection, Drills, Tubes—See *Heads, Furnaces, Injectors, Inspection, Drills, Tubes.*

Boiler Brace Iron—See *Iron, Boiler Brace.*

Boiler Braces—
Lukens Iron & Steel Co.
J. T. Ryerson & Son.

Boiler Feed Pumps — See *Pumps, Boiler Feed.*

Boiler Makers' Tools—
Hilles & Jones Co.
Prentice Bros.
Wm. Sellers & Co.
J. T. Ryerson & Son.

Boiler Stay Bolts—See *Bolts, Boiler Stay.*

Boiler Tube Cutters—See *Cutters, Boiler Tube.*

Boilers, Copper House—
Randolph & Clowes—

Boilers, Steam—
Edward P. Allis Co.
Babcock & Wilcox Co.
Brown Hoisting & Conveying Mach. Co.
Cahall Sales Department.
Thos. Carlin's Sons.
Harrison Safety Boiler Works.
Lane & Bodley Co.
Jas. Leffel & Co.
Lidgerwood Mfg. Co.

C. O. Lucas & Co.
Merrill-Stevens Engineering Co.
New Castle Engineering Works.
F. R. Patch Mfg. Co.
Pennsylvania Machine Co.
W. B. Pollock & Co.
Silver Mfg. Co.
Robert Wetherill & Co.

Bolster Plates—See *Plates, Bolster.*

Bolt and Nut Machinery—
Acme Machinery Co.
Detrick & Harvey Machine Co.
National Machinery Co.
Wiley & Russell Mfg. Co.

Bolt Clippers, Copper, Cutters, Headers, Holders, Pointers, Threaders, Wrenches—See *Clippers, Copper, Cutters, Headers, Holders, Pointers, Threaders, Wrenches.*

Bolt Head Milling Machines—See *Nut and Bolt Head Milling Machines.*

Bolt Head Trimmers—See *Trimmers, Bolt Head.*

Bolts, Agricultural—
W. H. Haskell Co.
Russell & Erwin Mfg. Co.

Bolts, Anchor—
American Bolt Co.

Bolts, Barn Door—
Enterprise Mfg. Co.

Bolts, Billiard Table—
Shelton Co.

Bolts, Boiler Patch—
Worcester Machine Screw Co.

Bolts, Boiler Stay—
J. H. Sternbergh & Son.

Bolts, Brass and Bronze—
J. H. Sternbergh & Son.
W. & J. Tiebout.

Bolts, Bridge and Roof—
American Bolt Co.
Pennsylvania Bolt & Nut Co.
Port Chester Bolt & Nut Co.
J. H. Sternbergh & Son.

***Bolts**, Carriage—*
Milton Mfg. Co.
Peck, Stow & Wilcox Co.
Pennsylvania Bolt & Nut Co.
Shelton Co.
J. H. Sternbergh & Son.

***Bolts**, Cupboard—*
Peck, Stow & Wilcox Co.

***Bolts**, Door—*
Arcade Mfg. Co.
Hobart B. Ives & Co.
Logan & Strobridge Iron Co.
Ney Mfg. Co.
Norwalk Lock Co.
Payson Mfg. Co.
Peck, Stow & Wilcox Co.
Reading Hardware Co.
Russell & Erwin Mfg. Co.
Stanley Works.
Taylor & Boggis Foundry Co.
Van Wagoner & Williams Hardware Co.
A. C. Williams.

***Bolts**, Elevator—*
Avery Stamping Co.
Wm. H. Haskell Co.
Pennsylvania Bolt & Nut Co.
J. H. Sternbergh & Son.

***Bolts**, Expansion—*
W. C. Boone Mfg. Co.
Isaac Church.
Steward & Romaine Mfg. Co.

***Bolts**, Eye—*
Billings & Spencer Co.
Bradlee & Co.
Rhode Island Tool Co.
J. H. Sternbergh & Son.
W. & J. Tiebout.
J. H. Williams & Co.
Wire Goods Co.

***Bolts**, Forged—*
Hartford Machine Screw Co.

***Bolts**, Galvanized—*
W. & J. Tiebout.

***Bolts**, King—*
E. D. Clapp Mfg. Co.

***Bolts**, Loom—*
American Bolt Co.

***Bolts**, Machine—*
American Bolt Co.
Wm. H. Haskell Co.
Milton Mfg. Co.
Pennsylvania Bolt & Nut Co.
Rhode Island Tool Co.
Shelton Co.
J. H. Sternbergh & Son.
Worcester Machine Screw Co.

***Bolts**, Patch—*
Hartford Machine Screw Co.
New Britain Hardware Mfg. Co.
Pennsylvania Bolt & Nut Co.
Port Chester Bolt & Nut Co.
J. H. Sternbergh & Son.

***Bolts**, Planer Head—*
Hartford Machine Screw Co.
New Britain Hardware Mfg. Co.
Worcester Machine Screw Co.

***Bolts**, Plow—*
Wm. H. Haskell Co.
Pennsylvania Bolt & Nut Co.
Shelton Co.
J. H. Sternbergh & Son.

***Bolts**, Ring—*
W. & J. Tiebout.

***Bolts**, Screen—*
J. H. Sternbergh & Son.

***Bolts**, Shackle—*
Port Chester Bolt & Nut Co.

***Bolts**, Shutter—*
Stanley Works.

***Bolts**, Sink—*
American Screw Co.
Port Chester Bolt & Nut Co
Russell & Erwin Mfg. Co.
Shelton Co.

***Bolts**, Sleigh Shoe—*
American Screw Co.
Shelton Co.

***Bolts**, Socket—*
Dover Iron Co.

Bolts, *Special (Coupling, Screen, Deck-hanger, Joint, Button Head, Bung Head, Boiler, Headless, Slotted Head, Hook Head, Cube Head, &c.)—*
American Bolt Co.
Cincinnati Screw & Tap Co.
Hartford Machine Screw Co.
Wm. H. Haskell Co.
Pennsylvania Bolt & Nut Co.
Port Chester Bolt & Nut Co.
Worcester Machine Screw Co.

Bolts, *Stay—*
Lockport Iron & Steel Co.
Pennsylvania Bolt & Nut Co.

Bolts, *Stove—*
American Screw Co.
Port Chester Bolt & Nut Co.
Russell & Erwin Mfg. Co.
Shelton Co.

Bolts, *Stud—*
American Bolt Co.
Wm. H. Haskell Co.
Milton Mfg. Co.
Pennsylvania Bolt & Nut Co.
Port Chester Bolt & Nut Co.
Rhode Island Tool Co.
J. H. Sternbergh & Son.
Worcester Machine Screw Co.

Bolts, *Tap—*
American Bolt Co.
Wm. H. Haskell Co.
Milton Mfg. Co.
Pennsylvania Bolt & Nut Co.
Rhode Island Tool Co.
J. H. Sternbergh & Son.

Bolts, *Tire—*
American Screw Co.
Pennsylvania Bolt & Nut Co.
Port Chester Bolt & Nut Co.
Russell & Erwin Mfg. Co.
Shelton Co.

Bolts, *Track—*
Allentown Rolling Mills.
American Bolt Co.
Milton Mfg. Co.
Pennsylvania Bolt & Nut Co.
J. H. Sternbergh & Son.

W. H. Thompson & Co.
Tudor Iron Works.

Bolts, *Whiffletree—*
Port Chester Bolt & Nut Co

Bolts, *Window Spring—*
Peck, Stow & Wilcox Co.
Reading Hardware Co.

Bolts, *Window, Ventilating—*
Hobart B. Ives & Co.

Bolts or Spikes, *Drift—*
J. H. Sternbergh & Son.

Bonds, *Rail—*
Forest City Electric Co.
Washburn & Moen Mfg. Co.

Bone, *Case Hardening—*
Rogers & Hubbard Co.

Bone Mills—See *Mills, Drug, Bone, Corn, &c.*

Bon Bon Dishes, *Silver Plated—*
Wallace Bros.

Book Racks—See *Racks, Book.*

Book Publishers — See *Publishers, Book.*

Boom Travelers—See *Travelers, Boom and Deck.*

Boot Jacks—See *Jacks, Boot.*

Boots, *Interfering—*
Covert Mfg. Co.

Borers, *Bung Hole—*
Enterprise Mfg. Co.

Borers, *Counter—*
Cleveland Twist Drill Co.

Boring Bars, *for Locomotive Cylinder—*
William Sellers & Co.

Boring Machines—
Baush & Harris Machine Tool Co.
Bement, Miles & Co.
Bullard Machine Tool Co.
Davis & Egan Machine Tool Co.
E. Harrington, Son & Co.
Lodge & Shipley Machine Tool Co
Newark Machine Tool Works.
Newton Machine Tool Works.

Niles Tool Works Co.
Pedrick & Ayer Co.
Pratt & Whitney Co.
Prentice Bros.
Wm. Sellers & Co.

Boring Machines, Carpenters'—

Millers Falls Co.
Snell Mfg. Co.

Boring Machines, Car Wheel—

Bement, Miles & Co.
Niles Tool Works Co.
Pond Machine Tool Co.
Prentice Bros.
Wm. Sellers & Co.

Boring Machines, Cylinder—

Bement, Miles & Co.
Lodge & Shipley Machine Tool Co.
Newark Machine Tool Works.
Niles Tool Works Co.
Pedrick & Ayer Co.
Wm. Sellers & Co.

Boring Machines, Hub—See *Hub Boring Machines.*

Boring Mills—See *Mills, Boring and Turning.*

Boring and Facing Machines, Cylinder—See *Cylinder Boring and Facing Machines.*

Botanizing Drums—See *Drums, Botanizing.*

Bottles, Steel—

Avery Stamping Co.
C. G. Eckstein & Co.
National Tube Works Co.

Bottoms, Copper—

Ansonia Brass & Copper Co.
Randolph & Clowes.

Box Chisels, Corners, Fasteners, Hooks, Openers, Scrapers, Straps, Stretchers—See *Chisels, Corners, Fasteners, Hooks, Openers, Scrapers, Straps, Stretchers.*

Boxes, Cigar, Silver Plated—

The Wm. Rogers Mfg. Co.

Boxes, Letter—

Norwalk Lock Co.

Boxes, Lock, Post Office—See *Post Office Equipment.*

Boxes, Mail—

Forest City Foundry & Mfg. Co.
W. C. Heller & Co.
Norwalk Lock Co.
Taylor & Boggis Foundry Co.

Boxes, Match, Aluminum—

Scovill Mfg. Co.

Boxes, Match, Silver Plated—

Wm. Rogers Mfg. Co.
Wallace Bros.

Boxes, Miter—

Millers Falls Company.
Stanley Rule & Level Co.

Boxes, Paper—

Folding Paper Box Co.
Jesse Jones Paper Box Co.

Boxes, Pin—See *Pin Trays and Boxes.*

Boxes, Shelf—

A. H. Green & Co.
W. C. Heller & Co.
Jesse Jones Paper Box Co.
C. P. Moore.

Boxes, Small Wood Packing—

A. H. Green & Co.

Boxes, Soap, Silver Plated—

The Wm. Rogers Mfg. Co.
Wallace Bros.

Boxes, Thimble Skein—See *Skeins Thimble, and Boxes.*

Boxes, Tin—

Sidney Shepard & Co.

Boxes, Tobacco, Aluminum—

Scovill Mfg. Co.

Boxes, Tobacco, Silver Plated—
The Wm. Rogers Mfg. Co.
Wallace Bros.

Boxes, Tote—
Avery Stamping Co.
Kilbourne & Jacobs Mfg. Co.

Boxes, Twine—
John Chatillon & Sons.
Peck, Stow & Wilcox Co.
Reading Hardware Co.
Russell & Erwin Mfg. Co.
A. C. Williams.

Boxwood Rules—See *Rules, Boxwood.*

Braces, Bit—
Bridgeport Mfg. Co.
John S. Fray & Co.
Goodell Bros. Co.
Mason & Parker.
H. H. Mayhew Co.
Millers Falls Co.
Peck, Stow & Wilcox Co.

Braces, Boiler—See *Boiler Braces.*

Braces, Extension—
John S. Fray & Co.

Braces, Rudder—
W. & J. Tiebout.

Braces and Rails, Top—
E. D. Clapp Mfg. Co.

Brackets, Axe—
W. & J. Tiebout.

Brackets, Flower Pot—
Peck, Stow & Wilcox Co.
Reading Hardware Co.
Russell & Erwin Mfg. Co.
Stover Mfg. Co.

Brackets, Hand Rail—
Norwalk Lock Co.
Pleuger & Henger Mfg. Co.
Reading Hardware Co.
Russell & Erwin Mfg. Co.

Brackets, Lamp—
Bevin Bros. Mfg. Co.
Bradley & Hubbard Mfg. Co.
Peck, Stow & Wilcox Co.

Reading Hardware Co.
Stover Mfg. Co.

Brackets, Office, Counter, &c.—See *Railing and Brackets, Office, Counter, &c.*

Brackets, &c., *Plumbing—*
Barnes Mfg. Co.
Logan & Strobridge Iron Co.
Pleuger & Henger Mfg. Co.
Southern Queen Mfg. Co.
E. C. Stearns & Co.

Brackets, Rafter—
Ney Mfg. Co.

Brackets, Roofing—
Berger Bros.
Peck, Stow & Wilcox Co.
Stanley Rule & Level Co.

Brackets, Shelf—
Atlas Mfg. Co.
Norwalk Lock Co.
Peck, Stow & Wilcox Co.
Pleuger & Henger Mfg. Co.
Reading Hardware Co.
Russell & Erwin Mfg. Co.
Stanley Works.
Stover Mfg. Co.
Stowell Mfg. & Foundry Co.

Brackets, Soap—See *Household Articles, Wire.*

Brackets, Store Fixture—
I. S. Spencer's Sons.

Brackets, *Window Screen Corner—*
Reading Hardware Co.

Brad Awls—See *Awls, Peg, Brad, &c.*

Brads, Tacks, Finishing Nails, &c.
—See *Tacks, Brads, Finishing Nails, &c.*

Braided Rope, Cotton, Linen, &c.—
See *Rope, Braided, Cotton, Linen, &c.*

Brake, *Fishing Reel—*
Payson Mfg. Co.

Brakes, Bicycle—
Bevin Bros. Mfg. Co.
Weedsport Drill Co.

Brands, Burning—
George M. Ness.

Brass Bedsteads, Bolts, Butts, Castings, Cocks, Hammers, Hinges, Kettles, Labels, Moldings, Pipe, Pumps, Ratchets, Rivets, Rods, Sheets, Studs, Tags, Tubing and Wire—See *Bedsteads, Bolts, Butts, Castings, Cocks, Hammers, Hinges, Kettles, Labels, Moldings, Pipe, Pumps, Ratchets, Rivets, Rods, Sheets, Studs, Tags, Tubing, Wire.*

Brass, Brazing—
Plume & Atwood Mfg. Co
Scovill Mfg. Co.

Brass, Embossed or Figured—
Ansonia Brass & Copper Co.
Bridgeport Brass Co.
Waterbury Brass Co.

Brass, Hoop—
Plume & Atwood Mfg. Co.

Brass, Perforated—
Bridgeport Brass Co.

Brass Quadrants, Skylight—See *Quadrants, Brass Skylight.*

Brass Rods—
Ansonia Brass & Copper Co.
Bridgeport Brass Co.
Plume & Atwood Mfg. Co.

Brass, Roll and Sheet—
Ansonia Brass & Copper Co.
Bridgeport Brass Co.
Plume & Atwood Mfg. Co.
Randolph & Clowes.
Scovill Mfg. Co.
Waterbury Brass Co.

Brass, Rule (Printers')—
Plume & Atwood Mfg. Co.

Brass Shells, Blanks, Seamless and Shot—See *Shells.*

Brass, Sign or Engravers'—
Ansonia Brass & Copper Co.
Randolph & Clowes.

Brass, Spring—
Plume & Atwood Mfg. Co

Brass, White—
Bridgeport Deoxidized Bronze & Metal Co.

Braziers' Rivets and Solder—See *Rivets, Solder.*

Brazing Brass, Furnaces—See *Brass, Furnaces.*

Bread Boards, Knives—See *Boards, Knives.*

Bread Coolers—See *Kitchen Articles, Wire.*

Break Arms, Pin—See *Pin Break Arms.*

Breakers, Ice—
Harrison Safety Boiler Works.

Breakers, Ice—See *Ice Harvesting Tools.*

Breast Drills—See *Drills, Breast.*

Brick, Fire—
Cyrus Borgner.
Edward J. Etting
James Gardner & Son.
C. B. Houston & Co.
Henry Maurer & Son.
Newton & Co.
Ostrander Fire Brick Co.
Presbrey Stove Lining Co.
M. D. Valentine & Bro. Co.

Brick Hoists, Hods, Stoves, Trowels—See *Hoists, Hods, Stoves, Trowels.*

Brick Machinery—
American Blower Co.
Thos. Carlin's Sons.
Chambers Bros. Co.
Eastern Machinery Co.

Brick, Stove Fire—
Huntington & Wyatt.
Presbrey Stove Lining Co.

Bridge Bolts, Flooring, Truss and Roof Rods, Turntables—See *Bolts Flooring, Rods, Turntables.*

Bridge Machinery—
Hilles & Jones Co.
Prentice Bros.
Wm. Sellers & Co.
Vulcan Iron Works.

Bridges—See *Buildings and Bridges.*

Bridle Bits—See *Bits, Bridle.*

Bright Wire Goods—See *Wire Goods, Bright.*

Brine Hooks—See *Hooks, Brine.*

Broaching Presses — See *Presses, Broaching.*

Broilers—
Edward Darby & Sons.
Estey Wire Works Co.
Fred. J. Meyers Mfg. Co.
Schneider & Trenkamp Co.
Wire Goods Co.

Brokers, Iron and Steel—See *Iron and Steel, Brokers and Merchants.*

Bronze Bolts, Butts, Castings, Hinges, Sheets, Tubing, Tuyeres, Wire—See *Bolts, Butts, Castings, Hinges, Sheets, Tubing, Tuyeres, Wire.*

Bronze Castings, Aluminum, Manganese, Phosphor—See *Castings, Bronze.*

Bronze Forgings, Manganese—See *Forgings, Manganese Bronze.*

Bronze, Manganese—
Bridgeport Deoxidized Bronze & Metal Co.
Wm. Cramp & Sons Ship & Engine Building Co.

Bronze Metal—
Ansonia Brass & Copper Co.
Plume & Atwood Mfg. Co.
Scovill Mfg. Co.

Bronze, Phosphor—
Bridgeport Deoxidized Bronze & Metal Co.
Phosphor Bronze Smelting Co.

Pope's Island Mfg. Corporation.
Paul S. Reeves.

Bronze, Roll and Sheet—
Ansonia Brass & Copper Co.
Pope's Island Mfg. Corporation.
Randolph & Clowes.

Broom Holders,—See *Holders, Broom.*

Brooms, Whisk, &c.—
Jos. Lay & Co.

Brush, Copper—See *Copper, Commutator Brush.*

Brushes, Billiard Table—
Osborn Mfg. Co.

Brushes, Butchers', Packers'—
Osborn Mfg. Co.

Brushes, Electroplating—
Hanson & Van Winkle Co.
Osborn Mfg. Co.

Brushes, Silver Plated—
The Wm. Rogers Mfg. Co.
Wallace Bros.

Brushes, Wire—
Chicago Flexible Shaft Co.
Edward Darby & Sons.
Estey Wire Works Co.
Jos. Lay & Co.
Fred. J. Meyers Mfg. Co.
Osborn Mfg. Co.
Wright & Colton Wire Cloth Co.

Brushes, Tumbler—
Osborn Mfg. Co.

Brushes, Whitewash, Horse, Shoe, &c.—
Jos. Lay & Co.
Osborn Mfg. Co.
Palmer Hardware Mfg. Co.

Bucket Blocks, Pumps—See *Blocks, Pumps.*

Buckets, Elevator—
Avery Stamping Co.
Bradford Mill Co.
W. J. Clark Co.
Jeffrey Mfg. Co.

Buckets, Fire—
Howard & Morse.
New York Belting & Packing Co.

Buckets, Self Dumping—
Brown Hoisting & Conveying Machine Co.
G. L. Stuebner.

Buckles, Belt—
W. & E. T. Fitch Co.

Buckles, Halter and Trace—
Covert's Saddlery Works.

Bucks, Wood Saw—
Henry Disston & Sons.

Buffers, Blacksmiths'—
Heller Bros.

Buffer Steels—See *Steels, Buffer and Scraper.*

Buffing and Polishing Machines—
Builders' Iron Foundry.
Chicago Flexible Shaft Co.
Diamond Machine Co.
Hanson & Van Winkle Co.
Northampton Emery Wheel Co.
Watson-Stillman Co.

Buffing Lathes—See *Buffing and Polishing Machines.*

Buffing Supplies—See *Polishing and Buffing Supplies.*

Buffs—
Compress Wheel Co.
Diamond Machine Co.
Hanson & Van Winkle Co.

Building Anchors— See *Anchors, Building.*

Building Material, Fire Proof—
Henry Maurer & Son.

Buildings and Bridges—
Berlin Iron Bridge Co.
Boston Bridge Co.
Moseley Iron Bridge & Roof Co.
Passaic Rolling Mill Co.
Pittsburgh Bridge Co.
Phœnix Iron Co.

Pottsville Iron & Steel Co.
A. & P. Roberts Co.
Shiffler Bridge Co.

Bull Leaders, Rings—See *Leaders, Rings.*

Bull's Eyes, Floor—
W. & J. Tiebout.

Bull's, Dead Eyes, &c.—See *Eyes, Dead, Bull's, &c.*

Bumpers, Wagon Spring—
New York Belting & Packing Co.

Bung Head Bolts—See *Bolts, Special.*

Bung Hole Borers—See *Borers, Bung Hole.*

Bung Starters—See *Starters, Bung.*

Burners, Kerosene—
Bridgeport Brass Co.
Plume & Atwood Mfg. Co.
Scovill Mfg. Co.
Taplin Mfg. Co.

Burners, Natural Gas—
Schneider & Trenkamp Co.

Burners, Paint—
Schneider & Trenkamp Co.

Burning Brands—See *Brands, Burning.*

Burnishers—
Buck Bros.
Tuck Mfg. Co.

Burring Machines, Nut—
The National Machinery Co.

Burrs, Copper—See *Rivets and Burrs, Copper.*

Bushings, Pulley—
Boston & Lockport Block Co.

Bush Hooks—See *Hooks, Bush.*

Bushed Chains—See *Chains, Bushed.*

Butcher Cleavers, Knives, Saws, Steels—See *Cleavers, Knives, Saws, Steels.*

Butchers' Tools—
L. & I. J. White Co.

Butt and Rabbet Gauges—See *Gauges, Butt and Rabbet.*

Butt Milling and Drilling Machines—See *Milling and Drilling Machines, Butt.*

Butter Spades, Triers—See *Spades, Triers.*

Butter Making Appliances — See *Cheese and Butter Making Appliances.*

Butterises, Blacksmiths'—
Peck, Stow & Wilcox Co.

Button Back Machines—
Mossberg & Granville Mfg. Co.

Button Head Bolts—See *Bolts, Special.*

Button Hooks, Silver Plated—See *Hooks, Button, Silver Plated.*

Buttons, Door—
Arcade Mfg. Co.
Ney Mfg. Co.
Peck, Stow & Wilcox Co.
Reading Hardware Co.
Russell & Erwin Mfg. Co.
Stover Mfg. Co.
W. & J. Tiebout.

Buttons, Push—
W. R. Ostrander & Co.
Reading Hardware Co.
Russell & Erwin Mfg. Co.
I. S. Spencer's Sons.

Butts and Hinges, Brass—
Plume & Atwood Mfg. Co.
Reading Hardware Co.
Russell & Erwin Mfg. Co.
Scovill Mfg. Co.
W. & J. Tiebout.
Union Mfg. Co.

Butts, Ball Bearing—
Stanley Works.

Butts, Bronze—
Norwalk Lock Co.
Reading Hardware Co.
Russell & Erwin Mfg. Co.

Butts, Cast Iron—
Norwalk Lock Co.
Peck, Stow & Wilcox Co.
Reading Hardware Co.
Russell & Erwin Mfg. Co.
Taylor & Boggis Foundry Co.
Union Mfg. Co.

Butts, Wrought Steel—
McKinney Mfg. Co.
Reading Hardware Co.
Stanley Works.

Cabinet Clamps, Locks, Scrapers, Vises—See *Clamps, Locks, Scrapers, Vises.*

Cable Chain—See *Chain, Crane, Cable, &c.*

Cable Railroads—See *Conveying Machinery.*

Cables, Electric—See *Wire and Cables, Electric.*

Cableways, Suspension—See *Tramways, Wire Rope.*

Cages, Bird and Animal—
Andrew B. Hendryx Co.
Fred J. Meyers Mfg. Co.

Cake Pans, Tins, Turners—See *Pans, Tins, Turners.*

Calendars, Silver Plated—See *Desk Specialties.*

Calf Weaners—See *Weaners, Calf.*

Caliper Gauges—See *Gauges, Caliper.*

Calipers,
Athol Machine Co.
Bemis & Call Hardware & Tool Co.
New England Specialty Co.
Peck, Stow & Wilcox Co.
L. S. Starrett Co.
J. Stevens Arms & Tool Co.

Calking Irons and Mallets—
W. & J. Tiebout.

Calking Irons—See *Irons, Calking.*

Calks, Toe—
P. F. Burke.
Rhode Island Perkins Horse Shoe Co.

Call Bells—See *Bells, Tea and Call.*

Calls, Dog—
 Waterbury Brass Co.

Cam Cutting Attachments—
 Cincinnati Milling Machine Co.

Cams—
 Newark Machine Tool Co.

Camp Stools—See *Stools, Camp.*

Candelabra—See *Candlesticks and Candelabra.*

Candlesticks—
 Logan & Strobridge Iron Co.
 North Bros. Mfg. Co.
 Peck, Stow & Wilcox Co.
 Russell & Erwin Mfg. Co.
 Turner & Seymour Mfg. Co.

Candlesticks and Candelabra, Silver Plated—
 The Wm. Rogers Mfg. Co.

Candy Pans, Scales, Scoops—See *Pans, Scales, Scoops.*

Cane Knives—See *Knives, Cane.*

Can Makers' Machinery—
 E. W. Bliss Co.

Canner, Fruit and Vegetable—
 John L. Gaumer Co.

Can Openers—See *Openers, Can.*

Canopies and Canopy Fixtures—
 I. E. Palmer.

Can Stock, Milk—See *Milk Can Stock.*

Cans, Ash—
 Howard & Morse.
 Sidney Shepard & Co.

Cans, Dredge Spice—
 Sidney Shepard & Co.

Cans, Milk—
 Sidney Shepard & Co.

Cans, Oil—
 Sidney Shepard & Co.

Cans, Paint and Varnish—
 Wilmot & Hobbs Mfg. Co.

Cans, Tin—
 Sidney Shepard & Co.

Cans, Waste—
 Howard & Morse.

Caps, Hose—See *Hose Attachments.*

Caps, Percussion—
 Union Metallic Cartridge Co.
 Waterbury Brass Co.

Cap Screws—See *Screws, Cap and Set.*

Caps and Ventilators—
 W. & J. Tiebout.

Car Axles, Bearings, Bells, Boxes, Coupler Knuckles, Doors, Heaters, Pushers, Trimmings, Ventilators, Wheels—See *Axles, Bearings, Bells, Boxes, Knuckles, Doors, Heaters, Pushers, Trimmings, Ventilators, Wheels.*

Car Door Plates—See *Plates, Car Door.*

Car Link Machines—
 National Machinery Co.

Car Pushers—
 Jos. F. McCoy Co.

Car Shop Tools—
 Prentice Bros.

Car Works Machinery—
 Hilles & Jones Co.

Car Wheel Boring Machines—See *Boring Machines, Car Wheel.*

Car Window Locks—See *Locks, Car Window.*

Carbines—See *Rifles, Carbines, &c.*

Carbon Tongs—See *Tongs, Carbon.*

Card Baskets, Cases, Frames—See *Baskets, Cases, Frames.*

Card Frames, Racks—See *Frames, Racks.*

Carpenters' Clamps, Slicks—See *Clamps, Slicks.*

THE IRON AGE INDEX.

Carpet Stretchers—See *Stretchers*.

Carpet Sweepers, Toy—See *Toy Carpet Sweepers*.

Carriage Axles, Bolts, Clamps, Fenders, Forgings, Lamps, Seats, Springs, Wrenches — See *Bolts, Clamps, Fenders, Forgings, Lamps, Seats, Springs, Wrenches*.

Carriage Trimmers' Clips—See *Clips, Carriage Trimmers'*.

Carriages, Tension—See *Tension Carriages*.

Carriages, Trolley—
Trenton Iron Co.

Carriers, Barb Wire—
Ludlow-Saylor Wire Co.

Carriers, Bicycle Luggage—
Wire Goods Co.

Carriers, Hand Hoist—
Stowell Mfg. & Foundry Co.

Carriers, Hay Fork—
Ney Mfg. Co.
J. E. Porter Co.
Stowell Mfg. & Foundry Co.
Syracuse Chilled Plow Co.

Carriers, Hay—See *Haying Tools*.

Carriers, Stove—
Lansing Wheelbarrow Co.

Carriers, Trunk—
Lansing Wheelbarrow Co.

Carrying Track, Overhead — See *Track, Overhead Carrying*.

Cars, Coal Mine, Pit, &c.—
Kilbourne & Jacobs Mfg. Co.
Lansing Wheelbarrow Co.
Link-Belt Engineering Co.

Cars, Dump—
Brown Hoisting & Conveying Machine Co.

Thos. Carlin's Sons.
Kilbourne & Jacobs Mfg. Co.
G. L. Stuebner.
Trenton Iron Co.

Cars, Elevator—
Columbus Wire & Iron Works.
Ludlow-Saylor Wire Co.
W. S. Tyler Wire Works Co.

Cars, Foundry—
Byram & Co.

Cars, Railroad—
J. W. Hoffman & Co.
Pierson & Co.

Cars, Skip—
Brown Hoisting & Conveying Machine Co.

Cars, Sugar—
Kilbourne & Jacobs Mfg. Co.

Cartridges—
Peters Cartridge Co.
Union Metallic Cartridge Co.

Carts and Wagons—See *Toy Carts and Wagons*.

Carts, Barrel—
Lansing Wheelbarrow Co.

Carts, Dump—
Kilbourne & Jacobs Mfg Co.
Lansing Wheelbarrow Co.

Carts, Lumber—
Lansing Wheelbarrow Co.

Carts, Pony—
Lansing Wheelbarrow Co.

Carts, Push—
Daln Mfg. Co.
Lansing Wheelbarrow Co.
Syracuse Chilled Plow Co.
R. W. Whitehurst & Co.

Carving Tools—
Buck Bros.
Millers Falls Co.

Case Hardening Bone, Furnaces—
See *Bone, Furnaces*.

Casement Adjusters, Fasteners—See
  Adjusters. Fasteners.
Cases, Card, Silver Plated—
  Wm. Rogers Mfg. Co.
  Wallace Bros.
Cases, Cigar and Cigarette—
  Scovill Mfg. Co.
  Wallace Bros.
Cases, Drill—
  Cleveland Twist Drill Co.
Cases, Screw and Bolt—
  A. H. Green.
  W. C. Heller & Co.
Cases, Seed—
  W. C. Heller & Co.
Casing, Wrought Iron—
  Kelly & Jones Co.
  National Tube Works Co.
Caskets, Jewel, Silver Plated—See
  Jewel Caskets. Silver Plated.
Cast Steel, Crucible—See *Steel, Crucible Cast.*
Cast Washers—See *Washers. Cast.*
Caster Bits—See *Bits, Caster.*
Casters, Bed, Plate, &c.—
  Palmer Hardware Mfg. Co.
  Payson Mfg. Co.
  Peck, Stow & Wilcox Co.
  Reading Hardware Co.
Casters, Truck—
  Payson Mfg. Co.
  Peck, Stow & Wilcox Co.
  Pleuger & Henger Mfg. Co.
  Reading Hardware Co.
  E. C. Stearns & Co.
Castings, Aluminum—
  Bridgeport Deoxidized Bronze & Metal Co.
  Haight & Clark.
  Andrew B. Hendryx Co.
  Pittsburgh Reduction Co.

Castings, Brass—
  Bridgeport Deoxidized Bronze & Metal Co.
  Builders' Iron Foundry.
  Eastwood Wire Co.
  Haight & Clark.
  Andrew B. Hendryx Co.
  Lorain Foundry Co.
  Mackintosh, Hemphill & Co.
  Edward Miller & Co.
  North Bros. Mfg Co.
  Paul S. Reeves.
  I. S. Spencer's Sons.
  Turner & Seymour Mfg. Co.
  Vulcan Iron Works.
Castings, Bronze—
  Bridgeport Deoxidized Bronze & Metal Co.
  Eastwood Wire Mfg. Co.
  Andrew B. Hendryx Co.
Castings, Composition—
  I. S. Spencer's Sons.
Castings, Copper—
  Bridgeport Deoxidized Bronze & Metal Co.
  Forest City Electric Co.
  Lorain Foundry Co.
Castings, Chrome Steel—
  Chrome Steel Works.
Castings, Gray Iron—
  American Foundry Co.
  Burr & Houston Co.
  S. Cheney & Sons.
  Forest City Foundry & Mfg. Co.
  North Bros. Mfg. Co.
  Palmers & DeMooy Foundry Co.
  Standard Foundry Co.
  Taylor & Boggis Foundry Co.
  Torrance Iron Co.
  Vulcan Iron Works.
Castings, Iron—
  American Foundry Co.
  Birmingham Iron Foundry.
  Baush & Harris Machine Tool Co
  Lloyd Booth Co.
  Thos. Carlin's Sons.
  Champion Iron Co.

Eastwood Wire Mfg. Co.
H. H. Franklin Mfg. Co.
Logan & Strobridge Iron Co.
Lorain Foundry Co.
Mackintosh, Hemphill & Co.
Wm. McFarland.
New Brunswick Foundry Co.
Ohio Pipe Co.
Pittsburgh Mfg. Co.
R. Poole & Sons Co.
Sessions Foundry Co.
I. S. Spencer's Sons.
Taylor & Boggis Foundry Co.
Turner & Seymour Mfg. Co.
Turner, Vaughn & Taylor Co.
Van Wagoner & Williams Hardware Co.
R. D. Wood & Co.
Robert Wetherill & Co.

Castings, Malleable Iron—
Acme Malleable Iron Works.
Arcade Malleable Iron Co.
W. & E. T. Fitch Co.
Hammer & Co.
Oriskany Malleable Iron Co.
Star Heel Plate Co.
Torrance Iron Co.

Castings, Manganese Bronze—
W. Cramp & Sons Ship & Engine Building Co.

*Castings, Ornamental—*See *Iron, Ornamental.*

Castings, Phosphor Bronze—
Pope's Island Mfg. Corporation.
Paul S. Reeves.

Castings, Rolling Mill—
Allentown Rolling Mills.
Lloyd Booth Co.
Thos. Carlin's Sons.
Frank-Kneeland Machine Co.
A. Garrison Foundry Co.
Leechburg Foundry & Machine Co.
Lorain Foundry Co.
Robinson-Rea Mfg. Co.
Totten & Hogg Iron & Steel Foundry Co.

Castings, Water Works—
Builders' Iron Foundry.
R. D. Wood & Co.

Castings, Steel—
Arcade Malleable Iron Co.
Birmingham Iron Foundry.
Chester Steel Casting Co.
Chrome Steel Works.
Denman & Davis.
Stanley G. Flagg & Co.
C. B. Houston & Co.
Mackintosh, Hemphill & Co.
Reliance Steel Casting Co.
Totten & Hogg Iron & Steel Foundry Co.

Castings, Tinned—
Logan & Strobridge Iron Co.
Turner & Seymour Mfg. Co.

Castings, White Metal—
Andrew B. Hendryx Co.

Catchers, Grass—
Enterprise Mfg. Co.

Catches, Cupboard—
Norwalk Lock Co.
Peck, Stow & Wilcox Co.
Reading Hardware Co.
Russell & Erwin Mfg. Co.
Taylor & Boggis Foundry Co.
W. & J. Tiebout.
Van Wagoner & Williams Hardware Co

Catches, Elbow—
Ney Mfg. Co.
Norwalk Lock Co.
Reading Hardware Co.
Russell & Erwin Mfg. Co.

Catches, Door—
Ney Mfg. Co.

Catches, Refrigerator—
W. & J. Tiebout.

Catches, Screen Door—
Norwalk Lock Co.
Peck, Stow & Wilcox Co.
Reading Hardware Co.
Russell & Erwin Mfg. Co.

Catches, *Showcase—*
Reading Hardware Co.
Stover Mfg. Co.

Catches, *Transom—*
Peck, Stow & Wilcox Co.
Reading Hardware Co.
Russell & Erwin Mfg. Co.

Catches, *Window—*
Norwalk Lock Co.
Reading Hardware Co.
Russell & Erwin Mfg. Co.
W. & J. Tiebout.

Cattle Leaders, Prods, Punches, Ties, Troughs—See *Leaders, Prods, Punches, Ties, Troughs.*

Cedar Kegs—See *Kegs, Cedar.*

Ceiling and Siding, *Iron and Steel—*
Ætna-Standard Iron & Steel Co.
American Steel Roofing Co.
Cambridge Roofing Co.
Cincinnati Corrugating Co.
Garry Iron Roofing Co.
Kansas City Metal Roofing & Corrugating Co.
Youngstown Iron & Steel Roofing Co.

Ceiling Pulleys—See *Pulleys, Ceiling.*

Cement, *Belting—*
Russia Cement Co.

Cement, *Roofing—*
Garry Iron Roofing Co.

Centering Chucks—See *Chucks, Centering.*

Centering Machines—
Niles Tool Works Co.
D. E. Whiton Machine Co.
Woodward & Rogers.

Center Drills, Gauges, Indicators, Testers—See *Drills, Gauges, Indicators, Testers.*

Center Grinders, *Lathe*—See *Grinders, Lathe Center.*

Centers, *Indexing—*
Cincinnati Milling Machine Co.

Centers, *Neck Yoke—*
Covert's Saddlery Works.

Centers, *Planer—*
C. O. Lucas & Co.

Centers, *Sash and Transom—*
Norwalk Lock Co.
Payson Mfg. Co.
Peck, Stow & Wilcox Co.
Reading Hardware Co.
Russell & Erwin Mfg. Co.

Centrifugal Pumps—See *Pumps, Centrifugal.*

Cesspools—
Southern Queen Mfg. Co.
E. C. Stearns & Co.

Chain Bars, *Bicycle*—See *Bicycle Chain Bars.*

Chain Belting, Hoists, Pipes, Pumps, Swivels—See *Belting, Hoists, Pipes, Pumps, Swivels.*

Chain, *Bicycle—*
Boston Gear Works.
Bridgeport Chain Co.
New Britain Hardware Mfg. Co.

Chain, *Binding—*
Garland Chain Co.

Chain, *Coil—*
Bradlee & Co.
Bridgeport Chain Co.
Garland Chain Co.
James McKay & Co.
Oneida Community.

Chain, *Crane, Cable, &c.—*
Bradlee & Co.
James McKay & Co.

Chain, *Hydrant—*
Bridgeport Chain Co.

Chain, *Jack, Safety, &c.—*
Bridgeport Brass Co.
Bridgeport Chain Co.
A. B. Hendryx & Co.
McNab & Harlin Mfg. Co.
Oneida Community.
Ossawan Mills Co.

Plume & Atwood Mfg. Co.
Russell & Erwin Mfg. Co.
Scovill Mfg. Co.
Turner & Seymour Mfg. Co.
Wire Goods Co.

Chain Links and Chain—
Wm. H. Haskell Co.
Rhode Island Tool Co.
J. H. Sternbergh & Son.
Stowell Mfg. & Foundry Co.

Chain Machinery, Bicycle—
Turner, Vaughn & Taylor Co.

Chain Pot Cleaners—See *Kitchen Articles, Wire.*

Chain Pump Fixtures—See *Pump Fixtures, Chain.*

Chains, Bushed—
Link Belt Engineering Co.

Chains, Dog and Halter—
Bridgeport Chain Co.
Covert Mfg. Co.
Garland Chain Co.
Oneida Community.
Wire Goods Co.

Chains, Flat Link—
Wm. H. Haskell Co.
Thomas Morton.
Smith & Egge Mfg. Co.

Chains, Harness—
Bridgeport Chain Co.
Covert's Saddlery Works.

Chains, Key—
Bridgeport Chain Co.
Oneida Community.

Chains, Ladder—
Ossawan Mills Co.
Turner & Seymour Mfg. Co.

Chains, Log, Detachable—
Stowell Mfg. & Foundry Co.

Chains, Log, Rafting, &c.—
Bradlee & Co.
Jas. McKay & Co.

Chains, Picket, Stake, &c.
Bridgeport Chain Co.
Garland Chain Co.

Chains, Picture—
Bridgeport Chain Co.

Chains, Sash, and Attachments—
Bridgeport Chain Co.
Thomas Morton.
Oneida Community.
Smith & Egge Mfg. Co.
Wire Goods Co.

Chains, Sling—
Bradlee & Co.

Chains, Stud—
Bradlee & Co.
Jas. McKay & Co.

Chains, Trace—
Bridgeport Chain Co.
Garland Chain Co.
Oneida Community.

Chains, Wagon and Fancy—
Bridgeport Chain Co.
Garland Chain Co.
Jas. McKay & Co.
Oneida Community.

Chains, Well—
W. & B. Douglas.
Garland Chain Co.

Chair Bottom Knives—See *Knives, Machine.*

Chairs and Settees, Lawn —
Columbus Wire & Iron Works.
Ellis & Halfenbarger:
Gilbert & Bennett Mfg. Co.
Howard & Morse.
Fred. J. Meyers Mfg. Co.
Scheeler's Sons.
Stewart Iron Works.
R. W. Whitehurst & Co.

Chalk Line Reels—See *Reels, Chalk Line.*

Chalk Lines—See *Lines, Chalk, Masons', &c.*

Chamfering Machines, Die—See *Die Chamfering Machines.*

Chandelier Hooks—See *Hooks, Chandelier.*

Chandeliers, Oil—
Bradley & Hubbard Mfg. Co.
Edward Miller & Co.

Chandlery, Ship, Hardware—See *Ship Chandlery Hardware.*

Channel, Shoe and Cobblers' Nails—See *Nails, Shoe, Cobblers', Channel, &c.*

Channels—See *Beams and Channels.*

Channeling Machines—
Ingersoll-Sergeant Drill Co.
F. R. Patch Mfg. Co.
Rand Drill Co.

Charcoal Blooms—See *Blooms, Charcoal.*

Charcoal Pig Iron—
Superior Charcoal Iron Co.

Check Rowers—
Challenge Corn Planter Co.

Check Springs, Valves—See *Springs, Valves.*

Checks, Baggage, Key, &c.—
Bridgeport Chain Co.
Geo. M. Ness.
Scovill Mfg. Co.
R. Woodman Mfg. & Supply Co.

Checks, Door—
Caldwell Sash Balance Co.
F. S. Hutchinson Co.
Norton Door Check & Spring Co.
Russell & Erwin Mfg. Co.
E. C. Stearns & Co.

Checks, Time—
R. Woodman Mfg. & Supply Co.

Cheese and Butter Making Appliances—
Moseley & Stoddard Mfg. Co.

Cheese Factory Scales—See *Scales, Cheese.*

Cheese Knives, Safes—See *Knives, Safes.*

Cheese Knives, Self Gauging—See *Knives, Cheese, Self Gauging.*

Cheese Triers—See *Triers, Butter and Cheese.*

Chemicals, Electro—
Hansen & Van Winkle Co.
Zucker & Levett & Loeb Co.

Chemists, Analytical—
J. Blodget Britton & Co.
Chas. F. McKenna.

Cherry Seeders and Stoners—See *Seeders, Stoners.*

Chest Handles and Hinges—See *Handles, Hinges.*

Chests, Tool—
American Tool Chest Co.
Millers Falls Co.

Children's Tricycles, Horse—See *Tricycles, Children's Horse.*

Child's Swings—See *Swings, Child's.*

Chilled Car Wheels—See *Wheels, Car.*

Chilled Rolls—See *Rolls, Sand and Chilled.*

Chimney Caps—See *Ventilators and Chimney Caps.*

Chimney Cleaners, Lamp—See *Cleaners, Lamp Chimney.*

Chimneys, Steel—
Thomas Carlin's Sons.
Philadelphia Engineering Co.

Chippers, Ice—
North Bros. Mfg. Co.

Chisel Gauges, Grinders, Handles—See *Gauges, Grinders, Handles.*

Chisels, Box—
Peck, Stow & Wilcox Co.
Russell & Erwin Mfg. Co.

Chisels, Cold—
Billings & Spencer Co.
Buck Bros.
Knapp & Cowles Mfg. Co.
Peck, Stow & Wilcox Co.
Snell Mfg. Co.
Tuck Mfg. Co.

Chisels, Ice—
Knapp & Cowles Mfg. Co.
Logan & Strobridge Iron Co.
A. C. Williams.

Chisels, Ice—See *Ice Harvesting Tools.*

Chisels, Toy—See *Toy Chisels.*

Chisels, Track—
Van Wagoner & Williams Hardware Co.

Chisels, Wire—
Peck, Stow & Wilcox Co.

Chisels and Gouges, Socket—
Buck Bros.
Peck, Stow & Wilcox Co.
L. & I. J. White Co.

Chisels and Gouges, Tanged—
Buck Bros.
Peck, Stow & Wilcox Co.
L. & I. J. White Co.

Christmas Tree Holders—See *Holders Christmas Tree.*

Chrome Steel—See *Steel, Chrome.*

Chucking Machines—
Brown & Sharpe Mfg. Co.

Chucks—
Cushman Chuck Co.
Dwight Slate Machine Co.
Morse Twist Drill & Machine Co.
Sebastian Lathe Co.
Skinner Chuck Co.
Standard Tool Co.
Union Mfg. Co.
D. E. Whiton Machine Co.

Chucks, Centering—
Cushman Chuck Co.

Chucks, Drill—
R. H. Brown & Co.
Cleveland Twist Drill Co.
Cushman Chuck Co.
Goodell Bros. Co.
William G. Le Count.
Millers Falls Co.
Morse Twist Drill & Machine Co.
Skinner Chuck Co.
Smith & Egge Mfg. Co.
Strange Forged Drill & Tool Co.
Union Mfg. Co.
D. E. Whiton Machine Co.
Wiley & Russell Mfg. Co.

Chucks, Lathe—
Cushman Chuck Co.
Hoggson & Pettis Mfg. Co.
Pratt & Whitney Co.
Skinner Chuck Co.
Union Mfg. Co.
D. E. Whiton Machine Co.

Chucks, Planer—
Geo. Burnham & Co.
Pedrick & Ayer Co.
Skinner Chuck Co.

Chucks, Wire—
T. F. Welch Mfg. Co.

Churns—
Moseley & Stoddard Mfg. Co.

Cider Mills—See *Mills, Cider.*

Cider Mill Teeth—See *Teeth, Cider Mill.*

Cigar Boxes, Cases, Cutters, Lighters—See *Boxes, Cases, Cutters, Lighters.*

Cinder, Mill—
Pilling & Crane.

Circular Saws—See *Saws, Circular.*

Cistern Pumps—See *Pumps, Cistern.*

Clam Hooks—See *Hooks, Clam.*

Clamp and Drill, Combined—
Weedsport Drill Co.

Clamp Dogs, Drills—See *Dogs, Drills.*

Clamps, Belt—
Billings & Spencer Co.

Clamps, Cabinet, Carpenters', Machinists', &c.
Armstrong Mfg. Co.
Billings & Spencer Co.
Hammer & Co.
Logan & Strobridge Iron Co.
G. A. Milbradt & Co.
Peck, Stow & Wilcox Co.
Reading Hardware Co.
E. C. Stearns & Co.
Stover Mfg. Co.
A. C. Williams.

Clamps, Carriage—
Reading Hardware Co.

Clamps, Handle Bar—
W. W. Shoe.

Clamps, Hose—See *Hose Attachments*.

Clamps, Key Seat—
Hoggson & Pettis Mfg. Co.

Clamps, Saw—
Henry Disston & Sons.
Reading Hardware Co.

Clamps, Steel—
W. G. Le Count.

Clamps, Toolmakers'—
J. Stevens Arms & Tool Co.

Clamps, Vise—
Prentiss Vise Co.

Clamps and Slides, Rope—
Covert's Saddlery Works.

Clapboard Gauges, Markers—See *Gauges, Markers*.

Clasps, Hoop and Pail—
Cary Mfg. Co.
E. H. Titchener & Co.

Claws,. Tack—
Bridgeport Mfg. Co.
Knapp & Cowles Mfg. Co.
H. H. Mayhew Co.
Peck, Stow & Wilcox Co.
J. H. Williams & Co.

Clay, Fire—
Ostrander Fire Brick Co.

Clay Mixing Pans—See *Pans, Clay Mixing and Ore*.

Cleaners, File—
Nicholson File Co.

Cleaners, Flue—
Jackson Flue Scraper Co.
Millers Falls Co.
Osborn Mfg. Co.
Pedrick & Ayer Co.
Wire Goods Co.

Cleaners, Lamp Chimney—
Fred. J. Meyers Mfg. Co.

Cleaners, Sidewalk—
Ely Hoe & Fork Co.
Iowa Farming Tool Co.
Palmer Hardware Mfg. Co.

Cleaners, Sink—
New York Stamping Co.
Osborn Mfg. Co.

Clearer Springs—See *Springs, Clearer*.

Cleats, Line—
Reading Hardware Co.
W. & J. Tiebout.

Cleavers, Butcher, &c.—
Geo. H. Bishop & Co.
John Chatillon & Sons.
C. A. Hoffman.
Knapp & Cowles Mfg. Co.
Mason & Parker.
National Saw Co.
Nichols Bros.
Peck, Stow & Wilcox Co.
L. & I. J. White Co.

Clevises, Malleable—
W. & J. Tiebout.

Clinch Rings, Rivets—See *Rings, Rivets*,

Clippers, Bolt and Rivet—
Chambers Bros. & Co.
Helwig Mfg. Co.
H. K. Porter.
Silver Mfg. Co.

Clippers, Horse and Toilet—
American Shearer Mfg. Co.
Chicago Flexible Shaft Co.

E. S. Hotchkiss.
Jos. F. McCoy Co.

Clips, Axle, Spring Bar, &c.—
E. D. Clapp Mfg. Co.
Richard Eccles.
Scranton Forging Co.
M. Seward & Son Co.

Clips, Carriage Trimmers' &c.—
United States Clothes Pin Co.

Clips, Damper—
Sidney Shepard & Co.
Stover Mfg. Co.
Troy Nickel Works.

Clips, Paper—See *Stationers' Hardware.*

Clips, Toe—
Bevin Bros. Mfg. Co.
Morgan & Wright.
Smith & Egge Mfg. Co.

Clock Bells, Springs—See *Bells, Springs.*

Clock Spring Steel—See *Steel, Clock Spring.*

Clocks—
Bradley & Hubbard Mfg. Co.

Clocks, Marine—
Ashcroft Mfg. Co.

Clocks, Watchman's—
W. R. Ostrander & Co.

Cloth, Emery—
Baeder, Adamson & Co.

Cloth, Window Screen—
Clinton Wire Cloth Co.
Fred. J. Meyers Mfg. Co.
New Jersey Wire Cloth Co.
New York Wire Cloth Co.
E. C. Stearns & Co.
W. S. Tyler Wire Works Co.
Wickwire Bros.

Cloth, Wire (see also *Cloth, Window Screen*)—
E. T. Barnum.
Bradford Mill Co.
Columbus Wire & Iron Works.

Edward Darby & Sons.
Eastwood Wire Mfg. Co.
Estey Wire Works Co.
Gilbert & Bennett Mfg. Co.
Ludlow-Saylor Wire Co.
Howard & Morse.
Fred. J. Meyers Mfg. Co.
New Jersey Wire Cloth Co.
New York Wire Cloth Co.
Scheeler's Sons.
W. S. Tyler Wire Works Co.
Wright & Colton Wire Cloth Co.
Wickwire Bros.

Clothes Dryers, Hangers, Horses, Lines, Pins, Wringers—See *Dryers, Hangers, Horses, Lines, Pins, Wringers.*

Clothes Line Holders, Hooks, Pulleys, Reels—See *Holders, Hooks, Pulleys, Reels.*

Clubs, Indian—
John Sommer's Son.

Clutch Couplings, Pulleys — See *Couplings, Pulleys.*

Clutches, Jaw—
Link-Belt Engineering Co.

Clutches, Wood Split Pulley—
Dodge Mfg. Co.
Reeves Pulley Co.

Coach Screws—See *Screws, Coach and Lag.*

Coal—
Ed. J. Etting.
C. D. Houston & Co.
Pilling & Crane.
W. H. Thompson & Co.
Francis Wister.

Coal Cars, Hods, Scales, Scoops, Screens, Shutes, Tongs, Vases—
See *Cars, Hods, Scales, Scoops, Screens, Shutes, Tongs, Vases.*

Coal Cutters—
General Electric Co.
Jeffrey Mfg. Co.

Coal Handling Machinery—
Brown Hoisting & Conveying Machine Co.
Thos. Carlin's Sons.
Jeffrey Mfg. Co.
Link-Belt Engineering Co.

Coal Holes—See *Iron Work, Builders'*.

Coal Lands—
J. H. Hillman & Co.

Coal Washing Machinery—
Jeffrey Mfg. Co.

Coasters and Lock, Combined Bicycle—See *Bicycle Lock and Coasters, Combined*.

Coat Hooks—See *Hooks, Coat and Hat*.

Cobblers' Kits—
Enterprise Mfg. Co.
Star Heel Plate Co.

Cobblers', Shoe Nails—See *Nails, Shoe, Cobblers', Channel, &c.*

Cockeyes, Swivel—See *Eyes, Cock, Swivel*.

Cocks, Brass—
Humphryes Mfg. Co.
McNab & Harlin Mfg. Co.
Pleuger & Henger Mfg. Co.

Cocks, Gauge—
Jenkins Bros.
McNab & Harlin Mfg. Co.

Coffin Hardware—
New Britain Hardware Mfg. Co.

Coffee Mills, Pot Stands, Roasters
—See *Mills, Roasters, Stands*.

Coil Chain—See *Chain, Coil*.

Coilers, Wire—
E. J. Manville Machine Co.
Mossberg & Granville Mfg. Co.
Stover Novelty Works.

Coils, Pipe—
Harrisburg Pipe Bending Co.
McNab & Harlin Mfg. Co.
National Pipe Bending Co.
Whitlock Coil Pipe Co.

Coiling Machines, Spring—See *Spring Coiling Machines*.

Coining Machinery—
Gould & Eberhardt.

Coke—
C. B. Houston & Co.
Jerome Keeley & Co
J. J. Mohr.
Pilling & Crane.
W. J. Rainey.
W. H. Thompson & Co.
Francis Wister.

Coke Forks—See *Forks, Coke*.

Cold Chisels—See *Chisels, Cold*.

Cold Rolled Steel—See *Steel, Cold Rolled*.

Cold Saw Cutting Off Machines—
See *Cutting Off Machines, Cold Saw*.

Collar Screws—See *Screws, Collar*.

Collars, Shafting—
Rhode Island Tool Co.
J. H. Williams & Co.

Collectors, Dust—
American Blower Co.

Colors, Mortar—
Garry Iron Roofing Co.

Colters, Plow—
Singer, Nimick & Co.

Columns—See *Buildings and Bridges*.

Columns, Veranda—See *Iron Work, Builders'*.

Combination Gauges—See *Gauges, Combination*.

Combs, Curry—
Bloomsburg Mfg. Co.
W. & E. T. Fitch Co.
Edward S. Hotchkiss.
Imperial Bit & Snap Co.
New York Stamping Co.
Stover Mfg. Co.

Commission Merchants, Hardware
—See *Agents, Hardware Manufacturers'*.

Commutator Brush Copper—See Copper, Commutator Brush.

Compasses, Dividers, &c.—
Athol Machine Co.
Bemis & Call Hardware & Tool Co.
Peck, Stow & Wilcox Co.
L. S. Starrett Co.
J. Stevens Arms & Tool Co.

Compound, Graphite Pipe Joint—
Jos. Dixon Crucible Co.

Compressed Air Tools—
Clayton Air Compressor Works.

Compression Pumps—See Pumps, Compression and Vacuum.

Compressors, Air—
Ed. P. Allis Co.
Barnes Mfg. Co.
Clayton Air Compressor Works.
Ingersoll-Sergeant Drill Co.
Norwalk Iron Works.
Pedrick & Ayer Co.
Philadelphia Engineering Works.
Rand Drill Co.
Henry R. Worthington.

Compressors, Gas—
Norwalk Iron Works.
Philadelphia Engineering Co.
Rand Drill Co.

Computing Scales—See Scales, Computing.

Condensers—
Union Steam Pump Co.
R. D. Wood & Co.
H. R. Worthington.

Conductor Elbows, Fasteners, Heads, Hooks, Punches, Reducers—See Elbows, Fasteners, Heads, Hooks, Punches, Reducers.

Conductors, Pipe—
American Steel Roofing Co.
Berger Bros.
Cambridge Roofing Co.
Garry Iron Roofing Co.

Cone Pulleys, Friction—See Pulleys, Friction Cone.

Confectioners' Hatchets—See Hatchets, Confectioners'.

Connecting Rods—See Rods, Connecting.

Constructing Engineers—See Engineers, Constructing.

Converters, Bessemer—
Mackintosh, Hemphill & Co.
New Castle Engineering Works.
W. B. Pollock & Co.
Wm. Tod & Co.

Conveying Machinery—
Bradford Mill Co.
Brown Hoisting & Conveying Machine Co.
Jeffrey Mfg. Co.
Link Belt Engineering Co.
R. Poole & Son Co.
Trenton Iron Co.

Cook Stoves—See Stoves, Cook.

Coolers, Milk and Aerator—
Champion Milk Cooler Co.

Coolers, Water—
Sidney Shepard & Co.

Cooling Towers—
H. R. Worthington.

Coopers' Tools—
L. & I. J. White Co.

Coops, Poultry—
Fred. J. Meyers Mfg. Co.

Copper—
American Metal Co.
Ansonia Brass & Copper Co.
Clendenin Bros.
John Davol & Sons.
W. S. Fearing.
Hendricks Bros.

Copper Bars—
Ansonia Brass & Copper Co.
Bridgeport Brass Co.

Copper, Braziers'—
Hendricks Bros.

Copper Boilers, Bottoms, Castings, Forgings, Furnaces, Hammers, Pipe, Rods, Sheathing, Shells, Tubing, Ware, Wire—See *Boilers, Bottoms, Castings, Forgings, Furnaces, Hammers, Pipe, Rods, Sheathing, Shells, Tubing, Ware, Wire.*

Copper, Bolt—
Ansonia Brass & Copper Co.
Bridgeport Brass Co.
Clendenin Bros.
Hendricks Bros.
U. T. Hungerford.
Randolph & Clowes.
Scovill Mfg. Co.

Copper, Commutator Brush—
Ansonia Brass & Copper Co.

Copper, Cornice—
Randolph & Clowes.

Copper, Roll and Sheet—
Ansonia Brass & Copper Co.
Bridgeport Brass Co.
Clendenin Bros.
U. T. Hungerford.
Randolph & Clowes.
Scovill Mfg. Co.

Coppering—
William N. Merriam.

Coppers, Soldering—
Ansonia Brass & Copper Co.
Bridgeport Brass Co.
Clendenin Bros.
Covert Mfg. Co.
Peck, Stow & Wilcox Co.
Union Hardware Co.

Copying Presses—See *Presses, Copying.*

Cord Adjusters, Electric—See *Electric Light Fittings.*

Cord, Electric—
Ossawan Mills Co.
Samson Cordage Works.

Cord Grips—See *Grips, Cord and Line.*

Cord, Picture—
Ossawan Mills Co.
Turner & Seymour Mfg. Co.

Cord, Sash—
Ossawan Mills Co.
Samson Cordage Works.
Silver Lake Co.

Cord, Shade and Ventilator—
Ossawan Mills Co.
Samson Cordage Works.
Silver Lake Co.

Cord, Signal—
Samson Cordage Works.
Silver Lake Co.

Cord, Wire, Picture—
Andrew B. Hendryx Co.
Ossawan Mills Co.
Wire Goods Co.

Cord, Wire, Sash—
Ossawan Mills Co.

Cordage Machinery—
W. C. Boone Mfg. Co.

Cords, Hammock—
I. E. Palmer.

Core Compound—
S. Obermayer Co.

Core Ovens—See *Ovens, Core.*

Cork Cutters, Presses, Pullers, Screws—See *Cutters, Presses, Pullers, Screws.*

Corn Cribs, Portable—See *Cribs, Corn, Portable.*

Corn Cutters, Hooks, Knives, Mills, Planters, Poppers, Shellers—See *Cutters, Hooks, Knives, Mills, Planters, Poppers, Shellers.*

Corner Irons—See *Irons, Corner and Brace.*

Corners, Box—
Cary Mfg. Co.

THE IRON AGE INDEX. 35

Cornice Copper—See *Copper, Cornice.*

Cornice, Galvanized Iron—
Garry Iron Roofing Co.

Corrugated Iron—
American Steel Roofing Co.
Berlin Iron Bridge Co.
Cincinnati Corrugating Co.
Garry Iron Roofing Co.
Kansas City Metal Roofing & Corrugating Co.
Moesley Iron Bridge & Roof Co.
Railway Supply Co.
Shiffler Bridge Co.
Youngstown Iron & Steel-Roofing Co.

Corrugating Machinery, Sheet—See *Sheet Corrugating Machinery.*

Corset Machinery—
A. L. Adams.

Corset Steel—See *Steel, Corset.*

Cotter Drills—See *Drills, Cotter.*

Cotters and Keys, Spring—
M. S. Brooks & Son.
E. Jenckes Mfg. Co.
Standard Tool Co.
Wire Goods Co.

Cotton Bale Snips—See *Snips, Cotton Bale.*

Cotton Hooks, Hose, Scales, Waste—See *Hooks, Hose, Scales, Waste.*

Counters, Revolution—
Ashcroft Mfg. Co

Counter Borers, Scales, Supports—See *Borers, Scales, Supports.*

Countershafts—
Builders' Iron Foundry.
Geo. V. Cresson Co.
Deming Co.
Dodge Mfg. Co.
W. & B. Douglas.
Mossberg & Granville Mfg. Co.
F. E. Myers & Bros.
B. F. Sturtevant Co.
Wiley & Russell Mfg. Co.

Countersinks—
Billings & Spencer Co.
Buck Bros.
Butterfield & Co.
Goodell Bros. Co.
H. H. Mayhew Co.
Stanley Rule & Level Co.
J. Stevens Arms & Tool Co.
Tuck Mfg. Co.
Wiley & Russell Mfg. Co.

Countersink Bits—See *Bits, Countersink.*

Countersinking Radial Machines—
Detrick & Harvey Machine Co.

Counting Machines—
W. N. Durant.
Pratt & Whitney Co.
C. H. Root.

Coupling Bolts—See *Bolts, Special.*

Couplings, Bell Cord—
Samson Cordage Works.
Silver Lake Co.
Stowell Mfg. & Foundry Co.

Couplings, Belt—
Samson Cordage Works.

Couplings, Flange—
Geo. V. Cresson Co.
Dodge Mfg. Co.
Fairmount Machine Co.

Couplings, Friction Clutch—
Geo. V. Cresson Co.
Dodge Mfg. Co.

Couplings, Hose—See *Hose Attachments.*

Couplings, Joint—
Boston Gear Works.

Couplings, Pump Rod—
Barnes Mfg. Co.

Couplings, Universal Joint—
Geo. V. Cresson Co.

Covers, Dish, Wire—See *Household Articles, Wire*

Covers, Barrel—
Columbus Wire & Iron Works.
Fred. J. Moyers Mfg. Co.
Wire Goods Co.
Wright & Colton Wire Cloth Co.

Covers, Pot—
Sidney Shepard & Co.

Covers, Truck Wheel, Rubber—
New York Belting & Packing Co.

Cow Bells—See *Bells, Cow.*

Crabs, Manhole—
J. T. Ryerson & Son.

Crackers, Nut—
Acme Shear Co.
Knapp & Cowles Mfg. Co.
Peck, Stow & Wilcox Co.
Reading Hardware Co.
Wm. Rogers Mfg. Co.
Turner & Seymour Mfg. Co.
Upson & Hart Co.
Wallace Bros.

Cradles, Grain—
Iowa Farming Tool Co.

Crane Chain—See *Chain, Crane, Cable, &c.*

Cranes, Hand Power—
Byram & Co.
Moore Mfg. Co.

Cranes, Hand Traveling—
Maris Bros.
Moore Mfg. Co.
Wm. Sellers & Co.

Cranes, Hydraulic—
Frank-Kneeland Machine Co.
Morgan Construction Co.

Cranes, Jib—
Maris Bros.
Craig Ridgway & Son.
Wm. Sellers & Co.

Cranes, Steam-Hydraulic—
Craig Ridgway & Son.

Cranes, Traveling, Power—
Alfred Box & Co.
Brown Hoisting & Conveying Machine Co.
Thomas Carlin's Sons.
Edwin Harrington, Son & Co.
Maris Bros.
Moore Mfg. Co.
Morgan Construction Co.
Pawling & Harnischfeger.
Reading Crane & Hoist Works.
Wm. Sellers & Co.
Craig Ridgway & Son.
J. G. Speidel.
R. D. Wood & Co.

Crank Pin Machines—
Pedrick & Ayer Co.

Crank Pins, Shafts—See *Pins, Shafts.*

Cranks, Bell—
Norwalk Lock Co.
W. R. Ostrander & Co.
Peck, Stow & Wilcox Co.
Reading Hardware Co.

Creasers, Blacksmiths'—
Heller Bros.

Cribs, Corn, Portable—
W. J. Adam.

Crimping Machines—
E. W. Bliss Co.
Peck, Stow & Wilcox Co.

Crimping Rolls—See *Rolls, Crimping.*

Crooks, Shepherd's—
Iowa Farming Tool Co.

Crosscut Saws—See *Saws, Mill, Mulay, Crosscut, &c.*

Crucible Cast Steel—See *Steel, Crucible Cast.*

Crucible Furnaces—See *Furnaces, Crucible.*

Crucibles—
Jos. Dixon Crucible Co.

Crushers, Ore and Rock—
E. P. Allis Co.
Robinson-Rea Mfg. Co.
Totten & Hogg Iron & Steel Foundry Co.

Crushing Rolls—See *Rolls, Crushing.*

Cube Head Bolts—See *Bolts, Special.*

Cultivators—
Iowa Farming Tool Co.
Syracuse Chilled Plow Co.

Cupboard Bolts, Catches, Turns—
See *Bolts, Catches, Turns.*

Cup Hooks—See *Hooks, Cup, Shoulder.*

Cupola Linings—
M. D. Valentine & Bro. Co.

Cupolas—
Byram & Co.
Thos. Carlin's Sons.
Wm. Sellers & Co.
Whiting Foundry Equipment Co.

Cups, Aluminum—
Scovill Mfg. Co.

Cups, Oil—
Lunkenheimer Co.
McNab & Harlin Mfg. Co.

Cups, Pocket—
Scovill Mfg. Co.

Cups, Shaving, Silver Plated—
Wm. Rogers Mfg. Co.
Wallace Bros.

Cups, Wax Melting—
Logan & Strobridge Iron Co.

Curbs, Well—
W. & B. Douglas.

Curled Hair—See *Hair, Curled.*

Curling Irons—See *Irons, Curling.*

Curry Combs—See *Combs, Curry.*

Curtain and Upholstery Fixtures—
M. S. Brooks & Son.
Ossawan Mills Co.
Turner & Seymour Mfg. Co.
Wire Goods Co.

Curtain Straps—See *Straps, Curtain.*

Cushions, Billiard Table—
New York Belting & Packing Co.

Cuspidors—
Bridgeport Brass Co.

Cutlery, Pocket—
John Chatillon & Sons.

Cutlery, Silver Plated.
Northampton Cutlery Co.
Wallace Bros.

Cutlery, Table—
Goodell Co.
Nichols Bros.
Northampton Cutlery Co.
Wm. Rogers Mfg. Co.
Upson & Hart Co.

Cutlery, Steel—See *Steel Cutlery.*

Cut Nail Machines—See *Nail Machines, Cut.*

Cut Nails—See *Nails, Cut.*

Cut-Offs—
American Steel Roofing Co.
Berger Bros.
Garry Iron Roofing Co.

Cutter Grinders—See *Grinders, Cutter.*

Cutters, Automatic Pinion—See *Pinion Cutters, Automatic.*

Cutters, Automatic Rack—
Gould & Eberhardt.

Cutters, Axle—
Butterfield & Co.

Cutters, Bar—
Buffalo Forge Co.

Cutters, Board—
Chambers Bros. Co.

Cutters, Boiler Tube—
D. Saunders' Sons.

Cutters, Bolt—
Davis & Egan Machine Tool Co.
Detrick & Harvey Machine Co.
Howard Iron Works.
National Machinery Co.
Pratt & Whitney Co.
Wm. Sellers & Co.
Wells Bros. & Co.

Cutters, Cigar—
Bradley & Hubbard Mfg. Co.
Erie Specialty Co.

Cutters, Coal—See *Coal Cutters.*

Cutters, Cork—
Simonds Mfg. Co.

Cutters, Corn—
Dain Mfg. Co.

Cutters, Feed and Ensilage—
Long & Allstatter Co.
Silver Mfg. Co.

Cutters, Gear—
Boston Gear Works.
Brown & Sharpe Mfg. Co.
Dwight Slate Machine Co.
Garvin Machine Co.
Gleason Tool Co.
Gould & Eberhardt.
Pratt & Whitney Co.
Wm. Sellers & Co.
Superior Machine Co.
D. E. Whiton Machine Co.

Cutters, Gear—See *Gear Cutters.*

Cutters, Glass—
W. L. Barrett.
H. H. Mayhew Co.
Millers Falls Co.
S. G. Monce.

Cutters, Glass Tube—
S. G. Monce.

Cutters, Gummer—
Butterfield & Co.

Cutters, Meat and Vegetable—
Athol Machine Co.
Colebrookdale Iron Co.
Enterprise Mfg. Co.
North Bros. Mfg. Co.

Peck, Stow & Wilcox Co.
Russell & Erwin Mfg. Co.
Silver Mfg. Co.
O. D. Woodruff.

Cutters, Milling—
Brown & Sharpe Mfg. Co.
Cleveland Twist Drill Co.
Morse Twist Drill & Machine Co.
Pratt & Whitney Co.
Standard Tool Co.
L. S. Starrett Co.

Cutters, Pipe—
Armstrong Mfg. Co.
Belden Machine Co.
Bignall & Keeler Mfg. Co.
Curtis & Curtis.
National Machine Co.
D. Saunders' Sons.
J. H. Williams & Co.

Cutters, Rod—
Belden Machine Co.
Buffalo Forge Co.

Cutters, Root—
Lane Bros.
R. W. Whitehurst & Co.

Cutters, Slaw—
Henry Disston & Sons.
Enterprise Mfg. Co.
National Saw Co.

Cutters, Tobacco—
Erie Specialty Co.
Logan & Strobridge Iron Co.
National Specialty Mfg. Co.
North Bros. Mfg. Co.
Peck, Stow & Wilcox Co.
Reading Hardware Co.

Cutters, Tobacco and Root—
Enterprise Mfg. Co.

Cutters, Washer—
Knapp & Cowles Mfg. Co.

Cutters, Wire—
Billings & Spencer Co.
J. M. King & Co.
H K. Porter.

Cutters and Lighters, Cigar—
Erie Specialty Co.

THE IRON AGE INDEX.

Cutting and Straightening Machines, Wire—See *Straightening and Cutting Machines, Wire.*

Cutting Attachments, Rack—
Cincinnati Milling Machine Co.

Cutting Dies, Nippers—See *Dies, Nippers.*

Cutting Machines—
Automatic Machine Co.

Cutting Machines, Rack—
Dwight Slate Machine Co.

Cutting Machines, Wire—
E. J. Manville Machine Co.

Cutting-Off Machines—
Hurlbut Rogers Machine Co.
Niles Tool Works Co.

Cutting-Off Machines, Cold Saw—
Newton Machine Tool Co.

Cutting-Off Tools—
Dwight Slate Machine Co.

Cycle Hangers—See *Hangers, Cycle.*

Cycle Wagons—See *Wagons, Cycle.*

Cyclometers—
Bridgeport Gun Implement Co.
Buffalo Meter Co.

Cylinder Boring and Facing Machines—
William Sellers & Co.

Cylinder Boring Bars, Locomotive—See *Boring Bars, Locomotive Cylinder.*

Cylinder Boring Machines—See *Boring Machines, Cylinder.*

Cylinders, Pump—See *Well Supplies and Tools.*

Cylinders, Pump—
Barnes Mfg. Co.

Cylinders, Steel—
Avery Stamping Co.
National Tube Works Co.

Dairy Supplies—
Moseley & Stoddard Mfg. Co.

Damper Clips and Regulators—See *Clips, Regulators.*

Dampers, Grate—
Southern Queen Mfg. Co.

Dampers, Pipe—
Arcade Mfg. Co.
Griswold Mfg. Co.
Peck, Stow & Wilcox Co.
Sidney Shepard & Co.
Stover Mfg. Co.
Troy Nickel Works.
Van Wagoner & Williams Hardware Co.
A. C. Williams.

Dandy Rolls—See *Rolls, Dandy.*

Dashes and Fenders—
McKinnon Dash & Hardware Co.

Daubers, Shoe—
Palmer Hardware Mfg. Co.

Dead Eyes—See *Eyes, Dead, Bull's, &c.*

Deckhanger Bolts—See *Bolts, Special.*

Deck Blocks, Lights, Plates, Pumps—See *Blocks, Lights, Plates, Pumps.*

Dehorning Saws—See *Saws, Dehorning.*

Dental Wheels—See *Wheels, Dental.*

Depth Gauges—See *Gauges, Depth.*

Derricks—
Thos. Carlin's Sons.

Desk Slides—See *Slides, Desk.*

Desk Specialties, Silver Plated (Inkstands, Calendars, Pen Wipers, Paper Files)—
Wm. Rogers Mfg. Co.

Diamond Tools—
Tanite Co.

Diaphragm Pumps—See *Pumps, Diaphragm*.

Dictionary Holders — See *Holders, Dictionary*.

Die Blocks—
Denman & Davis.
Frankfort Steel Co.
Wm. M. McFarland.

Die Holders, Plates—See *Holders, Plates*.

Die Chamfering Machines—
Hartford Machine Screw Co.

Die Heads, *Screw Cutting—*
Geometric Drill Co.

Die Sinkers—
Pratt & Whitney Co.
J. H. Williams & Co.

Dies and Stamps, Steel—See *Stamps and Dies, Steel*.

Dies and Taps—See *Stocks, Taps and Dies*.

Dies, *Adjustable Expanding—*
D. Saunders' Sons.
E. F. Reece Co.

Dies, *Chilled Cast Wire—*
Wm. McFarland.

Dies, *Cutting—*
Hoggson & Pettis Mfg. Co.
John Loyd.
L. & I. J. White Co.

Dies, *Sheet Metal—*
C. E. Coe.

Dies, *Solid Pipe—*
D. Saunders' Sons.

Dies, *Stamping—*
John Adt & Son.
Avery Stamping Co.
E. W. Bliss Co.
Erdle & Schenck.
I P. Richards.

Rudolphi & Krummel Machine Works.
J. H. Williams & Co.
Stiles & Fladd Press Co.
Vieillard & Osswald.
Waterbury Machine Co.

Dies, *Welding—*
P. F. Burke.

Differential Pulley Blocks — See *Blocks, Differential Pulley*.

Diggers, *Post Hole—*
Henry Disston & Sons.
Indiana Wire Fence Co.
Ludlow-Saylor Wire Co.
J. E. Porter Co.

Dimension Gauges—See *Gauges, Dimension*.

Dinner Pails—See *Pails, Dinner*.

Disc Notching Machines—See *Notching Machines, Armature Disc*.

Discs, *Armature—*
Avery Stamping Co.

Discs, *Harrow—*
Cambria Iron Co.
Singer, Nimick & Co.

Discs, Rubber—See *Washers and Discs, Rubber*.

Discs, *Valve—*
Jenkins Bros.

Dish Drainers—See *Drainers, Kitchen Articles*.

Dishes, *Soap—*
Reading Hardware Co.
A. C. Williams.

Ditching Shovels—See *Shovels, Tiling or Ditching*.

Ditching Tools—
St. Louis Shovel Co.

Dividers, Compasses, &c.—See *Compasses Dividers &c.*

Dividing Heads—See *Heads, Dividing, Indexing.*

Dock Spikes—See *Spikes, Dock, Wharf, &c.*

Dog Calls and Chain—See *Calls, Chain.*

Dog Furnishings—
Chapman Mfg. Co.
Oneida Community.
Smith & Egge Mfg. Co.
Turner & Seymour Mfg. Co.
Union Hardware Co.

Dogs, Clamp—
Billings & Spencer Co.

Dogs, Lathe—
Billings & Spencer Co.
Wm. G. Le Count.
Mark Mfg. Co.
W. T. Welch Mfg. Co.
J. H. Williams & Co.

Dogs, Saw Mill—
E. C. Atkins & Co.

Dogs, Timber—
American Bolt Co.

Door Bell Handles—See *Handles, Door Bell.*

Door Bells, Bolts, Catches, Hangers, Keys—See *Bells, Bolts, Catches, Hangers, Keys.*

Doors, Ash Pit—See *Iron Work, Builders'.*

Doors, Automatic Hatch—
Morse, Williams & Co.

Doors, Freight Car—
Q & C Co.

Doors, Screen—
Scheeler's Sons.

Doors and Shutters, Iron and Steel—
American Steel Roofing Co.
E. T. Barnum.
Berlin Iron Bridge Co.
Champion Iron Co.
Coburn Trolley Track Mfg. Co.
Garry Iron Roofing Co.

Kansas City Metal Roofing & Corrugating Co.
Mast, Foos & Co.
Fred. J. Meyers Mfg. Co.

Dormant Scales—See *Scales, Dormant.*

Double Pointed Tacks—See *Tacks, Double Pointed.*

Doublers, Sheet Mill—
Wais & Roos Punch & Shear Co.

Dowel Pins and Screws—See *Pins and Screws, Dowel.*

Dowels, Pattern Makers'—
New Britain Hardware Mfg. Co.

Drag Saws—See *Saws, Mill, Mulay, &c.*

Drainers, Barrel—
National Specialty Mfg. Co.

Drainers, Dish—
Fred. J. Meyers Mfg. Co.

Drain Spades and Cleavers—
St. Louis Shovel Co.

Draw Benches—See *Benches, Draw, Benches, Wire Draw.*

Drawer Handles, Knobs, Pulls—See *Handles, Knobs, Pulls.*

Drawing Knives, Presses—See *Knives, Presses.*

Drawing Machinery, Wire—
Morgan Construction Co.
Mossberg & Granville Mfg. Co.
Turner, Vaughn & Taylor Co.
Waterbury Machine Co.

Dredges—
Merrill Stevens Engineering Co.
Vulcan Iron Works.

Dressers, Emery Wheel—
Builders' Iron Foundry.
Diamond Machine Co.
W. & E. T. Fitch Co.
Hampden Corundum Wheel Co.
New Britain Hardware Mfg. Co.
Northampton Emery Wheel Co.
Standard Tool Co.

Dressing, Belt—See *Belt Dressing*.

Dried Fruit Augers—See *Augers, Dried Fruit*.

Drill and Clamp, Combined—See *Clamp and Drill, Combined*.

Drill, Anvil and Vise—See *Vise, Drill and Anvil*.

Drill Cases, Chucks, Gauges, Grinders—See *Cases, Chucks, Gauges, Grinders*.

Drill Grinding Machines, Twist—
Standard Tool Co.

Drill Rods, Steel—See *Rods, Steel Drill*.

Drill Sockets—See *Sockets, Drill*.

Drills—See *Taps and Drills*.

Drills, Automatic—
Goodell Bros. Co.

Drills, Bench—
George Burnham Co.
E. C. Stearns & Co.

Drills, Bicycle—
Bickford Drill & Tool Co.
Pratt & Whitney Co.

Drills, Bit Stock—
Cleveland Twist Drill Co.
New Process Twist Drill Co.

Drills, Blacksmith—
Buffalo Forge Co.
Champion Blower & Forge Co.
Peck, Stow & Wilcox Co.
Wells Bros. & Co.

Drills, Boiler Shell—
Thos. H. Dallett & Co.

Drills, Breast—
John S. Fray & Co.
Goodell Bros. Co.
Millers Falls Co.
Peck, Stow & Wilcox Co.
Seymour Smith & Son.

Drills, Clamp—
Geo. Burnham Co.

Drills, Combination Center—
J. T. Slocomb & Co.

Drills, Cotter—
Wm. Sellers & Co.

Drills, Fluted—
Cleveland Twist Drill Co.
Wiley & Russell Mfg. Co.

Drills, Geometric—
Geometric Drill Co.

Drills, Hand—
Thos. H. Dallett & Co.
Goodell Bros. Co.
Millers Falls Co.
Tower & Lyon.

Drills, Hollow—
Cleveland Twist Drill Co.
Morse Twist Drill & Machine Co.

Drills, Multiple—
Bickford Drill & Tool Co.
Newton Machine Tool Works.
Pratt & Whitney Co.
Prentice Bros.
Wm. Sellers & Co.

Drills, Portable—
Thos. H. Dallett & Co.
Stow Mfg. Co.

Drills, Rail—
Geo. Burnham Co.
Millers Falls Co.
Wm. Sellers & Co.
Stow Mfg. Co.

Drills, Ratchet—
Bignall & Keeler Mfg. Co.
Billings & Spencer Co.
Jos. F. McCoy Co.
Millers Falls Co.
Pratt & Whitney Co.

Drills, Rock—
Ingersoll-Sergeant Drill Co.
Jeffrey Mfg. Co.
Rand Drill Co.

Drills, Sensitive—
Geo. Burnham Co.
D'Amour & Littledale.
Davis & Egan Machine Tool Co.
Dwight Slate Machine Co.
Woodward & Rogers.

Drills, Suspension—
Cleveland Punch & Shear Works.

Drills, Tap—
Butterfield & Co.

Drills, Tire—
Pleuger & Henger Mfg. Co.

Drills, Turret—
A. D. Quint.

Drills, Twist—
Cleveland Twist Drill Co.
H. H. Mayhew Co.
Morse Twist Drill & Machine Co.
New Process Twist Drill Co.
J. T. Slocomb & Co.
Standard Tool Co.
Strange Forged Drill & Tool Co.

Drills, Universal—
Bickford Drill & Tool Co.
Detrick & Harvey Machine Co.
Wm. Sellers & Co.

Drilling and Milling Machines, Butt—See *Milling and Drilling Machines*.

Drilling Machines—
Ames Mfg. Co.
W. F. & John Barnes Co.
Baush & Harris Machine Tool Co.
Bement, Miles & Co.
Bickford Drill Co.
Geo. Burnham Co.
T. H. Dallett & Co.
D'Amour & Littledale.
Davis & Egan Machine Tool Co.
Diamond Drill & Machine Co.
Dreses, Mueller & Co.
Dwight Slate Machine Co.
Erdle & Schenck.
Garvin Machine Co.
Gould & Eberhardt.
Hamilton Machine Tool Co.
E. Harrington, Son & Co.
Mossberg & Granville Mfg. Co.
New Haven Mfg. Co.
Newton Machine Tool Co.
Niles Tool Works Co.
Norton & Jones Machine Tool Works.
Pawling & Harnischfeger.
Pond Machine Tool Co.
Pratt & Whitney Co.
Prentice Bros.
Prentiss Tool & Supply Co.
A. D. Quint.
D. Saunders' Sons.
Sebastian Lathe Co.
Wm. Sellers & Co.
Silver Mfg. Co.
Stover Novelty Works.
T. F. Welch Mfg. Co.
Wiley & Russell Mfg. Co.
Woodward & Rogers.

Drilling Machines, *Bicycle Rim*—
Pratt & Whitney Co.

Drilling Machines, *Gun Barrel*—
Pratt & Whitney Co.

Drilling and Tapping Machines—
Lodge & Shipley Machine Tool Co.
Woodward & Rogers.

Drinking Fountains—See *Fountains, Drinking*.

Drink Shakers—See *Shakers, Drink*.

Dripping Pans—See *Pans, Dripping*.

Drive Hooks, Punches, Screws—See *Hooks, Punches, Screws*.

Drivers, *Pile*—
Thos. Carlin's Sons.
Vulcan Iron Works.

Drivers, *Screw*—
Bemis & Call Hardware & Tool Co.
Billings & Spencer Co.
Bridgeport Mfg. Co.
Bridgeport Gun Implement Co.
R. H. Brown & Co.
Buck Bros.
Henry Disston & Sons.
Goodell Bros. Co.
Knapp & Cowles Mfg. Co.
H. H. Mayhew Co.

New England Specialty Co.
Peck, Stow & Wilcox Co.
Snell Mfg. Co.
Stanley Rule & Level Co.
Tower & Lyon.
Tuck Mfg. Co.

Drivers, Screw, Automatic—
Goodell Bros. Co.
Millers Falls Co.
X Ray Screw Driver Co.

Drivers, Screw, Ratchet—
Gay & Parsons.
Millers Falls Co.

Drivers, Screw, Spiral—
Decatur Coffin Co.

Drivers, Screw, and Holder—
Tower & Lyon.

Drivers, Staple—
I. S. Spencer's Sons.

Drop Forgings—See *Forgings, Drop.*

Drop Hammers, Presses, Tests—
See *Hammers, Presses, Tests.*

Drug Mills—See *Mills, Drug, Bone, Corn, &c.*

Drums, Botanizing—
Sidney Shepard & Co.

Dryers, Clothes—
Fairfield Lawn Swing Co.
Hill Dryer Co.

Dryers, Grain—
Pawling & Harnischfeger.

Dumb Bells, Waiters—See *Bells, Waiters.*

Dumb Waiter Pulleys—See *Pulleys, Dumb Waiter.*

Dumb Waiters—
Morse, Williams & Co.
J. G. Speidel.
Variety Machine Co.

Dump Cars and Carts—See *Cars and Carts, Dump.*

Dumping Buckets, Self—See *Buckets, Self Dumping.*

Dust Collectors—See *Collectors, Dust.*

Dust Pans—See *Pans, Dust.*

Dusters—See *Brushes, Whitewash, Horse, &c.*

Dusters, Turkey, Counter, &c.—
Osborn Mfg. Co.

Dynamos—
American Engine Co.
Chicago Flexible Shaft Co.
Thos. H. Dallett & Co.
General Electric Co.
Westinghouse Electric & Mfg. Co.

Dynamos, Electro Plating—
Eddy Electric Mfg. Co.
Hanson & Van Winkle Co.
Zucker & Levett & Loeb Co.

Ears, Brass Pail—
Bridgeport Brass Co.
Waterbury Brass Co.

Ears, Pail and Tub—
E. H. Titchener & Co.

Easels, Wire—See *Household Articles, Wire.*

Eave Trough Hangers—See *Hangers, Eave Trough.*

Eave Troughs and Gutters—
American Steel Roofing Co.
Berger Bros.
Cambridge Roofing Co.
Garry Iron Roofing Co.

Edgers, Turf—
Ely Hoe & Fork Co.
Iowa Farming Tool Co.
Knapp & Cowles Mfg. Co.

Edges, Straight—
Athol Machine Co.
Henry Disston & Sons.
L. S. Starrett Co.

Edges, Straight—See *Straight Edges.*

Edging Machines—
Seneca Falls Mfg. Co.

Egg Beaters and Poachers—See *Beaters and Poachers.*

Egg Boilers, Wire—See *Kitchen Articles, Wire.*

8 and S Hooks—See *Hooks, 8 and S.*

Ejectors—
McNab & Harlin Mfg. Co.

Elbow Catches—See *Catches, Elbow.*

Elbows, Pipe—
Berger Bros.
Sidney Shepard & Co.

Elbows and Shoes, Conductor—
American Steel Roofing Co.
Garry Iron Roofing Co.
Fred. J. Meyers Mfg. Co.

Electrical Alarms—See *Alarms, Electrical.*

Electrical Trolley Materials—See *Trolley Materials, Electrical.*

Electric Batteries, Bells, Cord, Pushes—See *Batteries, Bells, Cord, Pushes.*

Electric Bells and Supplies.
W. R. Ostrander & Co.

Electric Fixtures—See *Gas and Electric Fixtures.*

Electric Lamps, Bicycle—
Ohio Electric Works.

Electric Light Fittings (*Socket Bushings, Cord Adjusters, Socket Hooks, Lamp Attachments for Gas Fixtures*)—
W. R. Ostrander & Co.

Electric Lights, Necktie—
Ohio Electric Works.

Electric Motors, Transformers—See *Motors, Transformers.*

Electric Wire and Cables—See *Wire and Cables, Electric.*

Electric Woods—
Union Hardware Co.

Electro Chemicals—See *Chemicals, Electro.*

Electro Plating—See *Plating, Electro.*

Electro Plating Brushes, Dynamos—See *Brushes, Dynamos.*

Electro Plating Supplies—
Hanson & Van Winkle Co.
Zucker & Levett & Loeb Co.

Elevating Machinery—
Eastern Machinery Co.
F. S. Hutchinson Co.
Jeffrey Mfg. Co.
Lane & Bodley Co.
Link-Belt Engineering Co.
Roberts Mfg. Co.
Storm Mfg. Co.
Whiting Foundry & Equipment Co.

Elevator Bolts, Buckets, Cars, Guards, &c.—See *Bolts, Buckets, Cars, Guards.*

Elevator Enclosures—
E. T. Barnum.
Edward Darby & Sons.
Ludlow-Saylor Wire Co.
Fred. J. Meyers Mfg. Co.
Scheeler's Sons.

Elevators, Belt—
Morse, Williams & Co.

Elevators, Freight—
Fairmount Machine Co.
Morse, Williams & Co.
Springfield Elevator & Pump Co.
Variety Machine Co.

Elevators, Grain—
R. Poole & Son Co.

Elevators, Hand Power—
F. S. Hutchinson Co.
Morse, Williams & Co.
J. G. Speidel.
Storm Mfg. Co.

THE IRON AGE INDEX.

Elevators, Passenger—
Morse, Williams & Co.
Springfield Elevator & Pump Co.
Variety Machine Co.

Embossed Brass—See *Brass*.

Emery—
Tanite Co.

Emery Cloth—See *Cloth*.

Emery Grinding Pans, Stones, Wheel Dressers, Wheels — See *Dressers, Pans, Stones, Wheels*.

Enameling—
Avery Stamping Co.

Enameling Ovens, Stoves — See *Ovens, Stoves*.

Enclosures, Elevator—See *Elevators*.

End Mills—See *Mills*.

Engineers, Constructing—
Julian Kennedy.
Alex. Laughlin & Co.
G. W. McClure & Son.
Miller Bros. & Co.
New Castle Engineering Works.
S. R. Smythe Co.
Wm. Swindell & Bro.
Wellman-Seaver Engineering Co.

Engineers, Mechanical—
Henry Aiken.
Francis H. Richards.

Engineers, Metallurgical—
Huntington & Wyatt.
Julian Kennedy.
D. R. Lean & Co.
Wellman-Seaver Engineering Co.

Engine Bells, Governors, Indicators, Lathes—See *Bells, Governors, Indicators, Lathes*.

Engines, Blowing—
E. P. Allis Co.
Mackintosh, Hemphill & Co.
Philadelphia Engineering Works.
William Tod & Co.

Engines, Fire—
Deming Co.
W. & B. Douglas.

Engines, Gas and Gasoline—
J. I. Case Threshing Machine Co
Chicago Flexible Shaft Co.
Lambert Gas Engine Co.
New Era Iron Works.
J. J. Norman Co.
Otto Gas Engine Works.
Springfield Gas Engine Co.
Weber Gas & Gasoline Engine Co.

Engines, Hoisting—
E. P. Allis Co.
Brown Hoisting & Conveying Machine Co.
Lidgerwood Mfg. Co.
Pennsylvania Machine Co.

Engines, Logging—
Thos. Carlin's Sons.

Engines, Pumping—
E. P. Allis Co.
Pennsylvania Machine Co.
Henry R. Worthington.

Engines, Rolling Mill—
E. P. Allis Co.
Mackintosh, Hemphill & Co.
Philadelphia Engineering Works.
Wm. Tod & Co.
Totten & Hogg Iron & Steel Foundry Co.

Engines, Rotary—
Morse, Williams & Co

Engines, Steam—
E. P. Allis Co.
American Blower Co.
American Engine Co.
Buffalo Forge Co.
Thos. Carlin's Sons.
Howard & Morse.
Lane & Bodley Co.
Leechburg Foundry & Machine Co.
Jas. Leffel & Co.
C. O. Lucas & Co.

Mackintosh, Hemphill & Co.
F. R. Patch Mfg. Co.
Pawling & Harnischfeger.
Pennsylvania Machine Co.
Philadelphia Engineering Works.
Silver Mfg. Co.
B. F. Sturtevant Co.
Wm. Tod & Co.
Robt. Wetherill & Co.

Engravers' or Sign Brass—See *Brass, Sign.*

Engraving Lathes, Roll—See *Lathes, Roll Engraving.*

Engraving, Photo and Wood—
A. Mugford.

Ensilage and Feed Cutters—See *Cutters, Feed.*

Escapes, Fire—
E. T. Barnum.
Champion Iron Co.
Mast, Foos & Co.
Stewart Iron Works.

Escutcheon Pins—See *Pins.*

Escutcheons—
Norwalk Lock Co.
Peck, Stow & Wilcox Co.
Reading Hardware Co.
Russell & Erwin Mfg. Co.
Taylor & Boggis Foundry Co.

Exercisers—
Caldwell Mfg. Co.

Expanders, Tube—
Richard Dudgeon.
Jos. F. McCoy Co.
Watson-Stillman Co.

Expanding Dies, Adjustable—See *Dies.*

Expansion Augers, Bits, Bolts—See *Augers, Bits, Bolts.*

Express Wagons, Children's—See *Wagons.*

Extension Bit Holders, Braces, Gates—See *Holders, Braces, Gates.*

Extinguishers, Fire—
Randolph & Clowes.

Extractors, Juice—
Colebrookdale Iron Co.
Enterprise Mfg. Co.
Logan & Strobridge Iron Co.

Extractors, Spoke—
Butts & Ordway.

Eyelets, Metallic—
Waterbury Brass Co.

Eye Bolts—See *Bolts.*

Eyes, Cock—
Covert Mfg. Co.
Peck, Stow & Wilcox Co.

Eyes, Dead, Bull's, &c.—
Boston & Lockport Block Co.

Face Plate Jaws—See *Jaws, Face Plate.*

Facings, Foundry—
Jos. Dixon Crucible Co.

Family Grindstones, Scales— See *Grindstones, Scales.*

Fancy Chains—See *Chains, Wagon and Fancy.*

Fan Motors, Electric—See *Motors, Electric Fan.*

Fans—
American Blower Co.
Buffalo Forge Co.
Champion Blower & Forge Co.
Howard & Morse.
B. F. Sturtevant Co.

Fans, Fly—
Bridgeport Brass Co.

Farm Sleds—See *Sleds, Farm.*

Fasteners, Bed—
Pleuger & Henger Mfg. Co.
Quincy Hardware Mfg. Co.
Reading Hardware Co.
Russell & Erwin Mfg. Co.

Fasteners, Belt—
Billings & Spencer Co.
Bristol Co.
Samson Steel Belt Hook Co.
W. O. Talcott.

Fasteners, Blind—
Stanley Works.
W. & J. Tiebout.

Fasteners, Box—
Cary Mfg. Co.

Fasteners, Casement—
Reading Hardware Co.

Fasteners, Conductor—
Berger Bros.

Fasteners, Rope—
W. & E. T. Fitch Co.

Fasteners, Sash—
Logan & Strobridge Iron Co.
Norwalk Lock Co.
Payson Mfg. Co.
Peck, Stow & Wilcox Co.
Reading Hardware Co.
Russell & Erwin Mfg. Co.

Fasteners, Shutter—
Norwalk Lock Co.

Fasteners, Storm Sash, &c.—
A. A. Loetscher.
Stanley Works.

Fasteners, Tag—
E. H. Titchener & Co.

Fasteners and Hinges, Box—See *Hinges and Fasteners, Box*.

Faucets—
Boston & Lockport Block Co.
Mason & Parker.
North Bros. Mfg. Co.
John Sommer's Son.
E. C. Stearns & Co.

Faucets, Measuring—
Colebrookdale Iron Co.
Enterprise Mfg. Co.
Lane Bros.
National Specialty Mfg. Co.

Faucets, Suction—
Enterprise Mfg. Co.

Feed and Ensilage Cutters — See *Cutters, Ensilage.*

Feed Mills, Pumps, Boiler—See *Mills, Pumps, Boiler Feed.*

Feed Water Heaters, Purifiers, Regulators—See *Heaters, Purifiers, Regulators.*

Felloe Plates—See *Plates, Felloe.*

Felloe and Turning Webs—See *Webs, Turning, Felloe, &c.*

Felting, Hair—
Baeder, Adamson & Co.

Fence Machines—
Lansing Wheelbarrow Co.

Fence Posts, Post Tops—See *Posts, Post Tops.*

Fence Wire—See *Wire, Iron and Steel, Market, Fence, Stone, &c.*

Fence and Wire Stretchers—See *Stretchers, Fence and Wire.*

Fencing, Gates, &c.—
W. J. Adam.
E. T. Barnum.
Bradley & Hubbard Mfg. Co.
Champion Iron Co.
Clinton Wire Cloth Co.
Columbus Wire & Iron Works.
Edward Darby & Sons.
Dillon-Griswold Wire Co.
Ellis & Halfenbarger.
I. L. Ellwood Mfg. Co.
Gilbert & Bennett Mfg. Co.
Holmes & Ward Bros.
Howard & Morse.
Indiana Wire Fence Co.
International Steel Post Co.
Ludlow-Saylor Wire Co.
Mast, Foos & Co.
Fred. J. Meyers Mfg. Co.
New Jersey Wire Cloth Co.
Scheeler's Sons.
Stewart Iron Works.

Fender Nails—See *Nails, Fender.*

Fenders, Carriage—
McKinnon Dash & Hardware Co.

Fenders, Fire Place—
Bradley & Hubbard Mfg. Co.
Edward Darby & Sons.
Howard & Morse.
Fred. J. Meyers Mfg. Co.
Peck, Stow & Wilcox Co.

*Fenders and Dashes—*See *Dashes and Fenders.*

*Fenders and Tips, Rubber—*See *Tips, Fenders, Rubber.*

Ferro-Aluminum—
Pittsburgh Reduction Co.

Ferro-Chrome—
Pittsburgh Reduction Co.

Ferrules—
Bridgeport Brass Co.
William S. Fearing.
Iowa Farming Tool Co.
McNab & Harlin Mfg. Co.
Scovill Mfg. Co.
Union Hardware Co.
Waterbury Brass Co.

Fertilizer Machinery—
R. Poole & Son Co.

Fertilizers—
Russia Cement Co.

Field, Garden and Mortar Hoes—
See *Hoes, Garden, Field, Mortar.*

*Fifth Wheels—*See *Wheels, Fifth.*

*Figured or Embossed Brass—*See *Brass, Embossed or Figured.*

*Figures and Letters—*See *Letters, Figures, &c.*

*File, Chisel and Awl Handles—*See *Handles, Chisel, File, Awl, &c.*

*File Cleaners—*See *Cleaners, File.*

Files, Paper—
Arcade Mfg. Co.
Bradley & Hubbard Mfg. Co.

Fred. J. Meyers Mfg. Co.
Peck, Stow & Wilcox Co.
Stover Mfg. Co.
Turner & Seymour Mfg. Co.

Files, Planer Knife—
Simonds Mfg. Co.

Files and Rasps—
Arcade File Works.
G. & H. Barnett Co.
Henry Disston & Sons.
Heller Bros.
McCaffrey File Co.
National Saw Co.
Nicholson File Co.
Stokes Bros. Mfg. Co.

*Filing Machines, Band Saw—*See *Setting and Filing Machines, Band Saw*

Fillers, Bag—
John Chatillon & Sons.

Filters, Water—
Cleveland Safety Lock Co.
Cleveland Stamping & Tool Co.

*Finials, Iron—*See *Iron, Ornamental.*

*Finishing Nails—*See *Tacks, Brads, Finishing Nails, &c.*

*Fire Brick—*See *Brick, Fire.*

*Fire Brick, Stove—*See *Stove Fire Brick.*

*Fire Brick Stoves—*See *Stoves, Fire Brick—*

Fire Buckets, Clay, Engines, Escapes, Extinguishers, Pumps—
See *Buckets, Clay, Engines, Escapes, Extinguishers, Pumps.*

*Fire Place Fenders—*See *Fenders, Fire Place.*

*Fire Proof Building Material—*See *Building Material, Fire Proof.*

*Fire Sets—*See *Shovels, Tongs, Pokers, Fire Sets, &c.*

THE IRON AGE INDEX.

Fish Baskets, Plates, Scalers, Traps—See *Baskets, Plates, Scalers, Traps.*

Fishing Reels—See *Reels, Fishing.*

Fittings, Flanged—
Kelly & Jones Co.
McNab & Harlin Mfg. Co.
R. D. Wood & Co.

Fittings, Pipe—
Humphryes Mfg. Co.
Jarecki Mfg. Co.
Kelly & Jones Co.
McNab & Harlin Mfg. Co.
R. D. Wood & Co.

Fittings, Steam—
Eastwood Wire Mfg. Co.
McNab & Harlin Mfg. Co.

Fittings, Wire Rope—
Trenton Iron Co.

Fixtures, Grindstone, Stable, Store—See *Grindstone, Stable, Store.*

Flag Pole Sockets—See *Sockets, Flag Pole.*

Flagstaff Holders—See *Holders, Flagstaff.*

Flange Couplings—See *Couplings, Flange.*

Flange Wheels, Iron—See *Wheels, Iron Flange.*

Flanges, Steel—
Latrobe Steel Co.
Jos. T. Ryerson & Son

Flanging Presses—See *Presses, Flanging.*

Flasks, Powder—
Waterbury Brass Co.

Flat Link Chains—See *Chains, Flat Link.*

Flexible Shafts—See *Shafts, Flexible.*

Floats, Copper Ball—
McNab & Harlin Mfg. Co.
Naugatuck Mfg. Co.

Flooring, Bridge—
Youngstown Iron & Steel Roofing Co.

Floor and Base Knobs—See *Knobs, Base and Floor.*

Floor Bull's Eyes—See *Bull's Eyes, Floor.*

Floors, Wire Cloth—
Howard & Morse.

Floral Designs—
Fred. J. Meyers Mfg. Co.
W. W. Shoe.

Flour Mill Machinery—
E. P. Allis Co.
R. Poole & Son Co.

Flour Tester—See *Tester, Flour.*

Flour Sieves, Sifters—See *Sieves, Sifters.*

Flower Pot Brackets, Stands—See *Brackets, Stands.*

Flower Pickers—See *Pickers, Flower and Fruit.*

Flue Cleaners, Ventilators—See *Cleaners, Ventilators.*

Flush Rings—See *Rings, Flush.*

Fluted Drills—See *Drills, Fluted.*

Fluters—
North Bros. Mfg. Co.

Fly Fans, Traps—See *Fans, Traps.*

Fly Killer, Wire—
Osborn Mfg. Co.

Fodder Shredders, Dry—See *Shredders, Dry Fodder.*

Folding Machinery, Paper—
Chambers Bros. Co.

Foot Lathes, Presses, Scrapers—See *Lathes, Presses, Scrapers.*

Foot Rests, Shoeblacking—See *Rests, Foot, Shoeblacking.*

THE IRON AGE INDEX.

Force Pumps—See *Pumps, Force.*

Forcing Machines, Hand or Power—
Wm. Sellers & Co.

Forged Bolts, Unions—See *Bolts, Unions.*

Forges—
Bradley Co.
Buffalo Forge Co.
Champion Blower & Forge Co.
Miner & Peck Mfg. Co.
Pennsylvania Machine Co
B. F. Sturtevant Co.

Forging Machines—
Acme Machinery Co.
A. H. Merriman & Co.

Forging Presses—See *Presses, Forging.*

Forgings, Bicycle—
E. D. Clapp Mfg. Co.
Richard Eccles.
King Machine Screw Works.
M. Seward & Son Co.
J. H. Williams & Co.

Forgings, Carriage—
Butts & Ordway.
E. D. Clapp Mfg. Co.
Richard Eccles.
Scranton Forging Co.
M. Seward & Son Co.

Forgings, Copper—
Wyman & Gordon.

Forgings, Drop—
Belden Machine Co.
Billings & Spencer Co.
W. C. Boone Mfg. Co.
R. H. Brown & Co.
E. D. Clapp Mfg. Co.
Denman & Davis.
Richard Eccles.
National Tube Works Co.
Rhode Island Tool Co.
Scranton Forging Co.
Union Hardware Co.
Van Wagoner & Williams Hardware Co.
Waterbury Farrel Foundry & Machine Co.

J. H. Williams & Co.
Wyman & Gordon.

Forgings, Handle—
Billings & Spencer Co.

Forgings, Iron, Special—
Boston & Lockport Block Co.

Forgings, Manganese Bronze—
W. Cramp & Sons Ship & Engine Building Co.
Wyman & Gordon.

Forgings, Marine, Machine, Railroad and Shaft—
Avery Stamping Co.
Bethlehem Iron Co.
Cambria Iron Co.
Central Iron & Steel Co.
Cleveland City Forge & Iron Co.
Barclay W. Cotton & Co.
Crescent Steel Co.
Frankford Steel Co.
La Belle Steel Co.
Passaic Rolling Mill Co.
Pennsylvania Bolt & Nut Co.
Pierson & Co.
Pittsburgh Shear Knife & Machine Co.
Port Chester Bolt & Nut Co.
Samuel Trethewey & Co.
Vulcan Iron Works.
Wyman & Gordon.

Fork and Spade Handles—See *Handles, Fork, Spade, &c.*

Forks, Coke—
Iowa Farming Tool Co.
Osborn Mfg. Co.

Forks, Hay, Horse—
Ney Mfg. Co.
Syracuse Chilled Plow Co.

Forks, Ice—See *Ice Harvesting Tools.*

Forks, Hay, Manure, Spading, &c.—
Ely Hoe & Fork Co.
Iowa Farming Tool Co.

Forks, Kitchen—
H. H. Mayhew & Co.

Forks, Spoons, &c., Silver and Silver Plated—See *Spoons, Forks, &c., Silver and Silver Plated.*

Forks, Wood—
Iowa Farming Tool Co.

Forks and Spoons, Iron—See *Spoons and Forks, Iron.*

Forming Machines, Automatic—
Hartford Machine Screw Co.

Forming Machines, Sheet Metal—
John Adt & Son.

Forming Machines, Wire—
John Adt & Son.
American Wire Goods Co.
Automatic Machine Co.
E. J. Manville Machine Co.
Waterbury Machine Co.

Forming and Bending Machines—
National Machinery Co.

Forming and Blanking Sheet Metal—See *Blanking and Forming Sheet Metal.*

Foundation and Sewer Gratings—
See *Gratings, Foundation, Sewer, &c.*

Foundry Cars, Facings, Ladles, Trucks—See *Cars, Facings, Ladles, Trucks.*

Foundry Plants—
Byram & Co.
Whiting Foundry Equipment Co.

Foundry Supplies—
Justice Cox, Jr.
Osborn Mfg. Co.

Fountains, Drinking—
Plenger & Henger Mfg. Co.

Frames, Bracket Saw—
Millers Falls Co.

Frames, Card, Drawer—
Norwalk Lock Co.
Peck, Stow & Wilcox Co.
Reading Hardware Co.
Russell & Erwin Mfg. Co.

Frames, Door and Window Screen—
E. C. Stearns & Co.

Frames, Grindstone—
Athol Machine Co.
W. & B. Douglas.
Hamilton Machine Tool Co.

Frames, Hack Saw—
Knapp & Cowles Mfg. Co.
L. S. Starrett Co.

Frames, Photograph, Silver Plated—
Wm. Rogers Mfg. Co.

Frames, Wood Saw—
National Saw Co.

Frames and Summer Fronts, Grate—See *Grate Frames and Summer Fronts.*

Freezers, Ice Cream—
North Bros. Mfg. Co.
E. C. Stearns & Co.
White Mountain Freezer Co.

Freight Elevators—See *Elevators, Freight.*

Frogs, Railroad—See *Switches and Frogs, Railroad.*

Fruit Canners, Jar Rings, Steaming Racks—See *Canners, Rings, Racks.*

Fruit Pickers—See *Pickers, Fruit and Flower.*

Fruit Presses—See *Presses, Fruit and Meat.*

Fry Pans—See *Pans, Fry.*

Fuel Oil Equipment—
United States Fuel Oil Equipment Co.

Fuller Balls, Rubber—See *Balls, Fuller, Rubber.*

Furnace Blocks, Blast—See *Blocks, Blast Furnace.*

Furnace Charging Scales, Lamps—See *Scales, Lamps.*

Furnaces, *Annealing—*
Brown & Sharpe Mfg. Co.
Miller Bros. & Co.
Morgan Construction Co.
Wm. Swindell & Bros.
Turner, Vaughn & Taylor Co.
Waterbury Farrel Foundry & Machine Co.

Furnaces, *Blast—*
D. R. Lean & Co.
Julian Kennedy.
G. W. McClure & Son.
Mackintosh, Hemphill & Co.
New Castle Engineering Co.
Philadelphia Engineering Works.
W. B. Pollock & Co.

Furnaces, *Brazing—*
Waterbury Farrel Foundry & Machine Co.

Furnaces, *Case Hardening—*
Brown & Sharpe Mfg. Co.

Furnaces, *Corrugated Boiler—*
Barclay W. Cotton & Co.
Jos. T. Ryerson & Son.

Furnaces, *Copper—*
W. B. Pollock & Co.

Furnaces, *Crucible—*
Alex Laughlin & Co.

Furnaces, *Heating—*
Julian Kennedy.
Alex Laughlin & Co.
G. W. McClure & Son.
Miller Bros. & Co.
Morgan Construction Co.
S. R. Smythe Co.
Wm. Swindell & Bros.
Wellman-Seaver Engineering Co.

Furnaces, *Open Hearth—*
Julian Kennedy.
Alex Laughlin & Co.
G. W. McClure & Son.
Miller Bros. & Co.
Wm. Swindell & Bros.
Wellman-Seaver Engineering Co.

Furnaces, *Plumbers' and Tinners'—*
Peck, Stow & Wilcox Co.
Schneider & Trenkamp Co.

Furnaces, *Puddling—*
Alex Laughlin & Co.

Furnaces, *Roasting, Ore—*
E. P. Allis Co.

Furnaces, *Tube Welding—*
Alex Laughlin & Co.
Miller Bros. & Co.

Gadders—
Ingersoll-Sergeant Drill Co.
F. R. Patch Mfg. Co.
Rand Drill Co.

*Galley Sheets—*See *Sheets, Galley.*

*Galvanized Bolts—*See *Bolts, Galvanized.*

Galvanized Iron—
Apollo Iron & Steel Co.
Cambridge Iron & Steel Co.
Globe Iron Roofing & Corrugating Co.

Galvanizing—
Avery Stamping Co.
Champion Iron Co.
Sidney Shepard & Co.

Game Bags and Traps—See *Bags, Traps.*

Garden Hoes—See *Hoes, Garden, Field, Mortar, &c.*

Garden Lines, Line Reels, Rakes, Trowels, Weeders—See *Lines, Reels, Rakes, Trowels, Weeders.*

Garment Display Stands, Hooks and Eyes, Stand Bases—See *Stands, Hooks and Eyes, Bases.*

Garnet Paper—See *Papers, Sand, Garnet, &c.*

Gaskets and Rings, Rubber—
Boston Belting Co.
H. O. Canfield.
New York Belting & Packing Co.

Gas Attachments—
I. S. Spencer's Sons.

Gas and Electric Fixtures—
Bradley & Hubbard Mfg. Co.
Bridgeport Brass Co.
John L. Gaumer Co.

Gas Compressors, Engines, Heaters, Jet Guards, Lighters, Ovens, Producers, Radiators, Stoves, Tanks, Valves—See *Compressors, Engines, Guards, Heaters, Lighters, Ovens, Producers, Radiators, Stoves, Tanks, Valves.*

Gas Plant Machinery—
R. D. Wood & Co.

Gasoline Engines, Generators, Heaters, Stoves, Torches — See *Engines, Generators, Heaters, Stoves, Torches.*

Gate Hooks—See *Hooks, Gate and Door.*

Gates, Fence—See *Fencing, Gates, &c.*

Gates, Extension—
Ludlow-Saylor Wire Co.

Gate Hangers, Hinges, Latches—
See *Hangers, Hinges, Latches.*

Gates, Oil and Molasses—
Enterprise Mfg. Co.
E. C. Stearns & Co.
Taylor & Boggis Foundry Co.

Gauge Cocks, Saws—See *Cocks, Saws.*

Gauge and Square Combined—
H. H. Mayhew Co.
Stanley Rule & Level Co.

Gauges, Alarm—
Ashcroft Mfg. Co.

Gauges, Bit—
Millers Falls Co.

Gauges, Butt and Rabbet—
Stanley Rule & Level Co.

Gauges, Caliper—
Athol Machine Co.
Pratt & Whitney Co.

Gauges, Center—
Athol Machine Co.
Coffin & Leighton.
Henry Disston & Sons.

Gauges, Chisel—
Stanley Rule & Level Co.

Gauges, Clapboard—
Peck, Stow & Wilcox Co.
Stanley Rule & Level Co.

Gauges, Combination—
Henry Disston & Sons.

Gauges, Depth—
Athol Machine Co.
J. Stevens Arms & Tool Co
T. F. Welch Mfg. Co.
L. S. Starrett Co.

Gauges, Dimension—
E. C. Atkins & Co.

Gauges, Drill—
Cleveland Twist Drill Co.
T. F. Welch Mfg. Co.

Gauges, Hydraulic—
Ashcroft Mfg. Co.

Gauges, Jointer—
Millers Falls Co.

Gauges, Marking—
Henry Disston & Sons.
Knapp & Cowles Mfg. Co.
C. F. Richardson & Son.
Stanley Rule & Level Co.

Gauges, Micrometer—
Brown & Sharpe Mfg. Co
J. T. Slocomb & Co.

Gauges, Plug and Ring—
Pratt & Whitney Co.

Gauges, Pressure—
Ashcroft Mfg. Co.

Gauges, Recording—
Ashcroft Mfg. Co.
Bristol Co.

Gauges, Saw Tooth—
E. C. Atkins & Co.

Gauges, Scratch, Surface, &c.—
Billings & Spencer Co.
J. Stevens Arms & Tool Co.

Gauges, Screw Pitch—
Athol Machine Co.
Cincinnati Screw & Tap Co.

Gauges, Snap—
Cleveland Twist Drill Co.

Gauges, Steam and Vacuum—
Ashcroft Mfg. Co.

Gauges, Surface—
Athol Machine Co.
Hoggson & Pettis Mfg. Co.
J. Stevens Arms & Tool Co.
L. S. Starrett Co.

Gauges, Track—
Jos. F. McCoy Co.

Gauges, Water—
Lunkenheimer Co.
McNab & Harlin Mfg. Co.

Gauges, Wire—
Henry Disston & Sons.
Wright & Colton Wire Cloth Co.

Gauging Rods—See *Rods, Gauging.*

Gear Blanks, Cutters, Irons, Planers—See *Blanks, Cutters, Irons, Planers.*

Gears—
Boston Gear Works.
Brown & Sharpe Mfg. Co.
Chester Steel Casting Co.
Geo. V. Cresson Co.
Fairmount Machine Co.
Gleason Tool Co.
Link-Belt Engineering Co.
Morse, Williams & Co.
R. D. Nuttall Co.
F. R. Patch Mfg. Co.
R. Poole & Son Co.
Superior Machine Co.
T. F. Welch Mfg. Co.

Gem Pans—See *Pans, Gem.*

Generators, Gasoline—
Schneider & Trenkamp Co.

German Silver—
Bridgeport Brass Co.
Wm. S. Fearing.
Plume & Atwood Mfg. Co.
Pope's Island Mfg. Corporation.
Randolph & Clowes.
Scovill Mfg. Co.
Waterbury Brass Co.

German Silver Tubing—See *Tubing.*

Gimlets and Gimlet Bits—
Connecticut Valley Mfg. Co.
Goodell Bros. Co.
H. H. Mayhew Co.
Snell Mfg. Co.

Gins, Ice Hoisting—
W. T. Wood & Co.

Girder Rails—See *Rails, Girder.*

Girders—See *Buildings and Bridges—*

Girts, Web—
Covert Mfg. Co.

Glass Cutters, Tube Cutters—See *Cutters.*

Glasses Holders—See *Holders, Glasses.*

Glaziers' Points—See *Points, Glazier's, &c.*

Glue—
Baeder, Adamson & Co.
Russia Cement Co.

Gold Bronze Sheets—See *Sheets, Gold Bronze.*

Gold or Platers' Metal—See *Metal, Platers' or Gold.*

Gold Pans, Miners' — See *Pans, Miners' Gold.*

Gong Bells—See *Bells, Gong.*

Gougs—
U. T. Hungerford.
Wilmot & Hobbs Mfg. Co.

Gouges, Tanged, Socket—See *Chisels and Gouges.*

Governor Springs—See *Springs, Governor.*

Governors, Steam Engine—
H. C. Fish Machine Works.

Governors, Tank—
D'Este & Seeley Co.

Grabs, Rafter—
Ney Mfg. Co.

Graders, Road — See *Levelers and Graders, Road.*

Graduated Scales—See *Scales, Graduated.*

Grain Cradles, Elevators, Scales, Scoops—See *Cradles, Elevators, Scales, Scoops.*

Granaries, Portable—
W. J. Adam.

Grape Hoes—See *Hoes, Grape.*

Graphite—
Jos. Dixon Crucible Co.

Grapples, Ice — See *Ice Harvesting Tools.*

Grapples, Steel—
Stowell Mfg. & Foundry Co.

Grass Catchers—See *Catchers, Grass.*

Grate Ash Traps—
Southern Queen Mfg. Co.

Grate Dampers and Guards—See *Dampers, Guards.*

Grate Frames and Summer Fronts—
Southern Queen Mfg. Co.

Graters, Horse Radish, &c. —
Enterprise Mfg. Co.

Grates, Mantel -
Southern Queen Mfg. Co.

Gratings, Area — See *Iron Work Builders'.*

Gratings, Foundation, Sewer, &c.—
Champion Iron Co.
Pleuger & Henger Mfg. Co.
Schneider & Trenkamp Co.

Gray Iron Castings—See *Castings, Gray Iron.*

Grease, Axle—
Joseph Dixon Crucible Co.

Griddles, Soapstone—
Pike Mfg. Co.

Grilles, Iron—See *Iron, Ornamental.*

Grinders, Chisel—
Millers Falls Co.

Grinders, Cutter —
Cincinnati Milling Machine Co.
Gould & Eberhardt.
Norton Emery Wheel Co.
Pratt & Whitney Co.
Woodward & Rogers.

Grinders, Drill—
Cleveland Twist Drill Co.
Wm. Sellers & Co.
Standard Tool Co.

Grinders, Lathe—
Ball Bearing Co.

Grinders, Lathe Center —
Stow Flexible Shaft Co.

Grinders, Planer Knife—
Diamond Machine Co.
Northampton Emery Wheel Co.
Tanite Co.

Grinders, Portable—
Stow Flexible Shaft Co.
Stow Mfg. Co.

Grinders, Reamer—
Cincinnati Milling Machine Co.

Grinders, Roll—
E. Harrington, Son & Co.

THE IRON AGE INDEX.

Grinders, Surface—
Bignall & Keeler Mfg. Co.
Builders' Iron Foundry.
Diamond Machine Co.
Woodward & Rogers.

Grinders, Tool—
W. F. & J. Barnes Co.
Diamond Machine Co.
Dwight Slate Machine Co.
Gould & Eberhardt.
Hamilton Machine Tool Co.
Northampton Emery Wheel Co.
William Sellers & Co.
Tanite Co.

Grinders, Universal—
Cincinnati Milling Machine Co.
Diamond Machine Co.

Grinders' and Polishers' Supplies—
Northampton Emery Wheel Co.

Grinding Machines—
American Emery Wheel Works.
American Shearer Mfg. Co.
Brown & Sharpe Mfg. Co.
Builders' Iron Foundry.
Diamond Machine Co.
Dwight Slate Machine Co.
Garvin Machine Co.
Hampden Corundum Wheel Co.
Hanson & Van Winkle Co.
Kimball Bros. & Sprague.
Northampton Emery Wheel Co.
Norton Emery Wheel Co.
Pawling & Harnischfeger.
Pedrick & Ayer Co.
Pennsylvania Machine Co.
Sebastian Lathe Co.
Springfield Mfg. Co.
Tanite Co.

Grinding Machines, Drill—See *Drill Grinding Machines, Twist.*

Grinding Pans, Emery—See *Pans, Emery Grinding.*

Grindstone Fixtures—
Cleveland Stone Co.
W. & B. Douglas.
Peck, Stow & Wilcox Co.
Pleuger & Henger Mfg. Co.
Reading Hardware Co.
Stowell Mfg. & Foundry Co.

Grindstone Frames — See *Frames, Grindstone.*

Grindstones, Family—
Millers Falls Co.
Peck, Stow & Wilcox Co.
Pleuger & Henger Mfg. Co.
Reading Hardware Co.

Grindstones, Unmounted—
Cleveland Stone Co.

Grips, Bicycle—
Brockton Mallet Co.
J. S. Leng's Son & Co.

Grips, Cord and Line—
Samson Cordage Works.

Grips, Ice—
Erie Specialty Co.

Grooming Machines—
American Shearer Mfg. Co.

Grouting Pumps—See *Pumps, Grouting, Sewerage and Quarry.*

Guards, Bicycle—
Stover Mfg. Co.

Guards, &c., Elevator—
Howard & Morse.
W. S. Tyler Wire Works Co.

Guards, Gas Jet—
Gilbert & Bennett Mfg. Co.
Howard & Morse.

Guards, Grate—
E. T. Barnum.
Columbus Wire & Iron Works.
Edward Darby & Sons.
Gilbert & Bennett Mfg. Co.
Howard & Morse.
Fred. J. Meyers Mfg. Co.
Scheeler's Sons.

Guards, Grave—
Columbus Wire & Iron Works.
Gilbert & Bennett Mfg. Co.
Fred. J. Meyers Mfg. Co.

Guards, Skylight—See *Iron Work, Builders'.*

Guards, Tree—
Champion Iron Co.
Columbus Wire & Iron Works.
Howard & Morse.
Fred. J. Meyers Mfg. Co.
Scheeler's Sons.
Stewart Iron Works.

Guards, Trouser—
Bevin Bros. Mfg. Co.

Guards, Window, Iron—See *Iron, Ornamental.*

Guides, Band Saw—
Simonds Mfg. Co.

Guides, Sheet and Rope—
W. & J. Tiebout.

Gummer Cutters—See *Cutters, Gummer.*

Gummers, Saw—
Henry Disston & Sons.
National Saw Co.
Silver Mfg. Co.
Tanite Co.

Gun Barrel Drilling Machines—See *Drilling Machines, Gun Barrel.*

Gun Barrel Rifling Machines—See *Rifling Machines.*

Gun Implements—
Bridgeport Gun Implement Co.
Ideal Mfg. Co.
Remington Arms Co.
Union Hardware Co.
Waterbury Brass Co.

Gun Machinery—
Detrick & Harvey Machine Co.

Gun Wads—See *Wads, Gun.*

Guns, Shot—
Remington Arms Co.
J. Stevens Arms & Tool Co.

Gutters—See *Eave Troughs and Gutters.*

Hack Saws, Power—See *Saws, Power, Hack.*

Hack Saws and Hack Saw Blades—See *Saws, Hack, and Hack Saw Blades.*

Hair, Curled—
Baeder, Adamson & Co.

Hair Felting—See *Felting, Hair.*

Half Hatchets—See *Hatchets, Shingling, Half, &c.*

Half Soles—
Brandenburg & Co.

Halter Buckles, Chain, Leads, Snaps—See *Buckles, Chains, Leads, Snaps.*

Halters, Rope, Web, &c.—
Covert Mfg. Co.
Covert's Saddlery Works.

Hame Straps—See *Straps, Hame.*

Hammers—See *Sledges and Hammers.*

Hammers, Brass—
T. F. Welch Mfg. Co.

Hammers, Copper—
Clendenin Bros.
U. T. Hungerford.

Hammers, Drop—
Bement, Miles & Co.
Billings & Spencer Co.
E. W. Bliss Co.
Merrill Bros.
A. H. Merriman.
Miner & Peck Mfg. Co.
Pratt & Whitney Co.
Stiles & Fladd Press Co.

Hammers, Handled—
Billings & Spencer Co.
Heller Bros.
Logan & Strobridge Iron Co.
New England Specialty Co.
Peck, Stow & Wilcox Co.
Stover Mfg. Co.
A. C. Williams.

Hammers, Heavy and Sledges—
Van Wagoner & Williams Hardware Co.

Hammers, Magnet—
Arthur R. Robertson

Hammers, Paving—
E. C. Atkins & Co.

Hammers, Power—
Beaudry & Co.
Belden Machine Co.
Bradley Co.
Dienelt & Eisenhardt.
Dupont Mfg. Co.
Long & Allstatter Co.
Scranton & Co.

Hammers, Rawhide and Hide Faced—
Brockton Mallet Co.

Hammers, Saddlers' and Upholsterers'
Stanley Rule & Level Co.

Hammers, Shoe—
Logan & Strobridge Iron Co.
Peck, Stow & Wilcox Co.
Pleuger & Henger Mfg. Co.
Star Heel Plate Co.

Hammers, Steam—
Bement, Miles & Co.
Cleveland Punch & Shear Works.
Richard Dudgeon.
Pittsburgh Shear Knife & Machine Co.
William Sellers & Co.

Hammers, Tack—
Knapp & Cowles Mfg. Co.
Logan & Strobridge Iron Co.
New England Specialty Co.
Peck, Stow & Wilcox Co.
Stanley Rule & Level Co.
Stover Mfg. Co.
Troy Nickel Works.
Turner & Seymour Mfg. Co.
A. C. Williams.

Hammock Cords, Hooks, Rope Adjusters, Ropes—See *Adjusters, Cords, Hooks, Ropes.*

Hammocks—
I. E. Palmer.

Ham Preserving Pumps—See *Pumps, Ham Preserving*

Ham Stringers—See *Stringers, Ham.*

Hand Bells, Drills, Lamps, Saws—
See *Bells, Drills, Lamps, Saws.*

Hand Hoist Carriers—See *Carriers, Hand Hoist.*

Hand Power Elevators—See *Elevators, Hand Power.*

Hand and Power Punches — See *Punches, Hand and Power.*

Hand Rail Brackets, Screws—See *Brackets, Screws.*

Hand Vises—See *Vises, Hand*

Handle Bar Clamps—See *Clamps Handle Bar.*

Handle Forgings—See *Forgings.*

Handled Hammers—See *Hammers, Handled.*

Handles, Auger—
Millers Falls Co.

Handles, Basket, Wire—
E. H. Titchener & Co.

Handles, Chest, Shutter, &c —
Logan & Strobridge Iron Co.
Ney Mfg. Co.
Peck, Stow & Wilcox Co.
Reading Hardware Co.
Russell & Erwin Mfg. Co.
Stanley Works.
Taylor & Boggis Foundry Co.
W. & J. Tiebout.
A. C. Williams.

Handles, Chisel, File, Awl, &c.—
Brockton Mallet Co.
Buck Bros.
Knapp & Cowles Mfg. Co.
Northboro Tool Handle & Mfg. Co.
Peck, Stow & Wilcox Co.
Stanley Rule & Level Co.
E. C. Stearns & Co.
Union Hardware Co.

Handles, Crosscut Saw—
Simonds Mfg. Co.

Handles, Detachable Tool—
Brockton Mallet Co.
Millers Falls Co.
Nicholson File Co.

Handles, Door—
Norwalk Lock Co.
Taylor & Boggis Foundry Co.

Handles, Door Bell—
  Peck, Stow & Wilcox Co.
Handles, Drawer—
  Norwalk Lock Co.
  Reading Hardware Co.
Handles, Fork, Spade, &c.—
  Ely Hoe & Fork Co.
  Iowa Farming Tool Co.
Handles, Lifting—
  Peck, Stow & Wilcox Co.
Handles, Machine—
  J. H. Williams & Co.
Handles, Plane and Saw—
  E. C. Atkins & Co.
  Henry Disston & Sons.
  National Saw Co.
  Stanley Rule & Level Co.
Handles, Sad Iron—
  Colebrookdale Iron Co.
  Enterprise Mfg. Co.
Handles, Tub—
  Stanley Works.
Handles and Locks, Store Door—
  Reading Hardware Co.
  Russell & Erwin Mfg. Co.
Hanger Screws—See Screws, Hanger.
Hangers, Clothes—
  Van Wagoner & Williams Hardware Co.
Hangers, Cycle—
  Lane Bros.
  Miller & Van Winkle.
Hangers, Door—
  Chicago Spring Butt Co.
  Coburn Trolley Track Mfg. Co.
  Lane Bros.
  Lawrence Bros.
  Logan & Strobridge Iron Co.
  McKinney Mfg. Co.
  Moore Mfg. Co.
  Ney Mfg. Co.
  Norwalk Lock Co.
  Payson Mfg. Co.

  Peck, Stow & Wilcox Co.
  Pleuger & Henger Mfg. Co.
  Reading Hardware Co.
  E. C. Stearns & Co.
  Stowell Mfg. & Foundry Co.
  Van Wagoner & Williams Hardware Co.
  Wilcox Mfg. Co.
Hangers, Eave Trough—
  American Steel Roofing Co.
  Berger Bros.
Hangers, Gate—
  F. E. Myers & Bro.
Hangers, Pipe—
  Kelly & Jones Co.
  McNab & Harlin Mfg. Co.
Hangers, Shaft—
  Ball Bearing Co.
  Boston Gear Works.
  Brown & Sharpe Mfg. Co.
  Geo. V. Cresson Co.
  Dodge Mfg. Co.
  Fairmount Machine Co.
  Lane & Bodley Co.
  Link-Belt Engineering Co.
  Mossberg & Granville Mfg. Co.
  R. Poole & Son Co.
  B. F. Sturtevant Co.
Hangers and Rails, Suspended—See Rails and Hangers, Suspended.
Hanging Baskets, Lamps—See Baskets, Lamps.
Hanging Hopper Beam Scales—See Scales, Hanging Hopper Beam.
Hardening Furnaces, Case—See Furnaces, Case Hardening.
Hardies—.
  Heller Bros.
Hardware Commission Merchants
  —See Agents.
Hardware Jobbers—See Jobbers, Hardware, Cutlery, &c.
Hardware, Saddlery—See Saddlery Hardware.

Hardware Store Shelving—See *Shelving*.

Hardware, Upholstery—See *Upholstery Hardware*.

Harness Chains, Hooks, Repair Kits, Snaps—See *Chains, Hooks, Repair Kits, Snaps*.

Harpoons—
W. & J. Tiebout.

Harrow Discs, Teeth—See *Discs, Teeth*.

Harrows—
W. C. Heller & Co.
Long & Allstatter Co.
Syracuse Chilled Plow Co.

Hasps, Hinge—
McKinney Mfg. Co.
Reading Hardware Co.
Stanley Works.

Hatchets, Confectioners'—
Logan & Strobridge Iron Co.

Hatchets, Family—
Payson Mfg. Co.

Hatchets, Ice—
Logan & Strobridge Iron Co.
Mason & Parker.
A. C. Williams.

Hatchets, Shingling, Half, &c.—
Peck, Stow & Wilcox Co.
A. C. Williams.
L. & I. J. White Co.

Hatch Doors—See *Doors, Automatic Hatch*.

Hat Badges—See *Badges, Hat*.

Haulage Plants—
Thos. Carlin's Sons.
Roberts Mfg. Co.
Trenton Iron Co.

Hauls, Log—See *Log Hauls*.

Hay Forks—See *Forks, Hay. Manure, Spading, &c.*

Hay Fork Carriers, Pulleys—See *Carriers, Pulleys*.

Hay Knives, Stackers—See *Knives, Stackers*.

Haying Tools—
F. E. Myers & Bros.
J. E. Porter Co.

Header and Bender, Bicycle Spoke—See *Spoke Header and Bender, Bicycle*.

Headers, Bol —
Acme Machinery Co.
National Machinery Co.
Wells Bros. & Co.

Headers, Rod—
National Machinery Co.

Head Lights—See *Lights, Head*.

Heads, Kitchen Boiler—
Avery Stamping Co.

Heads, Conductor—
Berger Bros.

Heads, Indexing and Dividing—
Cincinnati Milling Machine Co.

Heads, Planer—
Frankford Steel Co

Headless Bolts—See *Bolts, Special*.

Headers, Barrel—
Variety Machine Co.

Heaters, Electric Car—
H. W. Johns Mfg. Co.

Heaters, Feed Water—
Harrisburg Pipe Bending Co.
Harrison Safety Boiler Works.
Hooker-Colville Steam Pump Co.
National Pipe Bending Co.
Warren Webster & Co.
Robt. Wetherill & Co.
Whitlock Coil Pipe Co.
Henry R. Worthington.

Heaters, Gas, Gasoline and Oil—
Bradley & Hubbard Mfg. Co.
Gilbert & Bennett Mfg. Co.
Edward Miller & Co.
Plume & Atwood Mfg. Co.
Schneider & Trenkamp Co.

THE IRON AGE INDEX.

Heaters, House—
Barbour, Stockwell & Co.
National Pipe Bending Co.

Heaters, Lamp Chimney—
Logan & Strobridge Iron Co.

Heaters, Lamp Chimney, Wire—See *Household Articles, Wire.*

Heaters, Sad Iron—
Enterprise Mfg. Co.
Schneider & Trenkamp Co.
Southern Queen Mfg. Co.
Van Wagoner & Williams Hardware Co.
A. C. Williams.

Heating and Ventilating Apparatus
American Blower Co.
Buffalo Forge Co.
H. C. Fish Machine Works.
Howard & Morse.
B. F. Sturtevant Co.

Heating Furnaces, Stoves—See *Furnaces, Stoves.*

Heavy Hammers—See *Hammers, Heavy, and Sledges.*

Heel Plates, Stiffeners—See *Plates, Stiffeners.*

Hens' Nests—See *Nests, Hens'.*

Hide Bound Mallets—See *Mallets, Raw Hide and Hide Bound.*

Hide Faced Hammers—See *Hammers, Raw Hide and Hide Faced.*

Hinge Plates—See *Plates, Hinge, Corner and Center.*

Hinge Hasps—See *Hasps, Hinge.*

Hinges, Blind—
Palmer Hardware Mfg. Co.
Pleuger & Henger Mfg. Co.
Reading Hardware Co.
Stanley Works.
Wire Goods Co.

Hinges, Brass—
Norwalk Lock Co.
C. J. Root.
Stanley Works.

Hinges, Brass, Bronze, &c.—See *Butts and Hinges, Brass, Bronze, &c.*

Hinges, Gate—
Logan & Strobridge Iron Co.
Peck, Stow & Wilcox Co.
Pleuger & Henger Mfg. Co.
Reading Hardware Co.

Hinges, Long Chest—
Stanley Works.

Hinges, Malleable Iron—
W. & J. Tiebout.

Hinges, Plate—
Peck, Stow & Wilcox Co.
Stanley Works.

Hinges, Refrigerator—
Reading Hardware Co.
Stanley Works.
W. & J. Tiebout.

Hinges, Screw Hook or Strap, and Eye—
McKinney Mfg. Co.
Peck, Stow & Wilcox Co.

Hinges, Shutter—
Norwalk Lock Co.

Hinges, Spring—
Arcade Mfg. Co.
Bommer Bros.
Chicago Spring Butt Co.
Payson Mfg. Co.
Peck, Stow & Wilcox Co.
Pleuger & Henger Mfg. Co.
Reading Hardware Co.
Scovill Mfg. Co.
E. C. Stearns & Co.
Stover Mfg. Co.
Union Mfg. Co.
Van Wagoner & Williams Hardware Co.

Hinges, Strap and T, &c.—
McKinney Mfg. Co.
Lawrence Bros.
Stanley Works.
W. & J. Tiebout.

Hinges, Strap and T, Corrugated—
Stanley Works.

Hinges, Trap Door—
Stanley Works.

Hinges, Trunk—
McKinney Mfg. Co.
Stanley Works.

Hinges, Water Closet—
Stanley Works.

Hinges and Fasts, Box—
Stanley Works.

*Hitching Hooks, Posts, Rings, Ropes, Weights—*See *Hooks, Posts, Rings, Ropes, Weights.*

Hitching Post, Rod—
Covert Mfg. Co.

*Hitching Post Tops—*See *Post Tops, Hitching.*

*Hitching Strap Adjusters—*See *Adjusters, Hammock Rope and Hitching Strap.*

Hods, Coal—
Cincinnati Screw & Tap Co.
Sidney Shepard & Co.

Hods, Mortar and Brick—
Lansing Wheelbarrow Co.

Hoes, Garden, Field, Mortar, &c.
Ely Hoe & Fork Co.
Iowa Farming Tool Co.

Hoes, Grape—
Syracuse Chilled Plow Co.

Hoes, Scuffle—
Ely Hoe & Fork Co.
Iowa Farming Tool Co.
Knapp & Cowles Mfg. Co.

*Hog Scrapers—*See *Scrapers, Hog.*

Hoisting Engines — See *Engines, Hoisting.*

Hoisting Machines—
Alfred Box & Co.
Thos. Carlin's Sons.
Lidgerwood Mfg. Co.
Jos. F. McCoy Co.
Wm. Sellers & Co.

J. G. Speidel.
R. D. Wood & Co.

Hoists, Brick and Mortar—
Thos. Carlin's Sons.

Hoists, Chain and Rope—
Gebr. Bolzani.
Alfred Box & Co.
Chas. G. Eckstein & Co.
Fulton Iron & Engine Works.
E. Harrington, Son & Co.
Jos. F. McCoy Co.
Maris Bros.
Moore Mfg. Co.
Ney Mfg. Co.
Reading Crane & Hoist Works.
J. G. Speidel.

Hoists, Pneumatic—
Pedrick & Ayer Co.
Rand Drill Co.
Craig Ridgway & Son.
Whiting Foundry Equipment Co.

Hoists, Portable—
Thos. Carlin's Sons.
Maris Bros.
Pedrick & Ayer Co.
Craig Ridgway & Son.

Hoists, Sidewalk –
F. S. Hutchinson & Co.
Variety Machine Co.

Holders, Bit, Brace, Die—
Butterfield & Co.

Holders, Broom—
Knapp & Cowles Mfg. Co.
A. C. Williams.

*Holders, Broom, Brush, Comb, Soap, Wire—*See *Household Articles, Wire.*

Holders, Card—
Logan & Strobridge Iron Co.
Stanley Works.

Holders, Christmas Tree—
Logan & Strobridge Iron Co.
North Bros. Mfg. Co.

Holders, Clothes Line—
Champion Safety Lock Co.

Holders, Dictionary—
E. C. Stearns & Co.
Stover Mfg. Co.

Holders, Die—
S. W. Card Mfg. Co.
J. M. Carpenter Tap & Die Co.
E. F. Reece Co.
Wiley & Russell Mfg. Co.

Holders, Divider Pencil—
Bemis & Call Hardware & Tool Co.

Holders, Door—
Caldwell Mfg. Co.
Wilcox Mfg. Co.

Holders, Drill—
Cleveland Twist Drill Co.

Holders, Extension Bit and Screw Driver—
Millers Falls Co.

Holders, Glasses—
Fred. J. Meyers Mfg. Co.

Holders, Flagstaff—
Enterprise Mfg. Co.

Holders, Hose—See Hose Attachments.

Holders, Nipple—
Armstrong Mfg. Co
Curtis & Curtis.
Wiley & Russell Mfg. Co.

Holders, Oil Stone—
Pike Mfg. Co.

Holders, Reamer—
Billings & Spencer Co.

Holders, Rubber Stamp—
R. Woodman Mfg. & Supply Co.

Holders, Sample—
Fred. J. Meyers Mfg. Co.

Holders, Sash—
Lawrence Bros.
Norwalk Lock Co.

Holders, Stake, Wagon—
Stanley Works.

Holders, Tap—
Ideal Machine Works.
A. D. Quint.
E. F. Reece Co.

Holders, Test Tube—
United States Clothes Pin Co.

Holders, Tire Bolt —
Wiley & Russell Mfg. Co.

Holders, Tool—
Gould & Eberhardt.
I. P. Richards.

Holders, Towel—
Turner & Seymour Mfg. Co.
Upson & Hart Co.

Holders, Twine—
Turner & Seymour Mfg. Co.

Holders, Wire Cloth—
Ossawan Mills Co.

Hollow Augers—See *Augers, Hollow.*

Hollow Drills—See *Drills, Hollow.*

Hollow Mills, Adjustable—See *Mills, Adjustable, Hollow.*

Hollow Ware — See *Ware, Hollow, Silver Plated, Steel, &c.*

Hones, Razor—
Pike Mfg. Co.

Hoof Knives, Parers—See *Knives, Parers.*

Hook Head Bolts—See *Bolts, Special.*

Hook and Eye Screws—See *Screws, Hook and Eye.*

Hooks, Awning—
W. & J. Tiebout.

Hooks, Bale, Box, Hogshead, &c.—
W. & J. Tiebout.

Hooks, Beam—
Stowell Mfg. & Foundry Co.

Hooks, Belt—
Bristol Co.
C. E. Coe.
E. Jenckes Mfg. Co.
Samson Steel Belt Hook Co.
Wire Goods Co.

Hooks, Bench—
Millers Falls Co.
Charles Morrill.
Peck, Stow & Wilcox Co.
Seymour Smith & Son.
E. C. Stearns & Co.

Hooks, Bird Cage—
Fred. J. Meyers Mfg. Co.
Peck, Stow & Wilcox Co.
Reading Hardware Co.
Russell & Erwin Mfg. Co.
Stover Mfg. Co.
Turner & Seymour Mfg. Co.
A. C. Williams.
Wire Goods Co.

Hooks, Boat—
W. & J. Tiebout.

Hooks, Box and Cotton—
Knapp & Cowles Mfg. Co.
Peck, Stow & Wilcox Co.
Russell & Erwin Mfg. Co.

Hooks, Brine—
Wire Goods Co.

Hooks, Bush—
Peck, Stow & Wilcox Co.

Hooks, Button, Silver Plated—
Wallace Bros.

Hooks, Cant—
Boston & Lockport Block Co.

Hooks, Chandelier—
Bradley & Hubbard Mfg. Co.
Peck, Stow & Wilcox Co.
Reading Hardware Co.
Russell & Erwin Mfg. Co.
A. C. Williams.
Wire Goods Co.

Hooks, Clam—
Ely Hoe & Fork Co.
Iowa Farming Tool Co.

Hooks, Clothes Line—
Logan & Strobridge Iron Co.
Peck. Stow & Wilcox Co.
Reading Hardware Co.
Russell & Erwin Mfg. Co.
W. & J. Tiebout.
Stowell Mfg. & Foundry Co.

Hooks, Coat, Hat, &c.—
Atlas Mfg. Co.
Brass Goods Mfg. Co.
E. Jenckes Mfg. Co.
Logan & Strobridge Iron Co.
Norwalk Lock Co.
Peck, Stow & Wilcox Co.
Reading Hardware Co.
Russell & Erwin Mfg. Co.
Stover Mfg. Co.
Stowell Mfg. & Foundry Co.
W. & J. Tiebout.
Van Wagoner & Williams Hardware Co.
A. C. Williams.
Wire Goods Co.

Hooks, Conductor—
American Steel Roofing Co.
Berger Bros.
Garry Iron Roofing Co.

Hooks, Corn and obacco—
Iowa Farming Tool Co.
Peck, Stow & Wilcox Co.

Hooks, Cup and Shoulder—
M. S. Brooks & Sons.
Peck, Stow & Wilcox Co.
Reading Hardware Co.
W. & J. Tiebout.

Hooks, Drive--
E. Jenckes Mfg. Co.

Hooks, 8 and S—
Bridgeport Chain Co.
Plume & Atwood Mfg. Co.
W. & J. Tiebout.

Hooks, Floor Pulley—
Ney Mfg. Co.
E. C. Stearns & Co.
Stowell Mfg. & Foundry Co.

Hooks, Gate and Door —
  Covert Mfg. Co.
  Covert's Saddlery Works.
Hooks, Guard Fishing—
  Payson Mfg. Co.
  Norwalk Lock Co.
  Peck, Stow & Wilcox Co.
  Reading Hardware Co.
  Russell & Erwin Mfg. Co.
Hooks, Gaff Topsail—
  W. & J. Tiebout.
Hooks, Hammock—
  M. S. Brooks & Sons.
  Peck, Stow & Wilcox Co.
  Russell & Erwin Mfg. Co.
  E. C. Stearns & Co.
  W. & J. Tiebout.
  Wire Goods Co.
Hooks, Harness—
  Arcade Mfg. Co.
  Logan & Strobridge Iron Co.
  Ney Mfg. Co.
  Peck, Stow & Wilcox Co.
  Pleuger & Henger Mfg. Co.
  Reading Hardware Co.
  Russell & Erwin Mfg. Co.
  Stowell Mfg. & Foundry Co.
  A. C. Williams.
Hooks, Hitching—
  Wire Goods Co.
Hooks, Ice—See *Ice Harvesting Tools.*
Hooks, Jamb—
  Russell & Erwin Mfg. Co.
Hooks, Meat—
  M. S. Brooks & Sons.
  Enterprise Mfg. Co.
  E. Jenckes Mfg. Co.
  Wire Goods Co.
Hooks, Picture—
  M. S. Brooks & Sons.
  Ossawan Mills Co.
  Peck, Stow & Wilcox Co.
  W. & J. Tiebout.
  Turner & Seymour Mfg. Co.

Hooks, Socket—
  I. S. Spencer's Sons.
Hooks, Staples, &c.—See *Wrought Iron Goods.*
Hooks, Ticket —
  Wire Goods Co.
Hooks, Weeding—
  Palmer Hardware Mfg. Co.
Hooks and Eyes, Garment—
  Turner & Seymour Mfg. Co.
Hooks and Eyes, Malleable—
  E. Jenckes Mfg. Co.
Hooks and Thimbles—
  W. & J. Tiebout.
Hoop Brass Clasps—See *Brass Clasps.*
Hoop Iron—
  Ogden & Wallace.
  A. R. Whitney & Co.
Horse Brushes, Clippers—See *Brushes, Clippers.*
Horse Hay Forks—See *Forks, Hay, Horse.*
Horse Radish Graters—See *Graters, Horse Radish, &c.*
Horse Tooth Rasps—See *Rasps, Horse Tooth.*
Horse Plumes—See *Plumes, Horse and Sleigh.*
Horses, Clothes —
  Hill Drier Co.
Horseshoe Nail Iron—See *Iron, Horseshoe Nail.*
Horseshoes—See *Shoes, Horse and Mule.*
Horseshoers' Vises—See *Vises, Horseshoers'.*
Hose Attachments (*Menders, Couplings, Bands, Holders, Reducers, Clamps, Caps, &c.*)—
  King & Knight.
  McNab & Harlin Mfg. Co.

THE IRON AGE INDEX. 67

Mast, Foos & Co.
New York Belting & Packing Co.
Pleuger & Henger Mfg. Co.

Hose, Cotton—
New York Belting & Packing Co.

Hose Reels—See *Reels, Hose.*

Hose, Rubber—
Boston Belting Co.
New York Belting & Packing Co.
Railway Supply Co.

Hot House Pulleys—See *Pulleys, Hot House.*

Hound Plates—See *Plates, Hound.*

House Bells, Heaters, Numbers—
See *Bells, Heaters, Letters.*

Household Articles, *Wire (Sponge Baskets, Dish Covers, Easels, Plate Handlers, Lamp Chimney Heaters, Broom Holders, Brush and Comb Holders, Soap Holders, Table Mats, Meat Rests, Shirt Rests, Stove Pipe Shelves, Soap Dishes and Brackets, Coffee Pot Stands, Tea and Coffee Pot Strainers)—*
Edward Darby & Sons.
Fred. J. Meyers Mfg. Co.
Turner & Seymour Mfg. Co.
Wickwire Bros.
Wire Goods Co.

Hub Boring Machines—
Silver Mfg. Co.

Hub Machines, Bicycle—
Dreses, Mueller & Co.
Hartford Machine Screw Co.
Pratt & Whitney Co.

Hubs, Bicycle—
New Britain Hardware Mfg. Co.

Hydrant Chain—See *Chain, Hydrant.*

Hydrants and Street Washers—
Chapman Valve Mfg. Co.
Deming Co.
W. & B. Douglas.
McNab & Harlin Mfg. Co.
Mast, Foos & Co.

F. E. Myers & Bro.
R. D. Wood & Co.

Hydraulic Accumulators, Cranes, Gauges, Jacks, Leather, Presses, Punches, Rams, Riveting, Shears
—See *Accumulators, Cranes, Gauges, Jacks, Leather, Presses, Punches, Rams, Riveting, Shears.*

Hydraulic Machinery—
Henry Aiken.
E. W. Bliss Co.
Lloyd Booth Co.
Julian Kennedy.
Mackintosh, Hemphill & Co.
Wm. Sellers & Co.
R. S. Smythe Co.
Wm. Tod & Co.
Waterbury Farrel Foundry & Machine Co.
Watson & Stillman Co.
R. D. Wood & Co.
Henry R. Worthington.

Ice Harvesting Tools *(Augers, Breakers, Chisels, Forks, Bars, Grapples, Hooks, Line Markers, Markers, Measuring Irons, Planes, Plows, House and Car Runs, Saws, Shavers, Scrapers, Adzes and Scoop Nets)—*
Wm. T. Wood & Co.

Ice Axes, Bars, Breakers, Chippers, Chisels, Cream Freezers, Grips, Hatchets, Picks, Saws, Shaves, Skates, Tongs—See *Axes, Bars, Breakers, Chippers, Chisels, Freezers Grips, Hatchets, Picks, Saws, Shaves, Skates, Tongs.*

Implements, Gun—See *Gun Implements.*

Incandescent Lamps—See *Lamps, Incandescent.*

Inclinometers—
L. S. Starrett Co.

Indicators, Center—
J. T. Slocomb & Co.
J. Stevens Arms & Tool Co.

Indicators, Speed—
Ashcroft Mfg. Co.
Cincinnati Screw & Tap Co.
Simonds Mfg. Co.
L. S. Starrett Co.
Tanite Co.
R. Woodman Mfg. & Supply Co.

Indicators, Steam Engine—
Ashcroft Mfg. Co.

Indexing Centers—See *Centers, Indexing.*

Indexing Heads—See *Heads, Indexing and Dividing.*

Indian Clubs—See *Clubs, Indian.*

Ingot Molds—See *Molds, Ingot.*

Injectors, Boiler—
Hayden & Derby Mfg. Co.
Jenkins Bros.
William Sellers & Co.

Inkstands—See *Stationers' Hardware.*

Inkstands, Silver Plated—See *Desk Specialties.*

Inspection, Steam Boiler—
Hartford Steam Boiler Inspection & Insurance Co.

Inspectors' Scales, Leather — See *Scales, Leather Inspectors'.*

Inspirators—See *Injectors, Boiler.*

Instruments, Leveling and Squaring—
Athol Machine Co.
C. F. Richardson & Son.
L. S. Starrett Co.

Insulators, Trolley—
H. W. Johns Mfg. Co.

Interfering Boots—See *Boots, Interfering.*

Iron Awnings—See *Awnings, Iron.*

Iron, Axle—
Lockhart Iron & Steel Co.

Iron Bedsteads, Lamps, Lathing, Pickets, Planes — See *Bedsteads, Lamps, Lathing, Pickets, Planes.*

Iron, Boiler Brace—
Lockhart Iron & Steel Co.

Iron Bars, Cold Rolled Sheet, Corrugated, Forgings, Hoop, Ore, Planished Sheet, Plates, Rivets, Roofing, Shapes, Squares — See *Bars, Corrugated, Forgings. Hoop, Ore, Plates, Rivets, Roofing, Shapes, Sheet, Squares.*

Iron Castings, Gray, Malleable—See *Castings.*

Iron Ceiling and Siding—See *Ceiling and Siding, Iron and Steel.*

Iron Cornice, Galvanized—See *Cornice, Galvanized Iron.*

Iron, Crowfeet—
I. S. Spencer's Sons.

Iron, Horseshoe—
Pierson & Co.

Iron Levels—See *Levels, Iron,* also *Plumbs and Levels.*

Iron Magazines—See *Magazines, Iron.*

Iron, Ornamental (Grilles, Crestings, Finials, Window Guards, Vanes, Wickets, &c.)—
E. T. Barnum.
J. G. Braun & Co.
Champion Iron Co.
Columbus Wire & Iron Works.
Edward Darby & Sons.
Estey Wire Works Co.
Garry Iron Roofing Co.
Gilbert & Bennett Mfg. Co.
Howard & Morse.
Kansas City Metal Roofing & Corrugating Co.
Ludlow-Saylor Wire Co.
Mast, Foos & Co.
Fred. J. Meyers Mfg. Co.
Scheeler's Sons.
Stewart Iron Works.
W. S. Tyler Wire Works Co.
Wright & Colton Wire Cloth Co.

Iron, Pig—
Allentown Rolling Mills.
Justice Cox, Jr.
Ed. J. Etting.
J. W. Hoffman & Co.
C. B. Houston & Co.
Junction Iron & Steel Co.
Jerome Keeley & Co.
Lake Superior Charcoal Iron Co.
J. Tatnall Lea & Co.
J. J. Mohr.
Nicolls, Wheeler & Co.
Ohio Iron & Steel Co.
Pilling & Crane.
Riverside Iron Works.
Frank Samuel.
E. H. Wilson & Co.
L. & R. Wister & Co.

Iron Ridging—See *Ridging, Iron.*

Iron, Rivet and Stay Bolt—
Lockhart Iron & Steel Co.

Iron Roofing—See *Roofing, Iron and Steel.*

Iron Rosettes—See *Rosettes, Iron.*

Iron Storage, Pig—See *Storage, Pig Iron.*

Iron Work, *Builders' (Veranda Columns, Ornamental, Porticoes, Coal Holes and Covers, Sidewalk Lights, Area Gratings, Ash Pit Doors, Ventilating Plates, Sash, Skylight Guards)—*

E. T. Barnum.
Champion Iron Co.
Columbus Wire & Iron Works.
Garry Iron Roofing Co.
Wm. H. Haskell Co.
Fred. J. Meyers Mfg. Co.
Port Chester Bolt & Nut Co.
J. H. Sternbergh & Son.
Stewart Iron Works.
Stowell Mfg. & Foundry Co.

Iron and Brass Studs—See *Studs, Brass and Iron.*

Iron and Steel Wire—See *Wire, Iron and Steel, Market, Fence, Stone, &c.*

Iron and Steel Stairs—See *Stairs, Iron and Steel.*

Iron and Steel, *Brokers and Merchants—*
Alphonse Bouchet.
Barclay W. Cotton & Co.
Justice Cox, Jr.
R. M. Cunliffe.
Edw. J. Etting.
Arthur C. Harvey Co.
Hiron & Co.
J. N. Hoffman & Co.
C. B. Houston & Co.
Jerome Keeley & Co.
J. Tatnall Lea & Co.
Henry Levis & Co.
A. Milne & Co.
J. J. Mohr.
Nicolls, Wheeler & Co.
Odgen & Wallace.
Pierson & Co.
Pilling & Crane.
Frank Samuel.
W. H. Thomson & Co.
W. H. Wallace & Co.
A. R. Whitney & Co.
E. H. Wilson & Co.
Francis Wister.
L. & R. Wister & Co.

Iron and Steel, Swedish—
Abbott, Wheelock & Co.
Arthur C. Harvey Co.
A. Milne & Co.

Ironing Boards, Stands, Tables—
See *Boards, Stands, Tables.*

Irons, Balling—
Covert Mfg. Co.

Irons, Calking—
L. & I. J. White Co.
W. & J. Tiebout.

Irons, Corner and Brace—
Stanley Works.
W. & J. Tiebout.
Wilcox Mfg. Co.

Irons, Curling—
Upson & Hart Co.

Irons, Gear—
E. D. Clapp Mfg. Co.

Irons, Measuring, Ice—See *Ice Harvesting Tools*.

Irons, Plane—
Buck Bros.
L. & I. J. White Co.

Irons, Rub—
Butts & Ordway.
Plenger & Henger Mfg. Co.

Irons, Sad, Laundry, &c.—
Colebrookdale Iron Co.
Enterprise Mfg. Co.
Plenger & Henger Mfg. Co.
Southern Queen Mfg. Co.
A. C. Williams.

Irons, Sash Cord—
Peck, Stow & Wilcox Co.
Reading Hardware Co.
Russell & Erwin Mfg. Co.

Irons, Tuyere—
Arcade Mfg. Co.
Logan & Strobridge Iron Co.
Plenger & Henger Mfg. Co.
Silver Mfg. Co.

Irons, Waffle—
Reading Hardware Co.
Schneider & Trenkamp Co.

Irrigation Pumps—See *Pumps, Irrigation*.

Ivory Rules—See *Rules, Ivory*.

Jack Chain, Screws—See *Chain, Jack*; *Jacks, Screw*.

Jacket Pumps—See *Pumps, Jacket*.

Jacks, Boot—
Logan & Strobridge Iron Co.
Peck, Stow & Wilcox Co.
Reading Hardware Co.
Russell & Erwin Mfg. Co.

Jacks, Hydraulic—
Dienelt & Eisenhardt.
Richard Dudgeon.
Jos. F. McCoy Co.
Watson-Stillman Co.

Jacks, Leveling—
Newark Machine Tool Works.

Jacks, Screw—
Wm. G. Le Count.
Jos F. McCoy Co.
Millers Falls Co.
Newark Machine Tool Works.
Peck, Stow & Wilcox Co.
E. C. Stearns & Co.

Jacks, Wagon—
Boston & Lockport Block Co.
Covert Mfg. Co.
Covert's Saddlery Works.
Knapp & Cowles Mfg. Co.
Lane Bros.
Lansing Wheelbarrow Co.
Millers Falls Co.
Silver Mfg. Co.

Jails, Jail Cells, &c.—
E. T. Barnum.
Champion Iron Co.
Mast, Foos & Co.
Fred. J. Meyers Mfg. Co.
Stewart Iron Works.

Jamb Hooks—See *Hooks, Jamb*.

Japanning—
Avery Stamping Co.
Forest City Foundry & Mfg. Co.
Haight & Clark.
Palmers & De Mooy Foundry Co.
I. S. Spencer's Sons.
Taylor & Boggis Foundry Co.
Turner & Seymour Mfg. Co.

Jaw Caps, Vise—See *Vise Jaw Caps*.

Jaw Clutches—See *Clutches, Jaw*.

Jaws, Face Plate—
Skinner Chuck Co.
Union Mfg. Co.

Jaws, Vise—
Prentiss Vise Co.

THE IRON AGE INDEX. 71

Jewel Caskets, Silver Plated—
The Wm. Rogers Mfg. Co.

Jewelers' Rolls, Saws—See *Rolls, Saws.*

Jib Cranes—See *Cranes.*

Jobbers, Hardware, Cutlery, Tools, Sporting Goods, &c.—
C. H. Besly & Co.
Dame, Stoddard & Kendall.
Dodge, Haley & Co.
Hartley & Graham.
U. T. Hungerford.
Russell & Erwin Mfg. Co.
Schroetter Bros.
Sickels-Nutting Co.
Supplee Hardware Co.

Joint Couplings—See *Couplings, Joint.*

Joints, Ball—
Boston Gear Works.

Joints, Step Ladder—
Stanley Works.

Joints, Stump—
E. D. Clapp Mfg. Co.

Jointer Gauges—See *Gauges, Jointer.*

Juice Extractors — See *Extractors, Juice.*

Kaolin—
Ostrander Fire Brick Co.

Kerosene Burners — See *Burners, Kerosene.*

Kettles, Brass—
Ansonia Brass & Copper Co.
Randolph & Clowes.
Waterbury Brass Co.

Kettles, Tea—
Cleveland Stamping & Tool Co.
Sidney Shepard & Co.

Key Chains, Checks, Rings, Seat Clamps—See *Chains, Checks, Clamps, Rings.*

Keys and Key Blanks—
Norwalk Lock Co.
Reading Hardware Co.
Russell & Erwin Mfg. Co.

Keys and Cotters, Spring—See *Cotters and Keys, Spring.*

Keys, Bed—
Van Wagoner & Williams Hardware Co.

Keys, Brake Shoe—
Q & C Co.

Keys, Flat Spring—
Standard Tool Co.

Keys, Riveted, Machine—
Wm. H. Haskell Co.

Kick Plates—See *Plates, Push, Pull, Kick.*

Kilns, Dry—
American Blower Co.

King Bolts—See *Bolts, King*

Kitchen Articles, Wire, (*Egg Boilers, Vegetable Boilers, Chain Pot Cleaners, Bread Coolers, Dish Drainers, Kitchen Forks, Vegetable Lifters, Potato Mashers, Skimmers, Strainers, Toasters, Potato Fryers, Berry Washers, &c.*)—
Carroll Muzzle Co.
Cleveland Stamping & Tool Co.
Edward Darby & Sons.
W. W. Shoe.
Wickwire Bros.
Wire Goods Co.

Kitchen Forks, Knives—See *Forks, Knives.*

Knife Grinders, Planer—See *Grinders, Planer Knife.*

Knife Sharpeners—See *Sharpeners, Knife.*

Knives, Angle—
Sam'l Trethewey & Co.

Knives, Butcher, Bread, Shoe, &c.—
John Chatillon & Sons.
Goodell Co.
New England Specialty Co.
Nichols Bros.
Northampton Cutlery Co.
Tuck Mfg. Co.

Knives, Butter and Cheese—
Nichols Bros.
John Wilson.

Knives, Cane—
★E. C. Atkins & Co.
Geo. H. Bishop & Co.
Henry Disston & Sons.
National Saw Co.

Knives, Cheese, Self Gauging—
Enterprise Mfg. Co.

Knives, Corn—
★E. C. Atkins & Co.
Geo. H. Bishop & Co.
Henry Disston & Sons.

Knives, Drawing—
Buck Bros.
Peck, Stow & Wilcox Co.
L. & I. J. White Co.

Knives, Hay and Straw—
Ney Mfg. Co.

Knives, Hoof—
Heller Bros.

Knives, Kitchen—
John Chatillon & Sons.
New England Specialty Co.
John Wilson.

Knives, Machine (*Planer, Paper Cutting, Leather Splitting, Chair Bottom, Washboard, Stave, Miter, &c.—*
John Loyd.
National Saw Co.
Simonds Mfg. Co.
Sam'l Trethewey & Co.
G. & C. Wardlow.
L. & I. J. White Co.

Knives, Metal Shear—See *Blades, Metal Shear.*

Knives, Mincing—
Geo. H. Bishop & Co.
Knapp & Cowles Mfg. Co.
Mason & Parker.
Fred. J. Meyers Mfg. Co.
National Saw Co.
New England Specialty Co.
Palmer Hardware Mfg. Co.
Sidney Shepard & Co.

Knives, Oyster—
Tuck Mfg. Co.

Knives, Paper Hangers', Oil Cloth, &c.—
Tuck Mfg. Co.

Knives, Putty—
Northampton Cutlery Co.

Knives, Rotary Slitting—
Samuel Trethewey & Co.

Knives, Saw—
Henry Disston & Sons.
National Saw Co.

Knives, Tobacco—
Tuck Mfg. Co.

Knobs, Base and Floor—
Union Hardware Co.

Knobs, Door—
Brass Goods Mfg. Co.
Norwalk Lock Co.
Peck, Stow & Wilcox Co.
Reading Hardware Co.
Russell & Erwin Mfg. Co.

Knobs, Drawer and Shutter—
Norwalk Lock Co.
Peck, Stow & Wilcox Co.
Reading Hardware Co.
Russell & Erwin Mfg. Co.
Stover Mfg. Co.
Turner & Seymour Mfg. Co.
Wire Goods Co.

Knob Screws—See *Screws, Knob.*

Knockers, Door—
Norwalk Lock Co.
Russell & Erwin Mfg. Co.
Van Wagoner & Williams Hardware Co.

Knuckles, Car Coupler—
Chester Steel Casting Co.

Labels, Brass—
George M. Ness.

Labels, Plant and Tree—
Boston & Lockport Block Co.

Lace Leather, Rawhide—See *Leather, Rawhide, Lace.*

Lacing, Leather, Rawhide, Steel—
See *Belt Lacing, Leather, Rawhide, Steel.*

Lacquers—
Hanson & Van Winkle Co.

Ladders, Rolling Store—
Bicycle Step Ladder Co.
Coburn Trolley Track Mfg. Co.
Lane Bros.
G. A. Milbradt & Co.
F. E. Myers & Bro.
Wilcox Mfg. Co.

Ladders, Steel—
E. T. Barnum.
F. E. Myers & Bro.

Ladders, Step—
Hill Dryer Co.
R. W. Whitehurst & Co.

Ladles, Foundry—
Byram & Co.
Thos. Carlin's Sons.
Whiting Foundry Equipment Co.

Ladles, Melting—
Logan & Strobridge Iron Co.
Peck, Stow & Wilcox Co.
Reading Hardware Co.
T. F. Welch Mfg. Co.

Lag and Coach Screws—See *Screws, Coach and Lag.*

Lamp Attachments, Electric, for Gas Fixtures—See *Electric Light Fittings.*

Lamp Brackets, Chimney Heaters, Posts, Reflectors, Trimmers—See *Brackets, Heaters, Posts, Reflectors, Trimmers.*

Lamps, Arc—
General Electric Co.
Westinghouse Electric & Mfg. Co.

Lamps, Bicycle—
Bridgeport Brass Co.
Bridgeport Gun Implement Co.
Edward Miller & Co.

Plume & Atwood Mfg. Co.
Scovill Mfg. Co.
Steam Gauge & Lantern Co.

Lamps, Furnace—
Taylor & Boggis Foundry Co.

Lamps, Hand—
Bridgeport Brass Co.

Lamps, Incandescent—
General Electric Co.
Westinghouse Electric & Mfg. Co.

Lamps, Iron, Malleable—
Hammer & Co.

Lamps, Miners'—
Sidney Shepard & Co.

Lamps, Miners' Safety—
Howard & Morse.

Lamps, Steel, Millyard, &c.—
Wilmot & Hobbs Mfg. Co.

Lamps, Signal—
Steam Gauge & Lantern Co.

Lamps, Street—
Steam Gauge & Lantern Co.

Lamps, Table, Banquet, Hanging, Piano, &c.—
Bradley & Hubbard Mfg. Co.
Bridgeport Brass Co.
Edward Miller & Co.
Plume & Atwood Mfg. Co.
Scovill Mfg. Co.
Turner & Seymour Mfg. Co.

Land Rollers—See *Rollers, Land.*

Lanterns—
Bridgeport Brass Co.
Edward Miller & Co.
Steam Gauge & Lantern Co.

Lapping Machines—
Brown & Sharpe Mfg. Co.
Builders' Iron Foundry.
Diamond Machine Co.
Mossberg & Granville Mfg. Co.
Northampton Emery Wheel Co.

Lard Presses—See *Presses, Lard.*

THE IRON AGE INDEX.

Lariats—
Samson Cordage Works.
Silver Lake Co.

Lariat and Picket Pins—
Covert Mfg. Co.
Imperial Bit & Snap Co.

Lashes, Whip, and Whips — See *Whips and Whip Lashes.*

Last Lathes, Stands —See *Lathes, Stands.*

Lasts and Stands, Shoe—
Logan & Strobridge Iron Co.
Southern Queen Mfg. Co.
Star Heel Plate Co.
Stowell Mfg. & Foundry Co.

Latches, Elevator Door—
Stowell Mfg. & Foundry Co.

Latches, Gate—
Logan & Strobridge Iron Co.
Peck, Stow & Wilcox Co.
Plenger & Henger Mfg. Co.
Reading Hardware Co.

Latches, Locks, &c. — See *Locks, Latches, &c.*

Latches, Night—
Reading Hardware Co.
Russell & Erwin Mfg. Co.

Latches, Refrigerator—
Payson Mfg. Co.
Norwalk Lock Co.
Reading Hardware Co.
Russell & Erwin Mfg. Co.

Latches, Thumb—
Arcade Mfg. Co.
Chicago Spring Butt Co.
Logan & Strobridge Iron Co.
Ney Mfg. Co.
Peck, Stow & Wilcox Co.
Plenger & Henger Mfg. Co.
Reading Hardware Co.
Russell & Erwin Mfg. Co.
Stover Mfg. Co.
Stowell Mfg. & Foundry Co.
Wilcox Mfg. Co.

Latches and Locks, Sliding Door, Barn Door—See *Locks and Latches.*

Lathe Chucks, Dogs, Grinders, Spindles—See *Chucks, Dogs, Grinders, Spindles.*

Lathe Tools, Thread-cutting—See *Tools, Thread-cutting, Lathe.*

Lathes—
Ames Mfg. Co.
W. F, & J. Barnes Co.
Bement, Miles & Co.
Brown & Sharpe Mfg. Co.
Bullard Machine Tool Co.
Detrick & Harvey Machine Co.
Draper Machine Tool Co.
Erdle & Schenck.
Florence Machine Co.
Garvin Machine Co.
Gleason Tool Co.
Gould & Eberhardt.
Hamilton Machine Tool Co.
Ed. Harrington, Son & Co.
Hendey Machine Co.
I. H. Johnson, Jr., & Co.
Jones & Lamson Machine Co.
Lodge & Shipley Machine Tool Co.
J. J. McCabe.
Millers Falls Co.
New Haven Mfg. Co.
Niles Tool Works.
Pawling & Harnischfeger.
Pond Machine Tool Co.
Pratt & Whitney Co.
Prentice Bros.
Prentiss Tool & Supply Co.
C. F. Richardson & Co.
Wm. Sellers & Co.

Lathes, Axle—
Niles Tool Works Co.
Pond Machine Tool Co.
Wm. Sellers & Co.

Lathes, Bench—
Dwight Slate Machine Co.

Lathes, Buffing and Polishing—See *Buffing and Polishing Machines.*

Lathes, Engine—
Ames Mfg. Co.
Bradford Mill Co.
Brown & Sharpe Mfg. Co.
Davis & Egan Machine Tool Co.
Detrick & Harvey Machine Co.
Fifield Tool Co.
H. C. Fish Machine Works.
Gould & Eberhardt.
Pond Machine Tool Co.
Sebastian Lathe Co.
Wm. Sellers & Co.
Seneca Falls Mfg. Co.
Wright Co.

Lathes, Foot—
W. F. & Jno. Barnes Co.
Sebastian Lathe Co.

Lathes, Lap—See *Buffing and Polishing Machines.*

Lathes, Last—
Kimball Bros. & Sprague.

Lathes, Pulley Turning—
Lodge & Shipley Machine Tool Co.
Newark Machine Tool Co.
Niles Tool Works Co.

Lathes, Roll—
Lloyd Booth Co.
Leechburg Foundry & Machine Co.
Totten & Hogg Iron & Steel Foundry Co.

Lathes, Roll Engraving—
Gould & Eberhardt.

Lathes, Shaft Turning—
Pond Machine Tool Co.

Lathes, Speed—
Diamond Machine Co.
Sebastian Lathe Co.
Seneca Falls Mfg. Co.
Wells Bros. & Co.

Lathes, Spinning—
E. W. Bliss Co.
Gould & Eberhardt.
A. H. Merriman.

Lathes, Turret—
Davis & Egan Machine Tool Co.
Dreses, Mueller & Co.

H. C. Fish Machine Works.
Jones & Lamson Machine Co.

Lathing, Iron—
American Steel Roofing Co.

Lathing, Wire—
Cincinnati Corrugating Co.
Clinton Wire Cloth Co.
Gilbert & Bennett Mfg. Co.
New Jersey Wire Cloth Co.
Scheeler's Sons.
W. S. Tyler Wire Works Co.
Wright & Colton Wire Cloth Co.

Laundry Irons, Tubs—See *Irons, Tubs.*

Lavatory Fittings and Legs—See *Plumbing Supplies.*

Lawn Mowers, Rakes, Rollers, Sprinklers, Swings, Vases—See *Mowers, Rakes, Rollers, Sprinklers, Swings, Vases.*

Lead—
American Metal Co.
John Davol & Sons.
Wm. S. Fearing.
Hendricks Bros.

Lead Blocks—See *Blocks, Lead.*

Lead Pencils, Pipe—See *Pencils, Pipe.*

Leaders, Cattle—
Covert Mfg. Co.
Peck, Stow & Wilcox Co.
Seymour Smith & Son.

Leads, Halter—
Covert's Saddlery Works.

Leather Belt Lacing—See *Belt Lacing, Leather.*

Leather Belting—See *Belting, Leather.*

Leather, Hydraulic—
Detroit Valve & Washer Co.

Leather, Raw Hide Lace—
Shultz Belting Co.

Leather Splitting Knives — See *Knives, Machine.*

Legs and Lavatory Fittings—See *Plumbing Supplies.*

Lemon Squeezers—See *Squeezers, Lemon.*

Letter Plates, Drop—See *Plates, Drop Letter.*

Letters, Cast Iron Sign—
Brown & Sharpe Mfg. Co.

Letters and Figures, House, &c.—
Chicago Spring Butt Co.
Norwalk Lock Co.
Payson Mfg. Co.
Reading Hardware Co.
Stover Mfg. Co.
W. & J. Tiebout.

Levelers and Graders, Road—
Kilbourne & Jacobs Mfg. Co.

Leveling Jacks—See *Jacks, Leveling.*

Leveling and Squaring Instruments—See *Instruments, Leveling and Squaring.*

Level Sights—
Stanley Rule & Level Co.

Levels, Bit and Square.—
Stanley Rule & Level Co.

Levels, Iron (*see also Plumbs and Levels*)—
Athol Machine Co.
Henry Disston & Sons.
Millers Falls Co.
C. F. Richardson & Son.
L. S. Starrett Co.

Levels, Pocket—
Athol Machine Co.
Stanley Rule & Level Co.
Tower & Lyon.

Levels and Plumbs—See *Plumbs and Levels.*

Lever Bells—See *Bells.*

Levers, Door Bell—
Peck, Stow & Wilcox Co.
Reading Hardware Co.
Russell & Erwin Mfg. Co.

Levers, Machine—
Wm. H. Haskell Co.

Library Shelving—See *Shelving, Library*

Lifters, Plug Tobacco—
Erie Specialty Co.

Lifters, Sash—
Arcade Mfg. Co.
Brass Goods Mfg. Co.
Hobart B. Ives & Co.
Logan & Strobridge Iron Co.
Norwalk Lock Co.
Peck, Stow & Wilcox Co.
Reading Hardware Co.
Russell & Erwin Mfg. Co.
Stanley Works.
Stover Mfg. Co.
Taylor & Boggis Foundry Co.
Van Wagoner & Williams Hardware Co.

Lifters, Screen—
Brass Goods Mfg. Co.

Lifters, Stove Lid—
Arcade Mfg. Co.
Logan & Strobridge Iron Co.
New York Stamping Co.
Peck, Stow & Wilcox Co.
Stover Mfg. Co.
Troy Nickel Works.
A. C. Williams.
Wire Goods Co.

Lifters, Transom—
Payson Mfg. Co.
Russell & Erwin Mfg. Co.

Lifting Handles, Scales—See *Handles, Scales.*

Lift Pumps—See *Pumps, Lift.*

Lighters, Cigar—
Bradley & Hubbard Mfg. Co.

Lighters, Gas, Electric—
W. R. Ostrander & Co.

THE IRON AGE INDEX.

Lights, Head—
 Steam Gauge & Lantern Co.
Lights, Side and Deck—
 W. & J. Tiebout.
Lights, Sidewalk—See *Iron Work, Builders'.*
Lights, Vault—See *Vault Lights.*
Line Cleats, Grips—See *Cleats, Grips.*
Lines, Chalk, *Masons', &c.—*
 Ossawan Mills Co.
 Samson Cordage Works.
 Silver Lake Co.
Lines, Clothes, Cotton, *&c.—*
 Ossawan Mills Co.
 Samson Cordage Works.
 Silver Lake Co.
Lines, Clothes, Wire—
 Fred. J. Meyers Mfg. Co.
 Ossawan Mills Co.
 Wire Goods Co.
 Wright & Colton Wire Cloth Co.
Lines, Garden—
 Samson Cordage Works.
 Silver Lake Co.
Linings, Cupola—See *Cupola Linings.*
Linings, Stove—
 Ostrander Fire Brick Co.
Link Belting, Chain—See *Belting, Chain Link.*
Link Machines, Car—See *Car Link Machines.*
Links, Bed—
 E. H. Titchener & Co.
Links, Chain—See *Chain Links.*
Links, Repair—
 Bridgeport Chain Co.
 Oneida Community.
 W. & J. Tiebout.
Loaders, Hay—
 Dain Mfg. Co.
Lock and Coasters, Combined, Bicycle—See *Bicycle Lock and Coasters, Combined.*

Lock Nuts—See *Nuts, Lock.*
Locks, Bicycle—
 Bridgeport Gun Implement Co.
 Smith & Egge Mfg. Co.
Locks, Cabinet, Trunk, *&c.—*
 Norwalk Lock Co.
Locks, Car Window—
 Russell & Erwin Mfg. Co.
Locks, Elevator Door—
 Moore Mfg. Co.
 Stowell Mfg. & Foundry Co.
Locks, Latches, &c.—
 Norwalk Lock Co.
 Reading Hardware Co.
 Russell & Erwin Mfg. Co.
 Taylor & Boggis Foundry Co.
 Warner Lock Co.
Locks and Handles, Store Door—
 See *Handles and Locks, Store Door.*
Locks and Latches, *Barn Door—*
 Stowell Mfg. & Foundry Co.
Locks and Latches, *Ship—*
 W. & J. Tiebout.
 Russell & Erwin Mfg. Co.
Locks and Latches, *Sliding Door—*
 Lane Bros.
 Reading Hardware Co.
 Russell & Erwin Mfg. Co.
 E. C. Stearns & Co.
Locks, Pad—
 Russell & Erwin Mfg. Co.
 Smith & Egge Mfg. Co.
 W. & J. Tiebout.
Locks, Sash—
 Caldwell Mfg. Co.
 Champion Safety Lock Co.
 W. & E. T. Fitch Co.
 Hobart B. Ives & Co.
 Stover Mfg. Co.
 Taylor & Boggis Foundry Co.
Locomotive Blocks, Reflectors, Transfer Tables—See *Blocks, Reflectors, Transfer Tables.*

Locomotives, Steam and Electric—
J. W. Hoffmann & Co.
General Electric Co.
Jeffrey Mfg. Co.

Locomotive Works Machinery—
Hilles & Jones Co.

Log Binders, Chains—See *Binders, Chains.*

Log Hauls—
Link-Belt Engineering Co.

Logging Engines—See *Engines, Logging.*

Loom Bolts—See *Bolts, Loom.*

Looms, Power—
Fairmount Machine Co.

Looms, Wire—
Turner, Vaughn & Taylor Co.

Loops, Furniture—See *Staples and Loops, Furniture.*

Loops, Mast—
W. & J. Tiebout.

Lubricants—
Jos. Dixon Crucible Co.

Lubricators—
Dodge Mfg. Co.
Kelly & Jones Co.
Lunkenheimer Co.
McNab & Harlin Mfg. Co.

Lumber Carts, Trucks—See *Carts, Trucks.*

Machine Bolts—See *Bolts, Machine.*

Machine Forgings—See *Forgings, Marine, Machine, Railroad and Shaft.*

Machine Handles, Knives, Levers, Screws—See *Handles, Knives, Levers, Screws.*

Machinery, Car Works, Cordage, Power Transmission, Elevating, Staple, Fertilizer, Flour Mill, Gas Plant, Gun, Hydraulic, Locomotive Works, Paper Folding, Phosphate, Plate Straightening, Rivet, Riveting, Rolling Mill, Rope Transmission, Sand Blast, Saw Mill, Sheet Corrugating, Special, Spike, Sugar, Tack, Tannery, Tin Plate, White Lead, Wood Screw—See *Car Works, Cordage, Power Transmission, Elevating, Staple, Fertilizer, Flour Mill, Gas Plant, Gun, Hydraulic, Locomotive Works, Folding, Paper, Phosphate, Straightening, Plate, Rivet, Riveting, Rolling Mill, Rope Transmission, Sand Blast, Saw Mill, Special, Spike, Sugar, Tack, Tannery, Tin Plate, White Lead.*

Machinery, Second Hand—See *Second Hand Machinery.*

Machinery for Handling Materials—
Brown Hoisting & Conveying Machine Co.
Jeffrey Mfg. Co.
Lidgerwood Mfg. Co.
Link-Belt Engineering Co.
Roberts Mfg. Co.
Trenton Iron Co.
Wellman-Seaver Engineering Co.

Machinery, Mining—
Allentown Rolling Mills.
E. P. Allis Co.

Machines to Set Bedstead Fastenings—
Quincy Hardware Mfg. Co.

Machines, Automatic Pin, Buffing, Band Saw Setting and Filing, Bicycle Hub, Bicycle Rim Drilling, Die Chamfering, Drilling, Edging, Forcing, Forging, Forming, Forming and Bending, Grinding, Grooming, Gun Barrel Drilling, Gun Barrel Rifling, Hand Shearing, Hoisting, Hub Boring, Key

Seating, Lapping, Marking, Metal Sawing, Metal Testing, Milling, Mortising, Molding, Multiple Spindle Drilling, Nut Tapping, Oil Testing, Perforating, Pickling, Pipe Cutting and Threading, Pipe Threading, Planing, Planishing, Plate Planing, Polishing, Portable Wood and Metal Polishing, Profiling, Pulley Molding, Quartering, Reeling, Riveting, Rod and Tube Pointing, Sand Mixing, Screw, Shaft Straightening, Shaping, Shearing, Sheep Shearing, Sheet Metal Forming, Soldering, Spooling, Spring Coiling, Stone Molding, Swaging, Tapping, Tapping and Reaming, Tenoning, Torsion Testing, Tufting, Twist Drill Grinding, Type Setting, Universal Drilling, Varnishing, Washer, Winding, Wire Forming, Wire Pointing, Wire Ring, Wire Straightening and Cutting—See Pin, Automatic, Buffing, Setting and Filing, Band Saw, Hub, Bicycle, Drilling, Bicycle Rim, Die Chamfering, Drilling, Edging, Forcing, Forging, Forming, Forming and Bending, Grinding, Grooming, Drilling, Gun Barrel, Rifling Gun Barrel, Shearing, Hoisting, Hub Boring, Lapping, Marking, Sawing, Testing, Milling, Mortising, Molding, Drilling, Tapping, Testing, Pickling, Pipe Cutting and Threading, Planishing, Planing, Polishing, Profiling, Molding, Quartering, Reeling, Riveting, Pointing, Mixing, Screw, Shaft Straightening, Shapers, Shears, Sheep Shearing, Soldering, Spooling, Spring Coiling, Molding, Swaging, Tapping, Tenoning, Testing, Tufting, Drill Grinding, Type Setting, Drilling, Varnishing, Washer, Winding, Forming, Pointing.

Machines, Tinners' — See *Tinners' Tools and Machines.*

Machinists' Clamps, Rules, Scrapers, Squares—See *Clamps, Rules, Scrapers, Squares.*

Magazines, Iron—
Garry Iron Roofing Co.

Magnet Hammers—See *Hammers.*

Mail Boxes—See *Boxes.*

Malleable Clevises, Hooks and Eyes, Rings—See *Clevises, Hooks and Eyes, Rings*

Malleable Iron Castings, Hinges—See *Castings, Hinges.*

Mallets, Calking—See *Calking Irons and Mallets.*

Mallets, Rawhide and Hide Bound—
Brockton Mallet Co.

Mallets, Rubber—
New York Belting & Packing Co.

Mallets, Wooden—
Boston & Lockport Block Co.
Knapp & Cowles Mfg. Co.
John Sommer's Son.
Stanley Rule & Level Co.
E. C. Stearns & Co.
Union Hardware Co.

Mandrels—
Cleveland Twist Drill Co.
Henry Disston & Sons.
W. G. Le Count.
Morse Twist Drill & Machine Co.
National Saw Co.
Peck, Stow & Wilcox Co.
Pleuger & Benger Mfg. Co.
Strange Forged Drill & Tool Co.
Wiley & Russell Mfg. Co.

Manganese Bronze, Castings, Forgings—See *Bronze, Castings, Forgings.*

Manheads—
Lukens Iron & Steel Co.
Jos. T. Ryerson & Son.

Manicure Goods—
Nicholson File Co.

Manicure Sets, *Silver Plated—*
Wm. Rogers Mfg. Co.

Mantel Grates—See *Grates.*

Manufacturing Properties—
J. H. Hillman & Co.

Manure Forks, Pumps—See *Forks, Pumps.*

Marine Clocks, —See *Clocks, Marine.*

Marine Forgings—See *Forgings, Marine, Machine, &c.*

Markers, Ice—See *Ice Harvesting Tools.*

Markers, Tire—
Wiley & Russell Mfg. Co.

Markers, Clapboard—
Stanley Rule & Level Co.

Market Wire — See *Wire, Iron and Steel, &c.*

Marking Gauges—See *Gauges.*

Marking Machines—
Dwight Slate Machine Co.

Mashers, Potato, &c.—
John Sommer's Son.

Masons' Chalk, &c., Lines—See *Lines, Chalk, &c.*

Match Boxes, Safes—See *Boxes, Safes.*

Material, Old—
M. & J. Blake.
Bridgeport Iron & Metal Co.
Justice Cox, Jr.
Ed. J. Etting.
Hirons & Co.
Jason Iron Co.
Jerome Keeley & Co.
Henry Levis & Co.
J. J. Mohr.
New Jersey Iron & Metal Co.
Nichols, Wheeler & Co.
Wm. H. Perry & Co.
Pilling & Crane.
Frank Samuel.

Morton B. Smith.
Walsh Bros. & Co.
E. H. Wilson & Co.
L. & R. Wister & Co.

Material, Structural—See *Structural Material.*

Mats, Rubber—
Boston Belting Co.
New York Belting & Packing Co.

Mats, Table, Wire — See *Household Articles, Wire.*

Mats, Wire and Steel—
E. T. Barnum.
Scheeler's Sons.
United States Wire Mat Co.
Wire Goods Co.

Mattocks—See *Picks.*

Mauls—
Plenger & Henger Mfg. Co.
Van Wagoner & Williams Hardware Co.
A. C. Williams.

Measures, Tape—
Bradley & Hubbard Mfg. Co.
Waterbury Brass Co.

Measures, Wood and Metal—
John Chatillon & Sons.
Stanley Rule & Level Co.

Measuring Faucets, Rods, Wheels —See *Faucets, Rods, Wheels.*

Meat Hooks—See *Hooks, Meat.*

Meat Presses—See *Presses, Fruit and Meat.*

Meat and Vegetable Cutters—See *Cutters, Vegetable.*

Mechanical Engineers — See *Engineers, Mechanical.*

Mechanical Rubber Goods, Stokers' —See *Rubber Goods, Stokers'.*

Melting Ladles—See *Ladles, Melting.*

Menders, Hose—See *Hose Attachments.*

Mending Plates—See *Plates, Mending.*

Merchant Pipe—See *Pipe, Merchant.*

Merchants, Iron and Steel—See *Iron and Steel Brokers and Merchants*.

Metal, Anti-Friction, Bronze, Babbitt, White — See *Anti Friction, Bronze, Babbitt, White Metal*.

Metal Forming Machines—See *Forming Machines, Sheet Metal*.

Metal Goods, Sheet, to Order—See *Sheet Metal Goods, to Order*.

Metal Pattern Making—See *Pattern Making, Metal*.

Metal Patterns—See *Patterns, Metal*.

Metal Planers, Sawing Machines, Shears, Shear Blades, Testing Machines—See *Planers, Sawing Machines, Shears, Blades, Metal Shear, Testing Machines*.

Metal Polish, Scribers—See *Polish, Scribers*.

Metal Stamping, Sheet—See *Stamping, Sheet Metal*.

Metal Work, Turned, to Order—See *Turned Metal Work, to Order*.

Metal and Wood Measures — See *Measures, Wood and Metal*.

Metal, Perforated—
Clinton Wire Cloth Co.
Erdle & Schenck.

Metal, Platers', or Gold—
Bridgeport Brass Co.
Scovill Mfg. Co.

Metal Specialties to Order—
Kevorkian Co.
W. C. Toles & Co.

Metal Work, Milled, Turned or Stamped, to Order—
Kevorkian Co.
Cincinnati Screw & Tap Co.

Metal Work, Ornamental Sheet—
W. H. Mullins.

Metal Work, Sheet, to Order—
C. J. Root.

Metallic Eyelets, Shingles—See *Eyelets, Shingles*.

Metallurgical Engineers — See *Engineers, Metallurgical*.

Meters, Ampere Recording—
The Bristol Co.

Meters, Fuel Oil—
Buffalo Meter Co.

Meters, Recording Watt—
The Bristol Co.

Meters, Water—
Buffalo Meter Co.
Builders' Iron Foundry.
Henry R. Worthington.

Mica, Molded—
H. W. Johns Mfg. Co.

Micrometers—
Athol Machine Co.
Brown & Sharpe Mfg. Co.
J. T. Slocomb & Co.
L. S. Starrett Co.

Milk Can Stock—
Sidney Shepard & Co.

Milk Cans and Coolers—See *Cans, Coolers*.

Mill Cinder—See *Cinder, Mill*.

Mill Saws—See *Saws, Mill, Mulay, Crosscut, Drag, &c.*

Mill Supplies—
New England Specialty Co.
W. S. Tyler Wire Works Co.

Mill Wire Goods—See *Wire Goods, Mill*.

Mill Yard Steel Lamps—See *Lamps, Steel Mill Yard, &c.*

Milled, Turned or Stamped Metal Work, to Order—See *Metal Work, Milled, Turned or Stamped, to Order*.

Milling Attachments—
Cincinnati Milling Machine Co.

Milling Cutters—See *Cutters, Milling.*

Milling Machines—
Ames Mfg. Co.
Baush & Harris Machine Tool Co.
Bement, Miles & Co.
E. W. Bliss Co.
Brown & Sharpe Mfg. Co.
Cincinnati Milling Machine Co.
Davis & Egan Machine Tool Co.
Garvin Machine Co.
Hilles & Jones Co.
Ingersoll Milling Machine Co.
Niles Tool Works Co.
Pedrick & Ayer Co.
Prentiss Tool & Supply Co.
Wm. Sellers & Co.
Waterbury Farrel Foundry & Machine Co.

Milling Machines, Bench and Hand—
Hartford Machine Screw Co.

Milling and Drilling Machines, Butt—
John Adt & Son.

Mills, Adjustable Hollow—
Morse Twist Drill & Machine Co.

Mills, Boring and Turning—
Baush & Harris Machine Tool Co.
Bement, Miles & Co.
Newark Machine Tool Works.
Newton Machine Tool Co.
Pedrick & Ayer Co.
Pratt & Whitney Co.
Pond Machine Tool Works.
Wm. Sellers & Co.

Mills, Car Wheel Boring—
Wm. Sellers & Co.

Mills, Cider—
R. W. Whitehurst & Co.

Mills, Coffee—
Arcade Mfg. Co.
Enterprise Mfg. Co.
Lane Bros.
Logan & Strobridge Iron Co.
National Specialty Mfg. Co.
Peck, Stow & Wilcox Co.

Mills, Drug, Bone, Corn, &c.—
Enterprise Mfg. Co.
Logan & Strobridge Iron Co.
National Specialty Mfg. Co.
R. W. Whitehurst & Co.

Mills, End—
Morse Twist Drill Co.

Mills, Feed—
Dain Mfg. Co.
Stover Mfg. Co.

Mills, Wind—
Mast, Foos & Co.
Stover Mfg. Co.

Mincing Knives—See *Knives, Mincing.*

Mine Pumps, Cars—See *Cars, Pumps.*

Miners' Lamps—See *Lamps, Miners'.*

Mining Machinery—See *Machinery, Mining.*

Miter Boxes, Rods—See *Boxes, Rods.*

Miter Planers—
Millers Falls Co.

Miter Squares—See *Squares, Try.*

Mixers, Concrete—
Thos. Carlin's Sons.

Mixing Machines, Sand—
Wm. Sellers & Co.

Molasses Gates—See *Gates, Oil and Molasses.*

Molded Mica—See *Mica.*

Molders' Bellows—See *Bellows, Blacksmiths', &c.*

Moldings, Brass—
Ansonia Brass & Copper Co.

Molding Machines—
Seneca Falls Mfg. Co.

Molding Machines, Stone—
F. R. Patch Mfg. Co.

THE IRON AGE INDEX.

Molds, Ingot—
Lorain Foundry Co.
Mossberg & Granville Mfg. Co.

Mole Traps—See *Traps, Mole.*

Mops, Sticks, &c.—
Arcade Mfg. Co.
Logan & Strobridge Iron Co.
Reading Hardware Co.
Stover Mfg. Co.

Mortar Colors—See *Colors.*

Mortar Hoes, Hoists—See *Hoes, Hoists.*

Mortising Machines—
W. F. & John Barnes Co.
Seneca Falls Mfg. Co.

Motors, Electric—
American Engine Co.
Chicago Flexible Shaft Co.
Thos. H. Dallett & Co.
Eddy Electric Mfg. Co.
General Electric Co.
B. F. Sturtevant Co.
Westinghouse Electric & Mfg. Co.

Motors, Electric Fan—
W. R. Ostrander & Co.

Motors, Electric Toy—
Ohio Electric Works.

Motors, Water—
Humphryes Mfg. Co.

Mouse Traps—See *Traps, Rat and Mouse.*

Mowers, Lawn—
Chadborn & Coldwell Mfg. Co.
Dain Mfg. Co.
Enterprise Mfg. Co.
Mast, Foos & Co.
Ney Mfg. Co.
E. C. Stearns & Co.
Supplee Hardware Co.

Muck Bars—See *Bars, Muck.*

Mucilage—
Russia Cement Co.

Mulay Saws—See *Saws, Crosscut, Drag, Mill, &c.*

Mule and Horse Shoes—See *Shoes, Horse and Mule.*

Music Wire—See *Wire, Music.*

Muzzles—
Carroll Muzzle Co.
Edward Darby & Sons.
Fred. J. Meyers Mfg. Co.
W. W. Shoe.
Wire Goods Co.
Wright & Colton Wire Cloth Co.

Nail Pullers, Rods, Sets—See *Pullers, Rods, Sets.*

Nail Machines, Cut—
Kimball Bros. & Sprague.
Pittsburgh Mfg. Co.
Totten & Hogg Iron & Steel Foundry Co.

Nail Machines, Shoe—
Kimball Bros. & Sprague.

Nail Machines, Wire—
Alexander & McLaughlin.
Cleveland Punch & Shear Works.
National Machinery Co.
Superior Machine Co.

Nails, Copper Shoe—See *Tacks and Nails.*

Nails, Cut—
Clendenin Bros.
Old Dominion Iron & Nail Works Co.
Pierson & Co.
Pottstown Iron Co.
Shelton Co.
Taunton Wire Nail Co.
Tower Co.
Wm. H. Wallace & Co.

Nails, Horseshoe—
Capewell Horse Nail Co.
W. M. Mooney & Co.
National Horse Nail Co.
Putnam Horse Nail Co.

Nails, Fender—
 H. O. Canfield.
 New York Belting & Packing Co.

Nails, Picture—
 Ossawan Mills Co.
 Turner & Seymour Mfg. Co.

Nails, Shoe, Cobblers', Channel, &c.—
 Clendenin Bros.
 Shelton Co.

Nails, Wire—
 American Screw Co.
 American Wire Co.
 Clendenin Bros.
 Consolidated Steel & Wire Co.
 Dillon-Griswold Wire Co.
 I. L. Ellwood Mfg. Co.
 Igoe Bros.
 Indiana Wire Fence Co.
 Ludlow-Saylor Wire Co.
 Milwaukee Tack Co.
 New Castle Wire Nail Co.
 Pittsburgh Wire Co.
 Quincy Hardware Mfg. Co.
 Russell & Erwin Mfg. Co.
 Salem Wire Nail Co.
 Geo. W. Stanley Co.
 E. H. Titchener & Co.
 Taunton Wire Nail Co.
 C. C. & E. P. Townsend.
 Wire Goods Co.
 A. R. Whitney & Co.

*Name Plates—*See *Plates, Name.*

*Natural Gas Burners—*See *Burners, Natural Gas.*

*Navy and Army Scales—*See *Scales, Army and Navy.*

*Neck Yoke Centers, Neck Yokes—*See *Centers, Yokes.*

*Necktie Lights, Electric—*See *Electric Lights, Necktie.*

*Needle Wire—*See *Wire, Needle.*

Needles, Machine—
 Excelsior Needle Co.

Nests, Hens', &c.—
 Gilbert & Bennett Mfg. Co.
 Wickwire Bros.

Netting, Wire—
 E. T. Barnum.
 Clinton Wire Cloth Co.
 Estey Wire Works Co.
 Gilbert & Bennett Mfg. Co.
 Howard & Morse.
 Ludlow-Saylor Wire Co.
 Fred. J. Meyers Mfg. Co.
 New Jersey Wire Cloth Co.
 W. S. Tyler Wire Works Co.
 Wright & Colton Wire Cloth Co.

Nets, Scoop—
 W. & J. Tiebout.

*Nets, Scoop, Ice—*See *Ice Harvesting Tools.*

Nickel—
 American Metal Co.

*Nickel Steel—*See *Steel, Nickel,*

Nickel and Brass, Electro Plated—
 See *Plating, Electro, Brass, Nickel, &c.*

Nickeline—
 Hermann Boker & Co.

*Night Latches—*See *Latches, Night.*

Nippers, Bicycle—
 Scovill Mfg. Co.
 J. Stevens Arms & Tool Co.

Nippers, Cutting—
 Bridgeport Mfg. Co.
 Peck, Stow & Wilcox Co.
 L. S. Starrett Co.
 Utica Drop Forge & Tool Co.

Nipple Holders, Wrenches — See *Holders, Wrenches.*

Nipples, Bicycle—
 Excelsior Needle Co.

Notching Machines, Armature Disk—
 E. W. Bliss Co.

Nozzles—
 Barnes Mfg. Co.
 The Deming Co.
 W. & B. Douglas.
 King & Knight.
 Mast, Foos & Co.
 F. E. Myers & Bro.
 H. F. Neumeyer Mfg. Co.
 New York Belting & Packing Co.
 Pleuger & Henger Mfg. Co.
 I. S. Spencer's Sons.

Nut Crackers, Picks, Tappers—See *Crackers, Picks, Tappers.*

Nut Burring, Nut Tapping Machines— See *Burring Machines, Tapping Machines.*

Nut Machinery, Automatic Cold Pressure—
 National Machinery Co.

Nut Machinery, Hot Forged—
 National Machinery Co.

Nut and Bolt Head Milling Machines—
 Dwight Slate Machine Co.

Nut and Bolt Machinery—See *Bolt and Nut Machinery.*

Nuts, Lock—
 National Elastic Nut Co.
 J. H. Sternbergh & Son.

Nuts, Pipe Sleeve—
 J. H. Sternbergh & Son.

Nuts, Square and Hexagon—
 American Bolt Co.
 American Screw Co.
 Cincinnati Screw & Tap Co.
 Hartford Machine Screw Co.
 William H. Haskell Co.
 Milton Mfg. Co.
 Pennsylvania Bolt & Nut Co.
 Pittsburgh Mfg. Co.
 Port Chester Bolt & Nut Co.
 Rhode Island Tool Co.
 Russell & Erwin Mfg. Co.
 J. H. Sternbergh & Son.

Nuts, Thumb—
 William H. Haskell Co.
 Logan & Strobridge Iron Co.
 Philadelphia Machine Screw Works.
 T. F. Welch Mfg. Co.

Oil Cans, Chandeliers, Cups, Heaters, Meters, Ovens, Pumps, Purifiers, Radiators, Separators, Stones, Stoves, Tanks, Testing Machines, Torches — See *Cans, Chandeliers, Cups, Heaters, Meters, Ovens, Pumps, Purifiers, Radiators, Separators, Stones, Stoves, Tanks, Testing Machines, Torches.*

Oil and Molasses Gates—See *Gates, Oil and Molasses*

Oil Cloth, Paper Hangers', &c., Knives—See *Knives, Paper Hangers', Oil Cloth, &c.*

Oil Equipment, Fuel—See *Fuel Oil Equipment.*

Oil Stone Holders—See *Holders, Oil Stone.*

Oil Well Supplies and Tools—See *Well Supplies and Tools.*

Oilers, Bicycle—
 Bridgeport Gun Implement Co.
 Scovill Mfg. Co.

Oilers, Shafting—
 Scovill Mfg. Co.
 Wilmot & Hobbs Mfg. Co.

Oilers, Spring—
 Bloomsburg Mfg. Co.
 Bridgeport Brass Co.
 Hammer & Co.
 Edward Miller & Co.
 Scovill Mfg. Co.
 Wilmot & Hobbs Mfg. Co.

Old Material—See *Material, Old.*

Onyx Tables—See *Tables, Onyx.*

Open Hearth Billets, Furnaces—See *Billets, Furnaces.*

Open Side Planers—See *Planers, Open Side.*

Openers, Box—
Bemis & Call Hardware & Tool Co.

Openers, Can—
W. L. Barrett.
Bridgeport Mfg. Co.
Goodell Co.
Knapp & Cowles Mfg. Co.
Logan & Strobridge Iron Co.
Fred. J. Meyers Mfg. Co.
New England Specialty Co.
Stowell Mfg. & Foundry Co.
Turner & Seymour Mfg. Co.

Openers, Cigar Box—
Erie Specialty Co.

Ordnance—
Bethlehem Iron Co.

Ore Crushers, Roasting Furnaces, Washer Screws—See *Crushers, Furnaces, Screws.*

Ore, Iron—
Justice Cox, Jr.
Jerome Keeley & Co.
J. Tatnall Lea & Co.
Pilling & Crane.
Frank Samuel.
Francis Wister.

Ornamental Sheet Metal Work—
See *Metal Work, Ornamental Sheet.*

Oven Stoves, Enameling—See *Stoves, Enameling Oven.*

Ovens, Core—
Byram & Co.
Millett Core Oven Co.
Whiting Foundry Equipment Co.

Ovens, Enameling—
G. S. Blodgett Co.

Ovens, Gas, Gasoline and Oil—
Schneider & Trenkamp Co.

Overhead Tramways—See *Tramways, Overhead.*

Ox Balls, Shoes, Yokes—See *Balls, Shoes, Yokes.*

Ox Bow Pins—See *Pins, Ox Bow.*

Oyster Knives, Rivets—See *Knives, Rivets.*

Package Protectors—See *Protectors, Package.*

Packing House Splitters—See *Splitters, Packing House.*

Packing, Valve, Rod and Piston—
Boston Belting Co.
Jenkins Bros.
H. W. Johns Mfg. Co.
Robert Morrison.
New York Belting & Packing Co.
Railway Supply Co.
Silver Lake Co.

Pad Locks—See *Locks, Pad.*

Pads, Horseshoe—
Butts & Ordway.

Pail Clasps, Ears—See *Clasps, Ears.*

Pails, Dinner—
Sidney Shepard & Co.

Pails, Foundry—
Osborn Mfg. Co.

Pails, Tin—
Sidney Shepard & Co.

Paint Burners, Cans—See *Burners, Cans.*

Paints—
Cambridge Roofing Co.
Cleveland Stone Co.
Jos. Dixon Crucible Co.
Garry Iron Roofing Co.
H. W. Johns Mfg. Co.

Panel Saws—See *Saws, Hand, Panel, Back, &c.*

Pans, Cake—
North Bros. Mfg. Co.

Pans, Candy—
John Chatillon & Sons.

Pans, Clay Mixing and Ore—
Thos. Carlin's Sons.

Pans, Dripping—
  Sidney Shepard & Co.
Pans, Dust—
  Monmouth Mfg. Co. Stamping Works.
Pans, Emery Grinding—
  Thos. Carlin's Sons.
Pans, Fry—
  New York Stamping Co.
  Sidney Shepard & Co.
Pans, Gem—
  Logan & Strobridge Iron Co.
  Russell & Erwin Mfg. Co.
  A. C. Williams.
Pans, Miners' Gold—
  Sidney Shepard & Co.
Pans, Roasting and Baking—
  Sidney Shepard & Co.
Pans, Sectional Stew—
  Schneider & Trenkamp Co.
Pans, Shop—
  Kilbourne & Jacobs Mfg. Co.
Pantry Steps—See *Steps, Pantry.*
Paper Boxes, Cutting Knives, Files, Racks — See *Boxes, Files, Knives, Racks.*
Paper Files—See *Desk Specialties.*
Paper Folding Machinery—See *Folding Machinery, Paper.*
Paper Hangers' Knives—See *Knives, Paper Hangers', Oil Cloth, &c.*
Paper Shells—See *Shells.*
Papers, *Sand, Garnet, &c.—*
  Baeder, Adamson & Co.
Parallel Vises—See *Vises, Parallel.*
Parers, *Apple and Potato—*
  Goodell Co.
  Reading Hardware Co.
Parers, *Hoof—*
  Heller Bros.
Parting Tools—See *Tools, Parting.*

Passenger Elevators—See *Elevators, Passenger.*
Patch Bolts—See *Bolts, Patch.*
Patent Attorneys—
  Dyer & Driscoll.
  Howson & Howson.
  H. W. S. Jenner.
  Francis H. Richards.
  E. B. Stocking.
  John Wedderburn & Co.
Pattern Makers' Dowels—See *Dowels, Pattern Makers'.*
Pattern Making—
  Forest City Foundry & Mfg. Co.
  Haight & Clark.
  A. P. Richmond.
  Whiting Foundry Equipment Co.
Pattern Making, *Metal—*
  Palmers & De Mooy Foundry Co.
Patterns, *Metal—*
  New Brunswick Foundry Co.
Paving Hammers — See *Hammers, Paving.*
Pawls, *Ratchet—*
  Boston Gear Works.
Pedal Rubbers—See *Rubbers, Pedal.*
Peg Awls—See *Awls, Peg.*
Pen Wipers—See *Desk Specialties, Silver Plated.*
Pencil Pointers—See *Pointers.*
Pencils, *Lead—*
  Jos. Dixon Crucible Co.
Percussion Caps—See *Caps, Percussion.*
Perforated Brass and *Metal—*See *Brass, Metal.*
Perforating Machines—
  R. Woodman Mfg. & Supply Co.

Pew Book Racks—See *Racks, Pew Book.*

Phosphate Machinery—
Merrill-Stevens Engineering Co.

Phosphor Bronze, Tin—See *Bronze, Tin.*

Phosphor Bronze Castings — See *Castings, Phosphor Bronze.*

Photo Engraving — See *Engraving, Photo and Wood.*

Photograph Frames — See *Frames, Photograph, Silver Plated.*

Photograph Trimmers — See *Trimmers, Photograph.*

Piano Lamps—See *Lamps, Table, Banquet, Hanging, Piano.*

Pickers, Flower and Fruit—
Acme Shear Co.
Turner & Seymour Mfg. Co.

Picket Chains—See *Chains, Picket.*

Picket Pointers—
I. S. Spencer's Sons.

Pickets, Iron—
Stowell Mfg. & Foundry Co.

Pickling Machines—
Leechburg Foundry & Machine Co.

Picks, Ice—
Knapp & Cowles Mfg. Co.
Mason & Parker.
Peck, Stow & Wilcox Co.
Snell Mfg. Co.
Stover Mfg. Co.
Tuck Mfg. Co.
A. C. Williams.

Picks, Nut—
Northampton Cutlery Co.
Wm. Rogers Mfg. Co.
Upson & Hart Co.
Wallace Bros.

Picks and Mattocks—
Van Wagoner & Williams Hardware Co.

Picture Chains, Cord, Hooks, Nails, Wire — See *Chains, Cord, Hooks, Nails, Wire.*

Picture Wire Reels—See *Reels, Picture Wire.*

Pie Racks, Tins—See *Racks, Tins.*

Pig Iron—See *Iron, Pig.*

Pig Iron Storage—See *Storage, Pig Iron.*

Pile Drivers—See *Drivers, Pile.*

Pillow Blocks—See *Blocks, Pillow.*

Pincers—
Heller Bros.
Logan & Strobridge Iron Co.
Peck, Stow & Wilcox Co.

Pinch Bars—See *Pushers, Car.*

Pinion Cutters, *Automatic—*
Dwight Slate Machine Co.

Pinions, *Roll—*
A. Garrison Foundry Co.
Seaman-Sleeth Co.

Pinking Rolls, Rawhide—See *Rolls, Rawhide Pinking.*

Pin Machines, *Automatic—*
Hartford Machine Screw Co.

Pin Trays and Boxes, *Silver Plated—*
Wm. Rogers Mfg. Co.

Pin Break Arms—
I. S. Spencer's Sons.

Pins, *Belaying—*
Boston & Lockport Block Co.
W. & J. Tiebout.

Pins, *Clothes—*
United States Clothes Pin Co.

Pins, *Crank—*
Central Iron & Steel Co
Frankford Steel Co.

Pins, *Domestic—*
Ossawan Mills Co.

Pins, Dowel—
American Screw Co.
Milwaukee Tack Co.
Salem Wire Nail Co.
Taunton Wire Nail Co.
E. H. Titchener & Co.

Pins, Escutcheon—
Bridgeport Brass Co.
Milwaukee Tack Co.
Plume & Atwood Mfg. Co.
Russell & Erwin Mfg. Co.
Scovill Mfg. Co.
Turner & Seymour Mfg. Co.
Wire Goods Co.

Pins, Ox Bow—
Peck, Stow & Wilcox Co.

Pins, Rolling—
John Sommer's Son.

Pins, Safety—
Turner & Seymour Mfg. Co.

Pins, Sash—
W. & J. Tiebout.

Pins, Shelf—
Norwalk Lock Co.

Pins, Taper—
Cincinnati Screw & Tap Co.
Hartford Machine Screw Co.
Worcester Machine Screw Co.

Pins, Ten—See *Ten Pins and Balls.*

Pipe Coils, Cutters, Dampers, Dies, Elbows, Fittings, Hangers, Swivels, Taps, Tongs, Vises, Wrenches—See *Coils, Cutters, Dampers, Dies, Elbows, Fittings, Hangers, Swivels, Taps, Tongs, Vises, Wrenches.*

Pipe, Brass and Copper—
U. T. Hungerford.
Randolph & Clowes.

Pipe, Cast Iron—
Chas. Millar & Son.
Ohio Pipe Co.
Pleuger & Henger Mfg. Co.
Whiting Foundry Equipment Co.
R. D. Wood & Co.

Pipe, Conductor—See *Conductor Pipe.*

Pipe Cutting and Threading Machines—
Bignall & Keeler Mfg. Co.
Curtis & Curtis.
Detrick & Harvey Machine Co.
Jarecki Mfg. Co.
Merrell Mfg. Co.
D. Saunders' Sons.

Pipe Hanger Tongs—See *Tongs, Pipe Hanger.*

Pipe Hook Plates, Steel—See *Plates, Pipe Hook, Steel.*

Pipe, Lead—
Chas. Millar & Son.

Pipe, Merchant—
National Tube Works Co.
Riverside Iron Works.
Frank Samuel.

Pipe, Riveted Water—
W. B. Pollock & Co.

Pipe, Sewer—
Columbus Sewer Pipe Co.
Turner, Vaughn & Taylor Co.

Pipe Sleeve Nuts—See *Nuts, Pipe Sleeve.*

Pipe, Steel—
Avery Stamping Co.
Barclay W. Cotton & Co.
National Tube Works Co.
Riverside Iron Works.

Pipe, Stove—
Globe Iron Roofing & Corrugating Co.

Pipe Strainers, Conductor — See *Strainers, Conductor Pipe.*

Pipe, Wrought Iron—
Kelly & Jones Co.
National Tube Works Co.

Pipes, Chain—
W. & J. Tiebout.

Pistols and Revolvers—
Iver Johnson's Arms & Cycle Works.
John P. Lovell Arms Co.
Remington Arms Co.
J. Stevens Arms & Tool Co.

Piston Packing, Rings, Rods—See *Packing, Rings, Rods.*

Pit Cars—See *Cars, Coal, Mine, Pit, &c.*

Pitcher Spout Pumps—See *Pumps, Cistern, Pitcher Spout, &c.*

Pits, Soaking—
G. W. McClure & Son.
Wm. Swindell & Bros.

Plane Irons, Handles—See *Irons, Handles.*

Plane Irons, Toy—See *Toy Plane Irons.*

Planes, Ice—See *Ice Harvesting Tools.*

Planes, Iron—
Stanley Rule & Level Co.
Tower & Lyon.

Planes, Wood—
Stanley Rule & Level Co.

Planer Centers, Chucks, Heads, Knives—See *Centers, Chucks, Heads, Knives.*

Planer Head Bolts—See *Bolts, Planer Head.*

Planer Knife Files—See *Files, Planer Knife.*

Planer Knife Grinders—See *Grinders, Planer Knife.*

Planers, Gear—
Gleason Tool Co.

Planers, Metal—
Ames Mfg. Co.
Davis & Egan Machine Tool Co.
Detrick & Harvey Machine Co.
Draper Machine Tool Co.
Edwin Harrington, Son & Co.
Hendey Machine Co.
New Haven Mfg. Co.
Niles Tool Works Co.
Pedrick & Ayer Co.
Pond Machine Tool Co.
Powell Planer Co.
Pratt & Whitney Co.
Sebastian Lathe Co.
Whitcomb Mfg. Co.
William Sellers & Co.

Planers, Miter—See *Miter Planers.*

Planers, Open Side—
Detrick & Harvey Machine Co.
Pedrick & Ayer Co.

Planers, Rotary—
Cleveland Punch & Shear Works.

Planers, Stone—
F. R. Patch Mfg. Co.

Planers, Wood—
Garvin Machine Co.

Planing Machines, Plate—
Bement, Miles & Co.
Hilles & Jones Co.

Planishing Machines—
A. H Merriman.

Planters, Corn—
Challenge Corn Planter Co.
J. E. Porter Co.
Variety Machine Co.

Plant Labels—See *Labels, Plant or Tree.*

Plaster, Asbestos—
H. W. Johns Mfg. Co.

Plastering Trowels—See *Trowels, Brick, Plastering, &c.*

Platers' Metal—See *Metal, Platers' or Gold.*

Plate, Black, for Tinning—
Ætna-Standard Iron & Steel Co.
Cambridge Iron & Steel Co.

Plate Casters—See *Casters.*

Plate Handlers, Wire—See *Household Articles, Wire.*

Plate Hinges,—See *Hinges, Plate.*

Plate Planing Machines—See *Planing Machines, Plate.*

Plate Straightening Machinery—See *Straightening Machinery, Plate.*

Plate, Tin and Terne—
Ætna-Standard Iron & Steel Co.
Atlanta Steel & Tin Plate Co.
Old Dominion Iron & Nail Works Co.

Platens and Rolls, *Typewriter—*
New York Belting & Packing Co.

Plates, *Bolster—*
Pleuger & Henger Mfg. Co.
Stover Mfg. Co.

Plates, *Brass Step—*
W. & J. Tiebout.

Plates, *Car Door—*
Russell & Erwin Mfg. Co.

Plates, *Deck or Manhole—*
W. & J. Tiebout.

Plates, *Die—*
Butterfield & Co.

Plates, *Drop Letter—*
Norwalk Lock Co.
Peck, Stow & Wilcox Co.
Reading Hardware Co.
Russell & Erwin Mfg. Co.

Plates, *Felloe—*
McKinney Mfg. Co.
Nut & Washer Mfg. Co.

Plates, *Fish—*
Allentown Rolling Mills.
Pierson & Co.
Tudor Iron Works.

Plates, *Hinge, Corner and Center—*
Norwalk Lock Co.
Reading Hardware Co.
Russell & Erwin Mfg. Co.

Plates, *Heel—*
Star Heel Plate Co.

Plates, *Hound—*
Pleuger & Henger Mfg. Co.

Plates, *Iron and Steel—*
Ætna-Standard Iron & Steel Co.
Bethlehem Iron Co.
Alphonse Bouchet.
Carbon Steel Co.
Barclay W. Cotton & Co.
Justice Cox, Jr.
J. W. Hoffman & Co.
C. B. Houston & Co.
Henry Levis & Co.
Lukens Iron & Steel Co.
Wm. McIlvain & Sons.
Nichols, Wheeler & Co.
Ogden & Wallace.
Pierson & Co.
Pottstown Iron Co.
Pottsville Iron & Steel Co.
Jos. T. Ryerson & Son.
W. H. Thomas & Co.
A. R. Whitney & Co.
Alan Wood Co.

Plates, *Mending—*
Stanley Works.
Wilcox Mfg. Co.

Plates, *Name—*
Norwalk Lock Co.
Reading Hardware Co.
I. S. Spencer's Sons.
E. C. Stearns & Co.

Plates, *Nickel Steel—*
Bethlehem Iron Co.
Carbon Steel Co.

Plates, *Pipe Hook, Steel—*
Avery Stamping Co.

Plates, *Push, Pull and Kick—*
Bommer Bros.
Chicago Spring Butt Co.
Reading Hardware Co.
Russell & Erwin Mfg. Co.
Stover Mfg. Co.
Taylor & Boggis Foundry Co.

Plates, *Railroad Tie—*
Q & C Co.

Plates, *Screw—*
Billings & Spencer Co.
Butterfield & Co.
S. W. Card Mfg. Co.

J. M. Carpenter Tap & Die Co.
Champion Blower & Forge Co.
Morse Twist Drill & Machine Co.
Oster Mfg. Co.
E. F. Reece Co.
Wells Bros. & Co.
Wiley & Russell Mfg. Co.

Plates, Stair—
U. T. Hungerford.

Plates, Ventilating—See Iron Work, Builders'.

Plates and Hooks, Window—
Norwalk Lock Co.
Peck, Stow & Wilcox Co.
Reading Hardware Co.
Russell & Erwin Mfg. Co.

Plates and Stubs, Store Shutter—
See *Stubs and Plates, Store Shutter.*

Plates and Washers, Floor—
Plume & Atwood Mfg. Co.

Platform Scales—See Scales, Platform.

Platforms, Iron, Pump—
Bucket Pump Co.

Plating, Electro—
John L. Gaumer Co.
Haight & Clark.
Kevorkian Co.
Ludlow-Saylor Wire Co.
New Britain Hardware Mfg. Co.
Pleuger & Henger Mfg. Co.
I. S. Spencer's Sons.
Taylor & Boggis Foundry Co.
Turner & Seymour Mfg. Co.

Plating Supplies, Electro — See Electro Plating Supplies.

Pliers—
Athol Machine Co.
Billings & Spencer Co.
Bridgeport Mfg. Co.
J. M. King & Co.
Logan & Strobridge Iron Co.
Fred. J. Meyers Mfg. Co.
Peck, Stow & Wilcox Co.
Tower & Lyon.
Utica Drop Forge & Tool Co.

Plow Bolts, Colters, Steel—See Bolts, Colters, Steel.

Plows—
American Steel Scraper Co.
W. C. Heller & Co.
Kilbourne & Jacobs Mfg. Co.
Long & Allstatter Co.
Sidney Steel Scraper Co.
Syracuse Chilled Plow Co.
R. W. Whitehurst & Co.

Plows, Ice—See Ice Harvesting Tools.

Plug Tobacco Lifters—See Lifters, Plug Tobacco.

Plug Gauges—See Gauges, Plug and Ring.

Plugs, Roll Turning—
Sam'l Trethewey & Co.

Plumbago—See Graphite.

Plumb Bobs—See Bobs, Plumb.

Plumbers' Furnaces, Pumps, Scrapers—See Furnaces, Pumps, Scrapers.

Plumbing Brackets—See Brackets, Plumbing.

Plumbing Supplies (Rubber Rings, Plunger Rubbers, Legs and Lavatory Fittings, Basin Plugs, &c.)—
H. O. Canfield.
Chas. Millar & Son.
Pleuger & Henger Mfg. Co.
Randolph & Clowes.
Smith & Egge Mfg. Co.

Plumbs and Levels—
Henry Disston & Son.
Millers Falls Co.
Stanley Rule & Level Co.
Tower & Lyon.

Plumes, Horse and Sleigh—
Bevin Bros. Mfg. Co.
Chapman Mfg. Co.

Plunger Rubbers—See Plumbing Supplies.

Pneumatic Call Bells, Hoists—See Bells, Hoists.

Poachers, Egg—
Sidney Shepard & Co.

THE IRON AGE INDEX. 93

Pocket Cups, Cutlery, Levels, Squares, Wrenches—See *Cups, Cutlery, Levels, Squares, Wrenches.*

Pod Bits—See *Bits, Pod.*

Pointers, Bolt—
National Machinery Co.

Pointers, Pencil—
Goodell Co.

Pointers, Picket—See *Picket Pointers.*

Pointers, Spoke—
E. C. Stearns & Co.

Pointers, Wire—
T. F. Welch Mfg. Co.

Pointing Machines, Rod and Tube—
Excelsior Needle Co.
Henderson Bros.

Pointing Machines, Wire—
Excelsior Needle Co.
Trenton Iron Co.
Waterbury Machine Co.

Points, Glaziers', &c.—
Shelton Co.

Points, Trammel—
Henry Disston & Sons.
Tower & Lyon.

Points, Well—See *Well Supplies and Tools.*

Pokes, Animal—
Iowa Farming Tool Co.
Lansing Wheelbarrow Co.

Pokers—See *Shovels, Tongs, Pokers, Fire Sets.*

Pokers, Stove—
Peck, Stow & Wilcox Co.

Pole Adjusters, Steps, Tips—See *Adjusters, Steps, Tips.*

Police Goods—
John P. Lovell Arms Co.
Tower & Lyon.

Polish, Metal—
Geo. W. Hoffman.

Polishers' Supplies—See *Grinders' and Polishers' Supplies.*

Polishing Belts, Wheels—See *Belts, Wheels.*

Polishing Machines—See *Buffing and Polishing Machines.*

Polishing Machines, Portable Wood and Metal—
Pawling & Harnischfeger.
Stow Flexible Shaft Co.

Polishing and Buffing Supplies—
Hanson & Van Winkle Co.
Zucker & Levett & Loeb Co.

Pony Carts—See *Carts, Pony.*

Poppers, Corn—
Edward Darby & Sons.
Estey Wire Works Co.
Gilbert & Bennett Mfg. Co.
Quincy Hardware Mfg. Co.
Fred. J. Meyers Mfg. Co.
Wickwire Bros.

Porch Supports—See *Supports, Porch.*

Portable Boring Machines, Drills, Granaries, Grinders—See *Boring Machines, Drills, Granaries, Grinders.*

Porticoes, Ornamental—See *Iron Work, Ornamental.*

Postal Scales—See *Scales, Postal.*

Post Hole Diggers—See *Diggers.*

Post Hole Spades—
St. Louis Shovel Co.

Post Tops, Fence—
Stowell Mfg. & Foundry Co.

Post Tops, Hitching—
E. C. Stearns & Co.

Posts, Binding—
Hartford Machine Screw Co.

Posts, Fence—
W. J. Adam.
Avery Stamping Co.
International Steel Post Co.
Stowell Mfg. & Foundry Co.
Wright & Colton Wire Cloth Co.

Posts, *Hitching—*
E. T. Barnum.
Covert Mfg. Co.
Ellis & Halfenbarger.
International Steel Post Co.
Logan & Strobridge Iron Co.
Ludlow-Saylor Wire Co.
Edward Darby & Sons.
Fred. J. Meyers Mfg. Co.

Posts, *Lamp—*
Stewart Iron Works.

Potato Fryers—See *Kitchen Articles, Wire.*

Potato Mashers, Wire—See *Kitchen Articles, Wire.*

Potato Mashers—See *Mashers, Potato*

Potato and Apple Parers—See *Parers, Apple and Potato.*

Pot Covers—See *Covers, Pot.*

Pots, *Tallow—*
Wilmot & Hobbs Mfg. Co.

Pouches, *Shot—*
Waterbury Brass Co.

Poultry Coops—See *Coops, Poultry.*

Pounders, *Steak—*
R. H. Brown & Co.
Logan & Strobridge Iron Co.
Peck, Stow & Wilcox Co.
Stanley Rule & Level Co.

Powder—
King Powder Co.

Powder Flasks—See *Flasks, Powder.*

Power Hammers, Presses, Pumps, Punches, Scales, Triplex Pumps—See *Hammers, Presses, Pumps, Punches, Scales.*

Power Transmission, *Electric—*
General Electric Co.

Power Transmission Machinery—
Bradford Mill Co.
Geo. V. Cresson Co.
Dodge Mfg. Co.
Jeffrey Mfg. Co.
Jas. Leffel & Co.

Power Transmission Sheaves—See *Sheaves, Power Transmission.*

Presses, *Baling—*
R. W. Whitehurst & Co.

Presses, *Broaching—*
Mossberg & Granville Mfg. Co.
Pratt & Whitney Co.
Rudolphi & Krummel.
Watson-Stillman Co.

Presses, *Copying—*
Whitcomb Mfg. Co.

Presses, *Cork—*
Enterprise Mfg. Co.
Russell & Erwin Mfg. Co.

Presses, Coining—See *Coining Machinery.*

Presses, *Drawing—*
John Adt & Son.
Avery Stamping Co.
E. W. Bliss Co.
Gould & Eberhardt.
A. H. Merriman.
Philadelphia Machine Tool Co.
Rudolphi & Krummel.
Stiles & Fladd Press Co.

Presses, *Drop—*
Billings & Spencer Co.
Gould & Eberhardt.
Miner & Peck Mfg. Co.
Mossberg & Granville Mfg. Co.
Philadelphia Machine Tool Co.
Waterbury Farrel Foundry & Machine Co.

Presses, *Flanging—*
Watson-Stillman Co.

Presses, *Foot—*
John Adt & Son.
Gould & Eberhardt.
E. J. Manville Machine Co.
Mossberg & Granville Mfg. Co.
Stiles & Fladd Press Co.
Waterbury Farrel Foundry & Machine Co

Presses, Forging—
Avery Stamping Co.
Beaudry & Co.
Cleveland Punch & Shear Works.
Watson-Stillman Co.

Presses, Fruit and Meat—
Athol Machine Co.
Enterprise Mfg. Co.
Logan & Strobridge Iron Co.

Presses, Hydraulic—
Mackintosh, Hemphill & Co.
Morgan Construction Co.
Waterbury Farrel Foundry & Machine Co.
Watson-Stillman Co.
R. D. Wood & Co.

Presses, Hydraulic Wheel—
Bement, Miles & Co.
Cleveland Punch & Shear Works.
Richard Dudgeon.
Niles Tool Works Co.
Pond Machine Tool Co.
Wm. Sellers & Co.

Presses, Lard—
Enterprise Mfg. Co.
Logan & Strobridge Iron Co.
Silver Mfg. Co.

Presses, Power—
Beaudry & Co.
E. W. Bliss Co.
C. E. Coe.
Gould & Eberhardt.
John Loyd.
E. J. Manville Machine Co.
A. H. Merriman.
Philadelphia Machine Tool Co.
Rudolphi & Krummel.
Stiles & Fladd Press Co.
Vieillard & Osswald.
Waterbury Farrel Foundry & Machine Co.
Waterbury Machine Co.

Presses, Punching—
Avery Stamping Co.
A. H. Merriman.
Philadelphia Machine Tool Co.
Rudolphi & Krummel.

Stiles & Fladd Press Co.
Wiley & Russell Mfg. Co.

Presses, Screw—
W. F. & John Barnes.
John Loyd.
Stiles & Fladd Press Co.
Waterbury Farrel Foundry & Machine Co.

Presses, Seal—
Charles Morrill.
Geo. M. Ness, Jr.

Presses, Tincture—
Enterprise Mfg. Co.

Presses, Trimming—
Billings & Spencer Co.
E. W. Bliss Co.
Philadelphia Machine Tool Co.
Pratt & Whitney Co.
Rudolphi & Krummel.
Stiles & Fladd Press Co.

Pressure Gauges—See *Gauges*.

Pressure Regulators—
D'Este & Seeley Co.

Primers—
Union Metallic Cartridge Co.
Waterbury Brass Co.

Printers' Rubber Blankets — See *Blankets, Printers' Rubber*.

Printers' Rule Brass—See *Brass, Rule, Printers'*.

Prods, Cattle—
Iowa Farming Tool Co.

Producers, Gas—
Duff Patents Co.
Alex Laughlin & Co.
G. W. McClure & Son.
Morgan Construction Co.
S. R. Smythe Co.
Wm. Swindell & Bro.
R. D. Wood & Co.

Professional Scales—See *Scales, Professional*.

Profiling Machines—
Ames Mfg. Co.
Garvin Machine Co.
Pratt & Whitney Co.

Protectors, *Package—*
Cary Mfg. Co.

Protectors, *Strap—*
Covert's Saddlery Works.

Protractors—
Athol Machine Co.
L. S. Starrett Co.

Prop Block Washers—See *Washers, Prop Block.*

Provision Safes—See *Safes, Provision.*

Pruners—
Fred. J. Meyers Mfg. Co.
Peck, Stow & Wilcox Co.
Seymour Smith & Son.

Pruning Saws, Shears—See *Saws, Shears.*

Publishers, *Book—*
Laborers' Instruction Publishing Co.
David Williams Co.

Puddle Ball Squeezers—See *Squeezers, Puddle Ball.*

Puddling Furnaces—See *Furnaces, Puddling.*

Puller, *Nail and Hammer Combined—*
Pelouze Scale & Mfg. Co.

Pullers, *Cork—*
Arcade Mfg. Co.
Enterprise Mfg. Co.
Erie Specialty Co.

Pullers, *Nail—*
Belden Machine Co.
Goodell Bros. Co.
Millers Falls Co.
National Specialty Mfg. Co.
Pelouze Scale & Mfg. Co.
Scranton & Co.

Pullers, *Tack—*
Bridgeport Mfg. Co.
Scranton & Co.

Pulley Bushings, Molding Machines, Turning Lathes—See *Bushings, Lathes, Molding Machines.*

Pulley Clutches, Wood Split—See *Clutches, Wood Split Pulley.*

Pulley Hooks, Floor —See *Hooks, Floor Pulley.*

Pulleys, *Ceiling—*
Reading Hardware Co.
Stowell Mfg. & Foundry Co.

Pulleys, *Clothes Line—*
Peck, Stow & Wilcox Co.
Reading Hardware Co.
Torrance Iron Co.

Pulleys, *Dumb Waiter—*
Peck, Stow & Wilcox Co.
Reading Hardware Co.
Russell & Erwin Mfg. Co.
Stowell Mfg. & Foundry Co.

Pulleys, *Electric Light—*
Reading Hardware Co.
Stowell Mfg. & Foundry Co.

Pulleys, *Friction Clutch—*
E. W. Bliss Co.
Brown Hoisting & Conveying Co.
Geo. V. Cresson Co.
Eastern Machinery Co.
Fairmount Machine Co.
Hartford Machine Screw Co.
Link-Belt Engineering Co.
New Haven Mfg. Co.
R. Poole & Son Co.

Pulleys, Friction Clutch—See *Pulleys, Friction Clutch.*

Pulleys, *Friction Cone—*
G. F. Evans.

Pulleys, *Hay Fork—*
Lawrence Bros.
Logan & Strobridge Iron Co.
Ney Mfg. Co.
Peck, Stow & Wilcox Co.
Pleuger & Henger Mfg. Co.
Reading Hardware Co.
E. C. Stearns & Co.
Stowell Mfg. & Foundry Co.

Pulleys, *Hot House—*
Peck, Stow & Wilcox Co.
Reading Hardware Co.

Pulleys, *Sash—*
Caldwell Mfg. Co.
Logan & Strobridge Iron Co.
Norwalk Lock Co.
Palmer Hardware Mfg. Co.
Peck, Stow & Wilcox Co.
Plenger & Henger Mfg. Co.
Reading Hardware Co.
Russell & Erwin Mfg. Co.
Smith & Egge Mfg. Co.
Stover Mfg. Co.
W. & J. Tiebout.

Pulleys, *Screw—*
Ney Mfg. Co.
Peck, Stow & Wilcox Co.
Reading Hardware Co.
Russell & Erwin Mfg. Co.
Stover Mfg. Co.

Pulleys, *Shaft—*
E. P. Allis Co.
American Pulley Co.
Boston Gear Works.
Geo. V. Cresson Co.
Dodge Mfg. Co.
Eastern Machinery Co.
Fairmount Machine Co.
Lane & Bodley Co.
F. R. Patch Mfg. Co.
R. Poole & Son Co.
Reeves Pulley Co.
Wm. Sellers & Co.
T. F. Welch Mfg. Co.

Pulleys, *Side—*
Ney Mfg. Co.
Peck, Stow & Wilcox Co.
Reading Hardware Co.
Russell & Erwin Mfg. Co.
W. & J. Tiebout.
Stowell Mfg. & Foundry Co.

Pulleys, *Tackle or Awning—*
Ney Mfg. Co.
Peck, Stow & Wilcox Co.
Reading Hardware Co.

Pulleys, *Upright—*
Peck, Stow & Wilcox Co.
Reading Hardware Co.
Russell & Erwin Mfg. Co.
W. & J. Tiebout.

Pulleys, *Wood Split—*
Dodge Mfg. Co.
Reeves Pulley Co.

Pull Plates—See *Plates, Pull, Push and Kick.*

Pulls, *Bell—*
Norwalk Lock Co.
W. R. Ostrander & Co.
Peck, Stow & Wilcox Co.
Reading Hardware Co.
Russell & Erwin Mfg. Co.
W. & J. Tiebout.

Pulls, *Door—*
Arcade Mfg. Co.
Chicago Spring Butt Co.
Ney Mfg. Co.
Norwalk Lock Co.
Peck, Stow & Wilcox Co.
Reading Hardware Co.
Russell & Erwin Mfg. Co.
Stover Mfg. Co.
W. & J. Tiebout.
Van Wagoner & Williams Hardware Co.

Pulls, *Drawer—*
Brass Goods Mfg. Co.
Logan & Strobridge Iron Co.
Norwalk Lock Co.
Peck, Stow & Wilcox Co.
Reading Hardware Co.
Russell & Erwin Mfg. Co.
Stanley Works.
Stover Mfg. Co..
Taylor & Boggis Foundry Co.
A. C. Williams.

Pulls, *Window—*
Norwalk Lock Co.

Pulverizers, *Ore and Clay—*
A. Garrison Foundry Co.

Pump Cylinders, Rods—See *Cylinders, Rods.*

Pump Fixtures, Chain—
Plenger & Henger Mfg. Co.

Pump Platforms, Iron—See *Platforms, Iron Pump.*

Pump Rod Couplings—See *Couplings, Pump Rod.*

Pumping Engines—See *Engines, Pumping.*

Pumps, Air—See *Compressors, Air.*

Pumps, Air Lift—
Clayton Air Compressor Works.
Ingersoll-Sergeant Drill Co.

Pumps, Artesian Well and Cylinders—
Deming Co.
Union Steam Pump Co.

Pumps, Bicycle—
Bridgeport Gun Implement Co.
Chapman Mfg. Co.
W. & B. Douglas.
Morgan & Wright.

Pumps, Boiler Feed—
E. P. Allis Co.
Barnes Mfg. Co.
Deming Co.
W. & B. Douglas.
Hooker-Colville Steam Pump Co.
C. O. Lucas & Co.
F. E. Myers & Bro.
Springfield Elevator & Pump Co.
Union Steam Pump Co.
Henry R. Worthington Co.

Pumps, Boiler Test—
Deming Co.
W. & B. Douglas.

Pumps, Brass—
Scovill Mfg. Co.

Pumps, Bucket—
Bucket Pump Co.

Pumps, Centrifugal—
Barnes Mfg. Co.
Deming Co.
W. & B. Douglas.
Humphryes Mfg. Co.
Union Mfg. Co.

Pumps, Chain—
Union Mfg. Co.

Pumps, Cistern, Pitcher Spout, &c.—
Barnes Mfg. Co.
Champion Iron Co.
Deming Co.
W. & B. Douglas.
F. E. Myers & Bro.
J. E. Porter Co.

Pumps, Compression and Vacuum—
Deming Co.

Pumps, Diaphragm—
Barnes Mfg. Co.
Boston & Lockport Block Co.
W. & B. Douglas.

Pumps, Electric—
W. & B. Douglas.
General Electric Co.
Henry R. Worthington.

Pumps, Fire—
Hooker-Colville Steam Pump Co.

Pumps, Force—
Barnes Mfg. Co.
Champion Iron Co.
Deming Co.
W. & B. Douglas.
Mast, Foos & Co.
McNab & Harlin Mfg. Co.
F. E. Myers & Bro.
J. E. Porter Co.
Union Mfg. Co.

Pumps, Grouting, Sewerage and Quarry—
Deming Co.
W. & B. Douglas.

Pumps, Ham Preserving—
Deming Co.
Silver Mfg. Co.

Pumps, Irrigation—
F. E. Myers & Bro.

Pumps, Jacket—
Barnes Mfg. Co.

Pumps, Lift—
Champion Iron Co.
W. & B. Douglas.

Mast, Foos & Co.
F. E. Myers & Bro.
J. E. Porter Co.

Pumps, *Manure, Liquid—*
W. & B. Douglas.

Pumps, *Mine (Cylinders and Heads)—*
Deming Co.

Pumps, *Oil—*
Deming Co.
W. & B. Douglas.

Pumps, *Plumbers' and Gas Fitters'—*
Barnes Mfg. Co.
Deming Co.
W. & B. Douglas.

Pumps, *Power—*
Deming Co.
W. & B. Douglas.
Hooker Colville Steam Pump Co
John H. McGowan Co.
F. E. Myers & Bro.
Springfield Elevator & Pump Co.
Union Steam Pump Co.
Henry R. Worthington.

Pumps, *Self Measuring—*
Enterprise Mfg. Co.

Pumps, *Ship and Deck—*
Deming Co.
W. & B. Douglas.

Pumps, *Siphon—*
Humphryes Mfg. Co.

Pumps, *Spraying—*
Barnes Mfg. Co.
Deming Co.
W. & B. Douglas.
Mast, Foos & Co.
F. E. Myers & Bro.
J. E. Porter Co.

Pumps, *Steam—*
Hooker-Colville Steam Pump Co.
Ingersoll-Sergeant Drill Co.
John H. McGowan Co.
Springfield Elevator & Pump Co.
Union Steam Pump Co.
Henry R. Worthington.

Pumps, *Tank—*
Barnes Mfg. Co.
Deming Co.
Humphryes Mfg. Co.
Mast, Foos & Co.
F. E. Myers & Bro.
J. E. Porter Co.

Pumps, *Water Works* –
E. P. Allis Co.
Deming Co.
Hooker-Colville Steam Pump Co.
Wm. Tod & Co.
Henry R. Worthington.

Pumps, *Windmill—*
Barnes Mfg. Co.
Champion Iron Co.
Deming Co.
W. & B. Douglas.
Humphryes Mfg. Co.
Mast, Foos & Co.
F. E. Myers & Bro.
J. E. Porter Co.

Punches, *Hand and Power—*
Bertsch & Co.
Bignall & Keeler Mfg. Co.
Buffalo Forge Co.
Cleveland Punch & Shear Works Co.
Davis & Egan Machine Tool Co.
Charles G. Eckstein & Co.
Erdle & Schenck.
Fulton Iron & Engine Works.
Hilles & Jones Co.
Long & Allstatter Co.
John Loyd.
Jos. F. McCoy Co.
Frank-Kneeland Machine Co.
Mackintosh, Hemphill & Co.
National Machinery Co.
Pittsburgh Mfg. Co.
Pond Machine Tool Co.
Wm. Sellers & Co.
Wais & Roos Punch & Shear Co.
Watson-Stillman Co.
Whitcomb Mfg. Co.
R. D. Wood & Co.

Punches, *Cattle—*
Fred. J. Meyers Mfg. Co.

Punches, Conductor, &c.—
Fred. J. Meyers Mfg. Co.
R. Woodman Mfg. & Supply Co.

Punches, Drive—
Bemis & Call Hardware & Tool Co.
Buck Bros.
Knapp & Cowles Mfg. Co.
H. H. Mayhew Co.
Peck, Stow & Wilcox Co.
Tuck Mfg. Co.

Punches, Hydraulic—
Richard Dudgeon.
Frank Kneeland Machine Co.
Mackintosh, Hemphill & Co.
Watson-Stillman Co.
R. D. Wood & Co.

Punches, Paper, Metal, &c.—
Charles Morrill.

Punches, Spiral Shear—
Pratt & Whitney Co.

Punches, Spring—
Fred. J. Meyers Mfg. Co.

Punches, Ticket—
Fred. J. Meyers Mfg. Co.

Punches, Triple—
Butts & Ordway.
I. P. Richards.

Punching Presses—See *Presses, Punching.*

Purifiers, Feed Water—
Harrisburg Pipe Bending Co.
Harrison Safety Boiler Works.
National Pipe Bending Co.
Warren Webster & Co.
Whitlock Coil Pipe Co.

Purifiers, Oil—
Q & C Co.

Push Buttons, Carts, Plates—See *Buttons, Carts, Plates.*

Pushers, Car—
Boston & Lockport Block Co.
R. Woodman Mfg. & Supply Co.

Pushes, Electric Bell—
Norwalk Lock Co.

Putty Knives—See *Knives, Putty.*

Putty, Store—
Cleveland Stone Co.

Pyrometers—
Ashcroft Mfg. Co.
Edward Brown.
Uehling, Steinbart & Co.

Quadrants, Brass Skylight—
W. & J. Tiebout.

Quarry Pumps—See *Pumps, Grouting and Quarry.*

Quartering Machines—
Wm. Sellers & Co.

Quoits—
Logan & Strobridge Iron Co.
Plenger & Henger Mfg. Co.
Reading Hardware Co.
A. C. Williams.

Rabbet and Butt Gauges — See *Gauges, Butt and Rabbet.*

Rack Cutters, Automatic—See *Cutters, Automatic Rack*

Rack Cutting Attachments, Cutting Machines—See *Cutting Attachments, Cutting Machines.*

Racks, Axe—
Weedsport Drill Co.

Racks, Card, Book and Paper—
Peck, Stow & Wilcox Co.

Racks, Fruit Steaming—
Sidney Shepard & Co.

Racks, Pew, Book—
Logan & Strobridge Iron Co.

Racks, Pie—
Wire Goods Co.

Racks, Steel Goods—
Iowa Farming Tool Co.

Racks and Rings, Towel—
Plenger & Henger Mfg. Co.

Radial Countersinking Machines—
See Countersinking Radial Machines.

Radiator Screens—See Screens, Radiator.

Radiators, Steam and Hot Water—
Jarecki Mfg. Co.

Radiators, Gas and Oil—
Schneider & Trenkamp Co.

Rafter Brackets, Grabs—See Brackets, Grabs.

Rail Benders, Bonds, Drills—See Benders, Bonds, Drills.

Rail, Door—
Bridgeport Brass Co.
Chicago Spring Butt Co.
Lane Bros.
Lawrence Bros.
McKinney Mfg. Co.
Peck, Stow & Wilcox Co.
Plenger & Henger Mfg. Co.
Plume & Atwood Mfg. Co.
Randolph & Clowes.
Reading Hardware Co.
Russell & Erwin Mfg. Co.
Scovill Mfg. Co.
Stanley Works.
Stowell Mfg. & Foundry Co.
Wilcox Mfg. Co.

Railing and Brackets, Office, Counter, &c.—
E. T. Barnum.
Bradley & Hubbard Mfg. Co.
Columbus Wire & Iron Works.
Edward Darby & Sons.
Ellis & Helfenberger.
Estey Wire Works Co.
Howard & Morse.
Gilbert & Bennett Mfg. Co.
Ludlow-Saylor Wire Co.
Fred. J. Meyers Mfg. Co.
Scheeler's Sons.
Stewart Iron Works.
W. S. Tyler Wire Works Co.
Wright & Colton Wire Cloth Co.

Railroad Cars, Forgings, Spikes, Tires, Track Scales, Turn Tables
—See Cars, Forgings, Spikes, Tires, Scales, Turn Tables.

Railroad Equipment—
Hirons & Co.
W. H. Thompson & Co.

Railroads, Cable—See Conveying Machinery.

Rails, Girder—
Cambria Iron Co.
Holland Co.

Rails, Light—
Allentown Rolling Mills.
Ætna-Standard Iron & Steel Co.
Bethlehem Iron Co.
Cambria Iron Co.
Riverside Iron Works.
Tudor Iron Works.

Rails, Old—See Material, Old.

Rails, Steel—
Bethlehem Iron Co.
Cambria Iron Co.
Hirons & Co.
J. W. Hoffman & Co.
Holland Co.
C. B. Houston & Co.
Henry Levis & Co.
Nicolls, Wheeler & Co.
Pierson & Co.
Riverside Iron Works.

Rails and Hangers, Suspended—
Ney Mfg. Co.
Trenton Iron Co.

Raisin Seeders—See Seeders, Raisin.

Rake Teeth—See Teeth, Rake.

Rakes, Garden—
Ely Hoe & Fork Co.
Iowa Farming Tool Co.

Rakes, Hay, Horse—
Long & Allstatter Co.

Rakes, Lawn—
Dain Mfg. Co.
Iowa Farming Tool Co.
Ney Mfg. Co.

Rams, Hydraulic—
  Barnes Mfg. Co.
  Deming Co.
  W. & B. Douglas.
  Humphryes Mfg. Co.
  Union Mfg. Co.

Ranges—See *Stoves and Ranges.*

Rasps and Files—See *Files and Rasps.*

Rasps, Horse Tooth—
  Heller Bros.
  Nicholson File Co.

Ratchets, Brass—
  Boston Gear Works.
  W. & J. Tiebout.
  T. F. Welch Mfg. Co.

Rachet Drills, Pawls—See *Drills, Pawls.*

Rat Traps—See *Traps.*

Rawhide Belting, Belt Lacing—See *Belting, Belt Lacing.*

Rawhide Hammers, Mallets—See *Hammers, Mallets.*

Razor Hones—See *Hones, Razor.*

Razors—
  Swedish Razor Co.

Reamer Grinders, Holders, Wrenches—See *Grinders, Holders, Wrenches.*

Reamers—
  Buck Bros.
  Butterfield & Co.
  S. W. Card Mfg. Co.
  J. M. Carpenter Tap & Die Co.
  Cincinnati Screw & Tap Co.
  Cleveland Twist Drill Co.
  Hartford Machine Screw Co.
  J. M. King & Co.
  H. H. Mayhew Co.
  Morse Twist Drill & Machine Co.
  Pratt & Whitney Co.
  Standard Tool Co.
  Strange Forged Drill & Tool Co.
  Tuck Mfg. Co.
  Wiley & Russell Mfg. Co.

Reamers, Pipe—See *Taps and Reamers, Pipe.*

Reaming Machines—See *Tapping and Reaming Machines.*

Receivers, Air—
  Clayton Air Compressor Works.

Recorders, Steam — See *Indicators, Steam.*

Recording Gauges—See *Gauges, Recording.*

Recording Instruments, Temperature—
  The Bristol Co.

Reducers, Conductor—
  Garry Iron Roofing Co.

Reducers, Hose — See *Hose Attachments.*

Reducing Rings, Valves—See *Rings Valves.*

Reeling Machines—
  Fairmount Machine Co.

Reels, *Chalk Line*—
  Stanley Rule & Level Co.
  Union Hardware Co.

Reels, *Clothes Line*—
  Plenger & Henger Mfg. Co.
  John Sommer's Son.
  E. C. Stearns & Co.

Reels, *Fishing*—
  Andrew B. Hendryx Co.
  John Sommer's Son.

Reels, *Garden Line*—
  Knapp & Cowles Mfg. Co.

Reels, *Hose*—
  The Hartzell Novelty Works.
  King & Knight.
  R. W. Whitehurst & Co.

Reels, *Picture Wire*—
  Ossawan Mills Co.

Reels, *Wire Rod*—
  Morgan Construction Co

Reels, *Wire*—
  Automatic Machine Co.

Reflectors, Lamp—
Plume & Atwood Mfg. Co.

Reflectors, Locomotive—
Waterbury Brass Co.

Refrigerator Catches, Hinges,—See *Catches, Hinges.*

Refrigerators—
Challenge Corn Planter Co.

Registers and Ceiling Plates, Stove Pipe—
Arcade Mfg. Co.
S. Cheney & Son.
E. C. Stearns & Co.
Stover Mfg. Co.
Stowell Mfg. & Foundry Co.

Registers and Ventilators—
Ferrosteel Co.
William Highton & Sons.
Plenger & Henger Mfg. Co.
Stowell Mfg. & Foundry Co.

Regulators, Damper—
D'Este & Seeley Co.
McNab & Harlin Mfg. Co.

Regulators, Feed Water—
D'Este & Seeley Co.

Regulators, Pressure—
D'Este & Seeley Co.

Regulators, Pressure—See *Pressure Regulators.*

Regulators, Upholsterers'—
Tuck Mfg. Co.

Regulators, Wind Mill—
Stover Mfg. Co.

Repair Kits, Cobblers'—See *Cobblers' Kits.*

Repair Kits, Stove and Harness—
Brandenburg & Co.

Repair Links—See *Links, Repair.*

Repair Outfits and Supplies, Tire—
See *Tire Repair Outfits and Supplies.*

Rests, Foot, Shoe Blacking—
Chicago Spring Butt Co.
Reading Hardware Co.

Rests, Meat, Wire—See *Household Articles, Wire.*

Rests, Shirt, Wire—See *Household Articles, Wire.*

Retorts, Clay—
Cyrus Borgner.
Henry Maurer & Son.

Revolution Counters—See *Counters, Revolution.*

Revolvers—See *Pistols and Revolvers.*

Ribbon, Sash—
Caldwell Mfg. Co.

Riddles and Sieves—
Edward Darby & Sons.
Estey Wire Works Co.
Gilbert & Bennett Mfg. Co.
Howard & Morse.
Ludlow-Saylor Wire Co.
Fred. J. Meyers Mfg. Co.
Osborn Mfg. Co.
Scheeler's Sons.
W. S. Tyler Wire Works.
Wright & Colton Wire Cloth Co.

Ridging, Iron—
American Steel Roofing Co.
Garry Iron Roofing Co.
Youngstown Iron & Steel Roofing Co.

Rifflers, Bent—
Nicholson File Co.

Rifles, Carbines, &c.—
Remington Arms Co.
J. Stevens Arms & Tool Co.

Rifling Machines, Gun Barrel—
Pratt & Whitney Co.

Rim Drilling Machines—See *Drilling Machines, Bicycle Rim.*

Ring Bolts, Gauges—See *Bolts, Gauges.*

Ring Machines, Wire—
E. W. Bliss Co.
Mossberg & Granville Mfg. Co.

Rings, Bull—
Peck, Stow & Wilcox Co.
Seymour Smith & Son.

Rings, Clinch—
Wm. H. Haskell Co.
Rhode Island Tool Co.

Rings, Flush—
Norwalk Lock Co.
Peck, Stow & Wilcox Co.
Reading Hardware Co.
Russell & Erwin Mfg. Co.
W. & J. Tiebout.

Rings, Fruit Jar—
New York Belting & Packing Co.

Rings, Hitching—
Ney Mfg. Co.
Peck, Stow & Wilcox Co.
E. C. Stearns & Co.
W. & J. Tiebout.
Wire Goods Co.

Rings, Key—
Billings & Spencer Co.

Rings, Malleable, Brass, &c.—
W. & J. Tiebout.

Rings on Plates—
W. & J. Tiebout.

Rings, Piston—
Samuel Trethewey & Co.

Rings, Reducing—
Stowell Mfg. & Foundry Co.

Rings, Rubber—See *Gaskets and Rings. Rubber.*

Rings, Towel—See *Racks and Rings.*

Riveted Work—See *Buildings and Bridges.*

Riveting Machinery—
John Adt & Son.
Bement, Miles & Co.
Garvin Machine Co.
Wm. Sellers & Co.
Watson-Stillman Co.
R. D. Wood & Co.

Rivet Clippers, Rods—See *Clippers, Rods.*

Rivet Iron—See *Iron, Rivet.*

Rivet Machinery—
Acme Machinery Co.
E. J. Manville Machine Co.
Waterbury Farrel Foundry & Machine Co.

Rivet Sets, Tongs—See *Sets, Tongs.*

Rivets, Brass—
Ansonia Brass & Copper Co.
Blake & Johnson.
Cobb & Drew.

Rivets, Braziers'—
Clendenin Bros.
Plume & Atwood Mfg. Co.
Scovill Mfg. Co.
Stover Mfg. Co.

Rivets, Clinch—
William N. Merriam.

Rivets, Iron and Steel—
American Rivet Co.
American Screw Co.
Blake & Johnson.
Burden Iron Co.
Clark & Cowles.
Clendenin Bros.
Cobb & Drew.
Dover Iron Co.
William N. Merriam.
Milwaukee Tack Co.
Port Chester Bolt & Nut Co.
Pennsylvania Bolt & Nut Co
Pittsburgh Mfg. Co.
Russell and Erwin Mfg. Co.
Jos. T. Ryerson & Son.
J. H. Sternbergh Mfg. Co.
C. C. & E. P. Townsend.

Rivets, Oyster—
W. & J. Tiebout.

Rivets and Burrs, Copper—
Ansonia Brass & Copper Co.
Bridgeport Brass Co.
Clendenin Bros.
Cobb & Drew.
Hendricks Bros.
U. T. Hungerford.
William N. Merriam.
Plume & Atwood Mfg. Co.
Waterbury Brass Co.

Road Rollers, Scrapers—See *Rollers, Scrapers.*

Roasters, Coffee—
Lane Bros.

Roasting and Baking Pans—See *Pans, Roasting and Baking.*

Rock Crushers—See *Crushers, Ore and Rock.*

Rock Drill Steel—See *Steel, Rock Drill.*

Rock Drills—See *Drills, Rock.*

Rod Cutters, Headers—See *Cutters, Headers.*

Rod Pointing Machines—See *Pointing Machines, Rod and Tube.*

Rod Reels, Wire—See *Reels, Wire Rod.*

Rods, Brass—See *Brass Rods.*

Rods, Connecting—
Frankford Steel Co.

Rods, Drill—
Hermann Boker & Co.
Crescent Steel Co.

Rods, Gauging, &c.—
Stanley Rule & Level Co.

Rods, Measuring—
Buffalo Scale Co.

Rods, Miter—
National Saw Co.

Rods, Nail and Rivet—
Abbott, Wheelock & Co.
Arthur C. Harvey Co.
A. Milne & Co.
Wm. & Harvey Rowland.

Rods, Piston—
Finished Steel Co.

Rods, Pump—
Finished Steel Co.

Rods, Saw—
Henry Disston & Sons.
National Saw Co.
Peck, Stow & Wilcox Co

Rods, Stove—
American Screw Co.

Rods, Roof, Bridge and Truss—
American Bolt Co.
Pennsylvania Bolt & Nut Co.

Rods, Steel Drill—
Cincinnati Screw & Tap Co.

Rods, Tie—
J. H. Sternbergh & Son.

Rods, Wire—
American Wire Co.
Consolidated Steel & Wire Co.
A. Milne & Co.
New Castle Wire Nail Co.
Pittsburgh Wire Co.

Roll Copper—See *Copper, Roll and Sheet.*

Roll Engraving Lathes—See *Lathes, Roll Engraving.*

Roll Grinders, Lathes, Pinions, Turning Plugs — See *Grinders, Lathes, Pinions, Plugs.*

Roll, Brass—See *Brass, Roll and Sheet.*

Roll, Bronze—See *Bronze, Roll and Sheet.*

Rolled Iron Shapes, Special—See *Shapes, Special Rolled Iron.*

Rolled Steel, Cold—See *Steel, Cold Rolled.*

Roller Bearings, Skates, Stays—See *Bearings, Skates, Stays.*

Rollers, Door—
Peck, Stow & Wilcox Co.
Reading Hardware Co.
Stowell Mfg. & Foundry Co.

Rollers, Land—
Lansing Wheelbarrow Co.
R. W. Whitehurst & Co.

Rollers, Lawn—
R. W. Whitehurst & Co.

Rollers, Road—
Thos. Carlin's Sons.

Rollers, Sash—
Ney Mfg. Co.
Peck, Stow & Wilcox Co.
Reading Hardware Co.
Russell & Erwin Mfg. Co.
W. & J. Tiebout.

Rollers, Stay—
Chicago Spring Butt Co.
Lawrence Bros.
Wilcox Mfg. Co.

Rollers, Towel—
Peck, Stow & Wilcox Co.

Rolling Mill Castings, Engines—
See *Castings, Engines.*

Rolling Mill Machinery—
Allentown Rolling Mills.
E. P. Allis & Co.
Birmingham Iron Foundry.
Lloyd Booth Co.
Frank-Kneeland Machine Co.
Leechburg Foundry & Machine Co.
Mackintosh, Hemphill & Co.
Morgan Construction Co.
New Castle Engineering Works.
Pittsburgh Shear Knife & Machine Co.
R. Poole & Son Co.
Robinson-Rea Mfg. Co.
Wm. Tod & Co.
Totten & Hogg Iron & Steel Foundry Co.
Waterbury Farrel Foundry & Machine Co.

Rolling Pins—See *Pins, Rolling.*

Rolls, Bending and Straightening—
Bement, Miles & Co.
Bertsch & Co.
Thos. Carlin's Sons.
Cleveland Punch & Shear Works.
Hilles & Jones Co.
Niles Tool Works Co.
Pittsburgh Mfg. Co.
Wm. Sellers & Co.
Wais & Roos Punch & Shear Co.
Whitcomb Mfg. Co

Rolls, Crimping—
Bertsch & Co.

Rolls, Crushing—
E. P. Allis Co.
Thos. Carlin's Sons.

Rolls, Dandy—
Eastwood Wire Mfg. Co.

Rolls, Hardened Forged Steel—
Samuel Trethewey & Co.

Rolls, Jewelers'—
E. J. Manville Machine Co.
Mossberg & Granville Mfg. Co.

Rolls, Rawhide Pinking—
Brockton Mallet Co.

Rolls, Rubber Covered—
New York Belting & Packing Co.

Rolls, Sand Chilled and Steel—
Birmingham Iron Foundry.
Lloyd Booth Co.
Frankford Steel Co.
Frank-Kneeland Machine Co.
A. Garrison Foundry Co.
Leechburg Foundry & Machine Co.
Lorain Foundry Co.
Robinson-Rea Mfg. Co.
Seaman-Sleeth Co.
Totten & Hogg Iron & Steel Foundry Co.

Rolls, Typewriter—See *Platens and Rolls, Typewriter.*

Roof Bolts, Rods—See *Bolts, Rods.*

Roofing, Asbestos—
H. W. Johns Mfg. Co.

Roofing Brackets, Cement, Tongs—
See *Brackets, Cement, Tongs.*

Roofing, Iron and Steel—
American Steel Roofing Co.
Berlin Iron Bridge Co.
Cambridge Roofing Co.
Cincinnati Corrugated Co.
Garry Iron Roofing Co.
Globe Iron Roofing & Corrugating Co.
Kansas City Metal Roofing and Corrugating Co.
Shiffler Bridge Co.
W. H. Thomas & Co.
Youngstown Iron & Steel Roofing Co.

Roofing, Metal—See *Corrugated Iron.*

Roofs—See *Buildings and Bridges.*

Root, Tobacco, Cutters—See *Cutters, Tobacco and Root.*

Rope, Braided Cotton, Linen, &c.—
Samson Cordage Works.
Silver Lake Co.

Rope Clamps, Fasteners, Fittings, Halters, Hoists, Stanchions, Swivels, Thimbles, Tramways.—See *Clamps, Fasteners, Fittings, Halters Hoists, Stanchions, Swivels, Thimbles, Tramways.*

Rope Transmission, Power—
Geo. V. Cresson Co.
Dodge Mfg. Co.
Fairmount Machine Co.
Link-Belt Engineering Co.

Rope, Wire—
Broderick & Bascom Rope Co.
Hazard Mfg. Co.
A. Leschen & Sons Rope Co.
Trenton Iron Co.
Washburn & Moen Mfg. Co.

Ropes, Hammock and Hitching—
Covert Mfg. Co.
Covert's Saddlery Works.

Rosettes, Iron—
Chas. G. Eckstein & Co.
Haight & Clark.
Stowell Mfg. & Foundry Co.

Rotary Engines, Planers, Shears, Slitting Knives—See *Engines, Knives, Planers, Shears.*

Rowlocks—
W. & J. Tiebout.

Rub Irons—See *Irons, Rub.*

Rubber Belting, Hose, Mallets, Mats, Stamps, Tiling, Tubing, Valves—See *Belting, Hose, Mallets, Mats, Stamps, Tiling, Tubing, Valves.*

Rubber Covered Rolls—See *Rolls, Rubber Covered.*

Rubber Goods, Mechanical—
H. O. Canfield.
New York Belting & Packing Co.

Rubber Rings—See *Plumbing Supplies*

Rubber Sheets, Vulcanized — See *Sheet Rubber, Vulcanized.*

Rubber, Tennis Soling—See *Tennis Soling Rubber.*

Rubber Tired Wheels—See *Wheels, Rubber Tired.*

Rubbers, Pedal—
Morgan & Wright.

Rudder Braces—See *Braces, Rudder.*

Rules, Boxwood—
Stanley Rule & Level Co.

Rules, Ivory—
Stanley Rule & Level Co.

Rules, Machinists'—
Athol Machine Co.
Coffin & Leighton.
Henry Disston & Sons.
L. S. Starrett Co.
J. Stevens Arms & Tool Co.

Rules, Tinners'—
Peck, Stow & Wilcox Co.
Russell & Erwin Mfg. Co.

Rumbling Barrels—See *Barrels, Tumbling.*

Runs, House and Car—See *Ice Harvesting Tools.*

Runways—
Lansing Wheelbarrow Co.

S & S Hooks—See *Hooks, S and S.*

Sad Iron Handles, Heaters, Stands—See *Handles, Heaters, Stands.*

Sad Irons—See *Irons, Sad, Laundry, &c.*

Saddlers' Hammers—See *Hammers, Saddlers' and Upholsterers'.*

THE IRON AGE INDEX.

Saddlery Hardware—
Chapman Mfg. Co.
Covert Mfg. Co.
Covert's Saddlery Works.
W. & E. T. Fitch Co.
Imperial Bit & Snap Co.

Saddles, Bicycle—
Bridgeport Gun Implement Co.
W. W. Shoe.

Safes, Cheese—
E. T. Barnum

Safes, Match—
Logan & Strobridge Iron Co.
Peck, Stow & Wilcox Co.
Reading Hardware Co.
Russell & Erwin Mfg. Co.
Scovill Mfg. Co.
A. C. Williams.

Safes, Provision—
Howard & Morse.

Safety Chain, Pins, Valves—See *Chain, Pins, Valves.*

Salts, Shaker—
Fred. J. Meyers Mfg. Co.

Sample Holders—See *Holders, Sample.*

Sand Blast Machinery—
Ward & Nash.

Sand Mixing Machines, Rolls, Sifters—See *Mixing Machines, Rolls, Sifters.*

Sand Screens—See *Screens, Sand, Coal, &c.*

Sand Paper—See *Papers, Sand, Garnet, &c.*

Sash Balances, Centers, Cord, Fasteners, Holders, Lifters, Locks, Pulleys, Ribbon, Rollers, Springs, Weights — See *Balances, Centers, Cord, Fasteners, Holders, Lifters, Locks, Pulleys, Ribbon, Rollers, Springs, Weights.*

Sash Centers—See *Centers, Sash and Transom.*

Sash Chains and Attachments—See *Chains, Sash, and Attachments.*

Sash Cord Irons—See *Irons, Sash Cord.*

Sash Holders, Pins — See *Holders, Pins.*

Sash, Iron—See *Iron Work, Builders'.*

Sausage Stuffers — See *Stuffers, Sausage.*

Savings Banks, Toy—See *Toy Savings Banks.*

Saw Arbors, Bucks, Clamps, Frames, Gummers, Handles, Knives, Rods, Screws, Sets, Sharpeners, Stretchers, Tables, Tools, Vises—See *Arbors, Bucks, Clamps, Frames, Gummers, Handles, Knives, Rods, Screws, Sets, Sharpeners, Stretchers, Tables, Tools, Vises.*

Saw Guides, Band—See *Guides, Band Saw.*

Saw Handles, Crosscut—See *Handles, Crosscut Saw.*

Saw Setting and Filing Machines, Band—See *Setting and Filing Machines, Band Saw.*

Saw Steel—See *Steel, Saw.*

Saw Tooth Gauges—See *Gauges, Saw Tooth.*

Saw Mill Machinery—
E. P. Allis Co.
Lane & Bodley Co.

Saw Mill Dogs, Trucks—See *Dogs, Trucks.*

Sawing Machines, Metal—
Cleveland Punch & Shear Works.
Newton Machine Tool Works.
Q & C Co.

Saws, Band—
E. C. Atkins & Co.
Henry Disston & Sons.
National Saw Co.

Silver Mfg. Co.
Simonds Mfg. Co.

Saws, Butcher—
Geo. H. Bishop & Co.
Henry Disston & Sons.
Millers Falls Co.
National Saw Co.

Saws, Circular—
E. C. Atkins & Co.
W. F. & John Barnes Co.
Henry Disston & Sons.
National Saw Co.
Seneca Falls Mfg. Co.
Simonds Mfg. Co.

Saws, Dehorning—
Henry Disston & Sons.
National Saw Co.

Saws, Gauge—
Henry Disston & Sons.

Saws, Hack, and Hack Saw Blades—
Cincinnati Screw & Tap Co.
Henry Disston & Sons.
Millers Falls Co.
Tower & Lyon.

Saws, Hand, Panel, Back, &c.—
E. C. Atkins & Co.
Geo. H. Bishop & Co.
Henry Disston & Sons.
National Saw Co.

Saws, Ice—
Geo. H. Bishop & Co.
Henry Disston & Sons.
National Saw Co.
W. T. Wood & Co.

Saws, Jewelers'—
Millers Falls Co.

Saws, Power, Hack—
Millers Falls Co.
Q & C Co.
Stover Novelty Works.

Saws, Mill, Mulay, Crosscut, Drag, &c.—
E. C. Atkins & Co.
Geo. H. Bishop & Co.
Henry Disston & Sons.
National Saw Co.
Simonds Mfg. Co.

Saws, Pruning—
Geo. H. Bishop & Co.
Henry Disston & Sons.
National Saw Co.

Saws, Scroll, and Scroll Saw Blades—
W. F. & John Barnes Co.
Henry Disston & Sons.
Millers Falls Co.
Seneca Falls Mfg. Co.

Saws, Slitting—
L. S. Starrett Co.

Saws, Stone—
F. R. Patch Mfg. Co.

Saws, Tube—
Waterbury Farrel Foundry & Machine Co.

Saws, Wood, and Wood Saw Blades—
Geo. H. Bishop & Co.
Henry Disston & Sons.
National Saw Co.
Stover Mfg. Co.

Scalers, Fish—
Covert's Saddlery Works.
Reading Hardware Co.

Scale Beams—
Buffalo Scale Co.
John Chatillon & Sons.
Peck, Stow & Wilcox Co.

Scales, Army and Navy—
Buffalo Scale Co.

Scales, Bicycle—
Buffalo Scale Co.

Scales, Candy—
John Chatillon & Sons.

Scales, Cheese—
Buffalo Scale Co.

Scales, Coal, Hay, &c.—
Buffalo Scale Co.

Scales, Computing—
Pelouze Scale & Mfg. Co.

Scales, Cotton—
Buffalo Scale Co.

Scales, *Counter—*
  Buffalo Scale Co.
  John Chatillon & Sons.
  Peck, Stow & Wilcox Co.
  Pelouze Scale & Mfg. Co.
  Reading Hardware Co.
  I. S. Spencer's Sons.

Scales, *Dormant—*
  Buffalo Scale Co.

Scales, *Family—*
  John Chatillon & Sons.
  Pelouze Scale & Mfg. Co.
  North Bros. Mfg. Co.
  I.S. Spencer's Sons.

Scales, *Furnace Charging—*
  John Chatillon & Sons.

Scales, *Graduated—*
  Brown & Sharpe Mfg. Co.

Scales, *Grain—*
  Buffalo Scale Co.
  Pratt & Whitney Co.

Scales, *Hanging Hopper Beam—*
  Buffalo Scale Co.

Scales, *Leather Inspectors'—*
  John Chatillon & Sons.

Scales *Lifting—*
  John Chatillon & Sons.

Scales, *Platform—*
  Buffalo Scale Co.
  John Chatillon & Sons.

Scales, *Postal—*
  Buffalo Scale Co.
  John Chatillon & Sons.
  Pelouze Scale & Mfg. Co.

Scales, *Power—*
  Florence Machine Co.

Scales, *Professional—*
  Pelouze Scale & Mfg. Co.

Scales, *R. R. Track—*
  Buffalo Scale Co.

Scales, *Reverse Acting Meat Beam—*
  Buffalo Scale Co.

Scales, *Stock—*
  Buffalo Scale Co.

Scales, *Suspended—*
  Buffalo Scale Co.
  John Chatillon & Sons.
  Pelouze Scale & Mfg. Co.

Scales, *Union—*
  Buffalo Scale Co.
  John Chatillon & Sons.

Scissors—See *Shears and Scissors.*

Scoop Nets—See *Nets, Scoop.*

Scoops, *Candy—*
  John Chatillon & Sons.

Scoops, *Grain, Coal, &c.—*
  St. Louis Shovel Co.

Scoops, *Wood—*
  John Sommer's Son.

Scrap—See *Material, Old.*

Scrapers, *Box—*
  Knapp & Cowles Mfg. Co.
  Peck, Stow & Wilcox Co.
  Stanley Rule & Level Co.

Scrapers, *Butchers' Block—*
  National Saw Co.

Scrapers, *Cabinet and Bench—*
  E. C. Atkins & Co.
  Geo. H. Bishop & Co.
  Henry Disston & Sons.

Scrapers, *Floor—*
  Osborn Mfg. Co.

Scrapers, *Foot—*
  Arcade Mfg. Co.
  Logan & Strobridge Iron Co.
  Peck, Stow & Wilcox Co.
  Pleuger & Henger Mfg. Co.
  Reading Hardware Co.
  Stover Mfg. Co.

Scrapers, *Hog—*
  Peck, Stow & Wilcox Co.

Scrapers, *Ice —* See *Ice Harvesting Tools.*

Scrapers, Machinists'—
Nicholson File Co.

Scrapers, Plumbers'—
Knapp & Cowles Mfg. Co.
Peck, Stow & Wilcox Co.

Scrapers, Road—
American Steel Scraper Co.
Kilbourne & Jacobs Mfg. Co.
Sidney Steel Scraper Co.
Syracuse Chilled Plow Co.

Scrapers, Ship—
Knapp & Cowles Mfg. Co.

Scrapers, Shovel—
Arcade Mfg. Co.

Scrapers, Tree—
Knapp & Cowles Mfg. Co.

Scrapers, Walk and Street—
Iowa Farming & Tool Co.

Scrapers, Wall—
National Saw Co.

Scrapers and Buffer Steels — See *Steels, Buffer and Scraper.*

Scratch Awls, Gauges — See *Awls, Gauges.*

Screen Bolts, Doors, Lifters—See *Bolts, Doors, Lifters.*

Screen Door Catches—See *Catches, Screen Door.*

Screen Wire Cloth—See *Cloth, Window Screen.*

Screens, Radiator—
E. T. Barnum.

Screens, Sand and Coal, &c.—
E. T. Barnum.
Columbus Wire & Iron Works.
Edward Darby & Sons.
Estey Wire Works Co.
Gilbert & Bennett Mfg. Co.
Howard & Morse.
Ludlow-Saylor Wire Co.
Fred. J. Meyers Mfg. Co.
W. S. Tyler Wire Works Co.
Wickwire Bros.
Wright & Colton Wire Cloth Co.

Screens, Window—
E. C. Stearns & Co.

Screens, Window, Lettered—
E. T. Barnum.

Screw Cases—See *Cases, Screw and Bolt.*

Screw Cutting Die Heads—See *Die Heads, Screw Cutting.*

Screw Drivers—See *Drivers, Screw.*

Screw Driver Bits, Holders—See *Bits, Holders.*

Screw Holder and Driver—See *Drivers, Screw and Holder.*

Screw Hook Hinges — See *Hinges, Screw Hook or Strap and Eye.*

Screw Jacks, Plates, Presses, Pulleys, Wrenches—See *Jacks, Plates, Presses, Pulleys, Wrenches.*

Screw Machines—
Brown & Sharpe Mfg. Co.
Davis & Egan Machine Tool Co.
Draper Machine Tool Co.
Dreses, Mueller & Co.
Garvin Machine Co.
Jones & Lamson Machine Co.
Hartford Machine Screw Co.
E. J. Manville Machine Co.
Niles Tool Works Co.
Pratt & Whitney Co.
Prentiss Tool & Supply Co.

Screw Pitch Gauges—See *Gauges, Screw Pitch.*

Screws, Bed—
Shelton Co.

Screws, Bench—
Peck, Stow & Wilcox Co.
Reading Hardware Co.

Screws, Cap and Set—
American Bolt Co.
American Screw Co.
Cincinnati Screw & Tap Co.
Hartford Machine Screw Co.
Wm. H. Haskell & Co.

Milton Mfg. Co.
New Britain Hardware Mfg. Co.
Pennsylvania Bolt & Nut Co.
Port Chester Bolt & Nut Co.
Rhode Island Tool Co.
J. H. Sternbergh & Son.
Worcester Machine Screw Co.

Screws, Coach and Lag—
American Bolt Co.
American Screw Co.
Hartford Machine Screw Co.
Wm. H. Haskell Co.
Milton Mfg. Co.
Pennsylvania Bolt & Nut Co.
Shelton Co.
J. H. Sternbergh & Son.

Screws, Collar—
Cincinnati Screw & Tap Co.
Hartford Machine Screw Co.
New Britain Hardware Mfg. Co.
Worcester Machine Screw Co.

Screws, Cork—
Erie Specialty Co.

Screws, Dowel—
American Screw Co.

Screws, Drive—
J. H. Sternbergh & Son.

Screws, Hand Rail—
American Screw Co.
Van Wagoner & Williams Hardware Co.
Wire Goods Co.

Screws, Hanger—
American Bolt Co.

Screws, Hook and Eye—
J. H. Sternbergh & Son.
W. & J. Tiebout.

Screws, Knob—
American Screw Co.
Russell & Erwin Mfg. Co.

Screws, Machine—
American Screw Co.
W. C. Boone Mfg. Co.
Cincinnati Screw & Tap Co.
Hartford Machine Screw Co.

Harvey Hubbell.
New Britain Hardware Mfg. Co.
Philadelphia Machine Screw Works.
Russell & Erwin Mfg. Co.
Worcester Machine Screw Co.

Screws, Ore Washer—
Pennsylvania Bolt & Nut Co.

Screws, Saw—
Henry Disston & Sons.
National Saw Co.

Screws, Shutter, Store Door—
Peck, Stow & Wilcox Co.
Reading Hardware Co.
Russell & Erwin Mfg. Co.

Screws, Special—
Blake & Johnson.
Franklin S. Miles.

Screws, Thumb—
American Screw Co.
Billings & Spencer Co.
Hartford Machine Screw Co.
Logan & Strobridge Iron Co.
T. F. Welch Mfg. Co.

Screws, Wood—
American Screw Co.
Russell & Erwin Mfg. Co.

Scribers, Metal—
J. Stevens Arms & Tool Co.

Scribes, Timber—
Bemis & Call Hardware & Tool Co.

Scribing Blocks—See *Blocks, Scribing*.

Scroll Saws and Scroll Saw Blades
—See *Saws, Scroll, and Scroll Saw Blades*.

Scrub Brushes—See *Brushes, Whitewash, Horse, &c.*

Scuffle Hoes—See *Hoes, Scuffle*.

Scythe Stones—See *Stones, Scythe*.

Seal Presses—See *Presses, Seal*.

Seals, Sealing Devices, &c.—
Theo. Hiertz & Son.
R. Woodman Mfg. & Supply Co.

Seals, Strap—
Cary Mfg. Co.

Seats, Agricultural, Steel—
Avery Stamping Co.

Seats, Child's Carriage—
Imperial Bit & Snap Co.

Second Hand Machinery—
American Tool Works.
C. R. Baird & Co.
U. Baird Machinery Co.
C. R. Bigelow.
Marvin Briggs.
Thos. Carlin's Sons.
T. P. Conrad.
R. M. Cunliffe.
Davis & Egan Machine Tool Co.
B. M. Everson.
Garvin Machine Co.
Henry F. Hill.
J. H. Hillman & Co
W. C. Johnson & Sons Machinery Co.
Lodge & Shipley Machine Tool Co.
S. T. Lund.
J. J. McCabe.
Frank McSwegan & Sons.
Machinists' Supply Co.
New York Machinery Depot.
Niles Tool Works Co.
Pennsylvania Machine Co.
Wm. H. Perry & Co.
Powell Planer Co.
Poulterer & Co.
Prentiss Tool & Supply Co.
Scranton Supply & Machine Co.
L. F. Seyfert's Sons.
J. Steptoe & Co.
Thomas & Lowe Machinery Co.
Frank Toomey.
Wilson & Roake.

Seed Cases, Sowers—See *Cases, Sowers*.

Seeders, Cherry—
Logan & Strobridge Iron Co.

Seeders, Raisin—
Enterprise Mfg Co

Self Measuring Pumps—See *Pumps, Self Measuring*.

Selling Agents, Hardware — See *Agents, Hardware Manufacturers'*.

Sensitive Drills—See *Drills, Sensitive*.

Separators, Oil—
Davis & Egan Machine Tool Co.
D'Este & Seeley Co.

Separators, Steam—
D'Este & Seeley Co.
Harrison Safety Boiler Works.

Set Screws—See *Screws, Cap and Set*.

Sets, Garden Tool—
Iowa Farming Tool Co.
Knapp & Cowles Mfg. Co.

Sets, Nail—
Buck Bros.
Goodell Bros. Co.
Knapp & Cowles Mfg. Co.
H. H. Mayhew Co.
Snell Mfg. Co.
Storm Mfg. Co.
Tuck Mfg. Co.

Sets, Rivet—
Peck, Stow & Wilcox Co.

Sets, Saw—
E. C. Atkins & Co.
Bemis & Call Hardware & Tool Co.
Henry Disston & Sons.
Fred. J. Meyers Mfg. Co.
Charles Morrill.
National Saw Co.
Peck, Stow & Wilcox Co.
Seymour Smith & Son.
Simonds Mfg. Co.
Taintor Mfg. Co.

Sets, Screw Driver and Tool—
Goodell Bros. Co.

Sets, Soldering—
Millers Falls Co.
Peck, Stow & Wilcox Co.
Stover Mfg. Co.

Sets, Smokers'—See *Smokers' Sets*.

Sets, Tool, Hollow Handle—
John S. Fray & Co.
Knapp & Cowles Mfg. Co.
Millers Falls Co.
Stanley Rule & Level Co.

Setting and Filing Machines, Band Saw—
Detrick & Harvey Machine Co.

Settees, Lawn—See *Chairs and Settees, Lawn.*

Sewer Gratings—See *Gratings, Foundation, Sewer, &c.*

Sewer Pipe, Traps—See *Pipe, Traps.*

Sewerage Pumps—See *Pumps, Grouting and Quarry.*

Sewing Machines—
Remington Arms Co.

Shade Cord—See *Cord, Shade and Ventilator.*

Shaft Adjusters, Hangers, Pulleys —See *Adjusters, Hangers, Pulleys.*

Shaft, Flexible—
Chicago Flexible Shaft Co.
Stow Flexible Shaft Co.
Stow Mfg. Co.

Shaft Straightening Machinery—
Niles Tool Works Co.

Shaft Trimmings, Leather — See *Trimmings, Shaft, Leather.*

Shaft Turning Lathes—See *Lathes, Shaft Turning.*

Shafting—
Allentown Rolling Mills.
E. P. Allis Co.
Bethlehem Iron Co.
Bradford Mill Co.
Cambria Iron Co.
Cleveland City Forge Co.
Geo. V. Cresson Co.
Denman & Davis.
Dodge Mfg. Co.
Fairmount Steel Co.
Finished Steel Co.
Frankford Steel Co.
Lane & Bodley Co.
Link-Belt Engineering Co.
F. R. Patch Mfg. Co.
Pierson & Co.
R. Poole & Son Co.
Roberts Mfg. Co.
Wm. Sellers & Co.

Shafting Collars, Oilers—See *Collars, Oilers.*

Shafts, Crank—
Bethlehem Iron Co.
Cleveland City Forge Co.
Frankford Steel Co.

Shaker Salts—See *Salts, Shaker.*

Shakers, Drink—
Erie Specialty Co.

Shapers—
Ames Mfg. Co.
W. F. & John Barnes Co.
Bement, Miles & Co.
Bignall & Keeler Mfg. Co.
Davis & Egan Machine Tool Co.
Detrick & Harvey Machine Co.
Gould & Eberhardt.
Hendey Machine Co.
New Haven Mfg. Co.
Niles Tool Works Co.
Pedrick & Ayer Co.
Pratt & Whitney Co.
Sebastian Lathe Co.
Wm. Sellers & Co.

Shapes, Agricultural—
Cambria Iron Co.
La Belle Steel Co
Singer, Nimick & Co.

Shapes, Special Rolled Iron—
J. G. Braun & Co.
Chas. G. Eckstein & Co.

Sharpeners, Dowel—
Stanley Rule & Level Co.

Sharpeners, Knife—
Millers Falls Co.
Pike Mfg. Co.
Star Heel Plate Co.
Tanite Co.

Sharpeners, Saw—
Diamond Machine Co.
Henry Disston & Sons.
Dupont Mfg. Co.

Sharpeners, Skate—
Osborn Mfg. Co.

Shavers, Beef—
Chadborn & Coldwell Mfg. Co.
Enterprise Mfg. Co.

Shavers, Ice—See *Ice Harvesting Tools.*

Shaves, Ice—
Enterprise Mfg. Co.
Erie Specialty Co.
Logan & Strobridge Iron Co.
North Bros. Mfg. Co.
Stover Mfg. Co.
A. C. Williams.

Shaves, Spoke—
Champion Safety Lock Co.
Millers Falls Co.
Seymour Smith & Son.
Stanley Rule & Level Co.
E. C. Stearns & Co.

Shaves, Tobacco—
North Bros. Mfg. Co.

Shaving Cups, Silver Plated—See *Cups, Shaving, Silver Plated.*

Shear Blades, Metal—See *Blades, Metal Shear.*

Shear Steel, Double—See *Steel, Double Shear.*

Shearing Machines, Hand—
Pond Machine Tool Co.

Shears, Beveling—
Hilles & Jones Co.

Shears, Hydraulic—
Henry Aiken.
Mackintosh, Hemphill & Co.
Morgan Construction Co.
Watson-Stillman Co.
R. D. Wood & Co.

Shears, Metal—
Henry Aiken.
Bertsch & Co.
E. W. Bliss Co.
Lloyd Booth Co.
Buffalo Forge Co.
Butts & Ordway.
Cleveland Punch & Shear Works.
Davis & Egan Machine Tool Co.
Chas. G. Eckstein & Co.
Fulton Iron & Engine Works.
Hilles & Jones Co.
Long & Alstatter Co.
Mackintosh, Hemphill & Co.
A. H. Merriman.
C. S. Mersick & Co.
Morgan Construction Co.
National Machinery Co.
Philadelphia Machine Tool Co.
Pittsburgh Foundry & Machine Co.
Wm. Sellers & Co.
Smith & Egge Mfg. Co.
Totten & Hogg Iron & Steel Foundry Co.
Wais & Roos Punch & Shear Co.
Watson-Stillman Co.
R. D. Wood & Co.

Shears, Pruning—
Knapp & Cowles Mfg. Co.
Fred. J. Meyers Mfg. Co.
New England Specialty Co.

Shears, Rotary—
Detrick & Harvey Machine Co.
Mossberg & Granville Mfg. Co.

Shears, Sheep—
Seymour Cutlery Co.

Shears, Tinners'—
Peck, Stow & Wilcox Co.

Shears, Wire—
J. M. King & Co,

Shears and Scissors—
Acme Shear Co.
Bridgeport Mfg. Co.
Farwell, Ozmun, Kirk & Co.
R. Heinisch's Sons Co.
Seymour Cutlery Co.

Sheathing, Asbestos—
H. W. Johns Mfg. Co.

Sheathing, Copper—
Hendricks Bros.

Sheaves, Door—
Norwalk Lock Co.
Peck, Stow & Wilcox Co.
Reading Hardware Co.
Russell & Erwin Mfg. Co.
E. C. Stearns & Co.
Stowell Mfg. & Foundry Co.
W. & J. Tiebout.

Sheaves, Power Transmission—
Thos. Carlin's Sons.
Geo. V. Cresson Co.
Dodge Mfg. Co.
Jeffrey Mfg. Co.
Link-Belt Engineering Co.
Trenton Iron Co.

Sheaves, Shutter—
Peck, Stow & Wilcox Co.
Reading Hardware Co.

Sheaves, Tackle Block—
Boston & Lockport Block Co.
W. & J. Tiebout.
Union Hardware Co.

Sheep Bells, Shears—See *Bells, Shears*.

Sheep Shearing Machines—
American Shearer Mfg. Co.

Sheet Copper—See *Copper, Roll and Sheet*.

Sheet Corrugating Machinery—
Frank-Kneeland Machine Co.

Sheet Guides—See *Guides, Sheet and Rope*.

Sheet Iron, *Cold Rolled—*
Cambridge Iron & Steel Co.

Sheet Iron, *Planished—*
W. Dewees Wood Co.

Sheet Iron Ware—See *Ware, Sheet Iron*.

Sheet Metal Dies—See *Dies, Sheet Metal*.

Sheet Metal Goods to Order—
Taplin Mfg. Co.

Sheet Metal Stamping—See *Stamping, Sheet Metal*.

Sheet Metal Work, Ornamental—
See *Metal Work, Ornamental Sheet*.

Sheet Metal Work, to order— See *Metal Work, Sheet, to order*.

Sheet Mill Doublers—See *Doublers, Sheet Mill*.

Sheet Rubber, *Vulcanized—*
New York Belting & Packing Co.

Sheet Steel, *Cold Rolled—*
Jonas & Colver Continental Steel Works.
Wm. Jessop & Sons.
Singer, Nimick & Co.
S. & C. Wardlow.

Sheet Steel, *Hot Rolled—*
Crescent Steel Co.
Jonas & Colver Continental Steel Works.
Wm. Jessop & Sons.
Singer, Nimick & Co.
S. & C. Wardlow.

Sheet and Roll Bronze—See *Bronze, Roll and Sheet*.

Sheets, *Aluminum—*
Pittsburgh Reduction Co.
Scovill Mfg. Co.

Sheets, *Brass—*
John Davol & Sons.
Wm. S. Fearing.
Pope's Island Mfg. Corporation.
See also *Brass, Roll and Sheet*.

Sheets, *Galley—*
Ansonia Brass & Copper Co.

Sheets, *Gold Bronze—*
Pope's Island Mfg. Corporation.

Sheets, *Iron and Steel—*
Ætna-Standard Iron & Steel Co.
Cambridge Iron & Steel Co.
Carbon Steel Co.

Justice Cox. Jr.
Crescent Steel Co.
J. W. Hoffman & Co.
William Jessop & Sons
Henry Levis & Co.
Railway Supply Co.
Wm. & Henry Rowland.
Jos. T. Ryerson & Son.
Scottdale Iron & Steel Co.
S. & C. Wardlow.
Wilmot & Hobbs Mfg. Co.
Alan Wood Co.
W. Dewees Wood Co.

Sheets and Roll Brass—See *Brass, Roll and Sheets.*

Shelf Boxes, Brackets, Pins, Supports—See *Boxes, Brackets, Pins, Supports.*

Shellers, Corn—
Garry Iron Roofing Co.
Stover Mfg. Co.
R. W. Whitehurst & Co.

Shells, *Brass, Seamless*—
Randolph & Clowes.

Shells, *Brass Shot*—
Union Metallic Cartridge Co.
Waterbury Brass Co.

Shells, Copper, Seamless—
Randolph & Clowes.

Shells, Paper, Loaded—
Peters Cartridge Co.
Union Metallic Cartridge Co.

Shells, Paper Shot—
Union Metallic Cartridge Co.
Waterbury Brass Co.

Shelves, Stove Pipe, Wire—See *Household Articles, Wire.*

Shelving, Hardware Store—
The Hartzell Novelty Works.

Shelving, Library—
The Hartzell Novelty Works.

Shepherds' Crooks—See *Crooks, Shepherds'.*

Shifters, Belt—See *Belt Shifters.*

Shingles, Metallic—
American Steel Roofing Co.
Garry Iron Roofing Co.
Kansas City Metal Roofing & Corrugating Co.

Shingling Hatchets— See *Hatchets, Shingling, Half, &c.*

Ship Anchors, Pumps, Scrapers—
See *Anchors, Pumps, Scrapers.*

Ship Carpenters' Tools—See *Tools, Ship Carpenters'.*

Ship Chandlery Hardware—
Boston & Lockport Block Co.
W. & J. Tiebout.

Ship Locks and Latches—See *Locks and Latches.*

Shoe Blacking Brushes, Daubers, Hammers, Knives, Nails, Stretchers—See *Blacking, Brushes, Daubers, Hammers, Knives, Nails, Stretchers.*

Shoe Nail Machines—See *Nail Machines, Shoe.*

Shoe and Last Stands—See *Stands, Lasts, Shoe.*

Shoes, Horse and Mule—
Burden Iron Co.
Crescent Works.
Old Dominion Iron & Nail Works.
Phœnix Horse Shoe Co.
Rhode Island Perkins Horse Shoe Co.

Shoes, Wagon Lock—
Pleuger & Henger Mfg. Co.

Shoes, Ox—
Millers Falls Co.
Scranton Forging Co.

Shoes, Sleigh—
Pleuger & Henger Mfg. Co.

Shop Pans—See *Pans, Shop.*

Shot Guns, Pouches, Spreaders—
See *Guns, Pouches, Spreaders.*

Shoulder Hooks—See *Hooks, Cup and Shoulder.*

Shovel Handles, Scrapers—See *Handles, Scrapers.*

Shovel Steel—See *Steel, Shovel.*

Shovels, Snow—
Avery Stamping Co.

Shovels, Steam—
Vulcan Iron Works.

Shovels, Stove—
New York Stamping Co.
Peck, Stow & Wilcox Co.
Sidney Shepard & Co.
Stover Mfg. Co.
Troy Nickel Works.

Shovels, Tiling or Ditching—
Ney Mfg. Co.
St. Louis Shovel Co.

Shovels, Tongs, Pokers, Fire Sets, &c.—
Bradley & Hubbard Mfg. Co.
Logan & Strobridge Iron Co.
Peck, Stow & Wilcox Co.
Russell & Erwin Mfg. Co.

Shovels, Wood—
John Sommer's Son.

Shovels and Spades—
St. Louis Shovel Co.

Showcase Catches—See *Catches, Showcase.*

Shredders, Dry Fodder—
Silver Mfg. Co.

Shrinkers, Tire—
Champion Blower & Forge Co.
Wells Bros. & Co.
Wiley & Russell Mfg. Co.

Shutes, Coal—
Lansing Wheelbarrow Co.

Shutter Bars, Bolts, Fasteners, Handles, Hinges, Knobs, Sheaves—See *Bars, Bolts, Fasteners, Handles, Hinges, Knobs, Sheaves.*

Shutters, Iron and Steel—See *Doors and Shutters, Iron and Steel.*

Side Pulleys—See *Pulleys, Side.*

Sidewalk Cleaners, Hoists—See *Cleaners, Hoists*

Siding, Iron and Steel—See *Ceiling and Siding, Iron and Steel.*

Sieves—See *Riddles and Sieves.*

Sieves, Ash—
Wickwire Bros.

Sieves, Flour—
Estey Wire Works Co.
Gilbert & Bennett Mfg. Co.
Fred. J. Meyers Mfg. Co.
Sidney Shepard & Co.

Sifters, Ash—
W. S. Tyler Wire Works Co.
Wright & Colton Wire Cloth Co.

Sifters, Flour—
Edward Darby & Sons.
Fred. J. Meyers Mfg. Co.
Sidney Shepard & Co.

Sifters, Sand—
Byram & Co.
Whiting Foundry Equipment Co.

Signal Cord, Lamps—See *Cord, Lamps.*

Sign Letters—See *Letters, Cast Iron Sign.*

Sign or Engravers' Brass—See *Brass, Sign or Engravers'.*

Signs, Wire, &c.—
E. T. Barnum.
Columbus Wire & Iron Works.
Ludlow-Saylor Wire Co.
Fred. J. Meyers Mfg. Co.

Silver, German—See *German Silver.*

Silver Plated Brushes—See *Brushes, Silver Plated.*

Silver Tubing—See *Tubing, Silver.*

Sink Bolts, Cleaners—See *Bolts, Cleaners.*

Sinkers, Die—See *Die Sinkers.*

Sinks, Cast—
Barnes Mfg. Co.
Humphryes Mfg. Co.

Sinks, *Wrought Steel*—
Kilbourne & Jacobs Mfg. Co.

Siphon Pumps—See *Pumps, Siphon.*

Sizing—
Russia Cement Co.

Skate Steel—See *Steel, Skate.*

Skates, Ice—
Union Hardware Co.

Skates, *Roller*—
Union Hardware Co.
Upson & Hart Co.

Skeins, *Thimble and Boxes*—
Colebrookdale Iron Co.
A. C. Williams.

Skelp, *Steel*—
Riverside Iron Works.

Skids,
Boston & Lockport Block Co.

Skimmers—See *Kitchen Articles, Wire.*

Skip Cars—See *Cars, Skip.*

Skylights—
American Sheet Roofing Co.
Brown Bros. Mfg. Co.
Garry Iron Roofing Co.

Slaters' Tools—
Belden Machine Co.

Slaw Cutters—See *Cutters, Slaw.*

Sleds, Farm—
Sidney Steel Scraper Co.

Sledges—See *Hammers, Heavy, and Sledges.*

Sledges and Hammers—
Heller Bros.
Van Wagoner & Williams Hardware Co.

Sleigh Bell Straps—See *Straps, Sleigh Bell.*

Sleigh Bells, Plumes, Shoes—See *Bells, Plumes, Shoes.*

Sleigh Shoe Bolts—See *Bolts, Sleigh Shoe.*

Slicers, *Vegetable*—
Knapp & Cowles Mfg. Co.

Slicks, *Carpenters'*—
Buck Bros.
L. & I. J. White Co.
Peck, Stow & Wilcox Co.

Slides, *Desk*—
Stanley Works.

Slides, Rope—See *Clamps and Slides Rope.*

Sling Chains—See *Chains, Sling.*

Slings, *Hay*—
F. E. Myers & Bro.
Ney Mfg. Co.

Slitting Knives, Rotary—See *Knives, Rotary Slitting.*

Slitting Machines—
Kimball Bros. & Sprague.
Waterbury Farrel Foundry & Machine Co.
Waterbury Machine Co.

Slitting Saws—See *Saws, Slitting.*

Slotted Head Bolts—See *Bolts, Special.*

Slotting Machines—
Ames Mfg. Co.
Bement, Miles & Co.
Garvin Machine Works.
Newark Machine Tool Works.
New Haven Mfg. Co.
Newton Machine Tool Works.
Niles Tool Works Co.
Wm. Sellers & Co.

Slotting and Slabbing Machines, Bicycle Nipple—
Garvin Machine Co.
Hartford Machine Screw Co.

Slotting Machines, Screw Head—
Hartford Machine Screw Co.

Smokers' Sets, Aluminum—
Scovill Mfg. Co.

Smokers' Sets, Silver Plated—
Wm. Rogers Mfg. Co.

Snap Gauges, Gauge Blanks—See *Gauges, Blanks.*

Snaps, Halter, Harness, &c.—
Bridgeport Chain Co.
Covert Mfg. Co.
Covert's Saddlery Works.
W. & E. T. Fitch Co.
Imperial Bit & Snap Co.

Snaps and Swivels, Halter, Harness, &c.—
Oneida Community.

Snatch Blocks—See *Blocks, Deck and Snatch.*

Snaths—
Iowa Farming Tool Co.

Snips, Cotton Bale—
Peck, Stow & Wilcox Co.

Snips, Tinners'—
Acme Shear Co.
R. Heinisch's Sons Co.
Peck, Stow & Wilcox Co.

Snow Shovels—See *Shovels, Snow.*

Soaking Pits—See *Pits, Soaking.*

Soap Boxes, Silver Plated — See *Boxes, Soap, Silver Plated.*

Soap Dishes, Trays—See *Dishes, Trays.*

Soapstone Griddles — See *Griddles, Soapstone.*

Socket Bolts, Hooks — See *Bolts, Hooks.*

Socket Bushings and Hooks, Electric—See *Electric Light Fittings.*

Sockets, Drill—
Billings & Spencer Co.
Cleveland Twist Drill Co.
Imperial Bit & Snap Co.
Oneida Community.
Stow Flexible Shaft Co.

Sockets, Flag Pole—
W. & J. Tiebout.

Sockets, Whip—
W. & E. T. Fitch Co.
Imperial Bit & Snap Co.
Peck, Stow & Wilcox Co.

Sockets and Standards, Canopy Top—See *Standards and Sockets, Canopy Top.*

Society Ballots—See *Ballots, Society.*

Soda Tanks—See *Tanks, Gas, Air, Soda, &c.*

Solder—
Theo. Hiertz & Son.

Solder, Braziers'—
U. T. Hungerford.
Scovill Mfg. Co.

Soldering Coppers, Sets—See *Coppers, Sets.*

Soldering Machines—
E. W. Bliss Co.

Soles, Boot and Shoe—See *Half Soles.*

Solid Box Vises—See *Vises, Solid Box.*

Sowers, Seed—
Goodell Co.

Spacing Tables, Automatic—
Long & Allstatter Co.

Spade Handles—See *Handles, Fork, Spade, &c.*

Spades—See *Shovels and Spades.*

Spades, Butter—
Knapp & Cowles Mfg Co.

Spades, Post Hole—See *Post Hole Spades.*

Spading Forks—See *Forks, Hay, Manure, Spading, &c.*

Spark Arresters — See *Arresters, Spark.*

Speaking Tube Hardware—
W. R. Ostrander & Co.
Reading Hardware Co.

Speaking Tubes—See *Tubes, Speaking.*

Special Machinery—
R. D. Nuttall Co.
A. P. Richmond.

Special Screws, Wire—See *Screws, Wire.*

Specialties, Wooden — See *Wooden Specialties.*

Specialties to Order, Metal — See *Metal Specialties to Order.*

Speed Indicators or Recorders, Lathes—See *Indicators, Lathes.*

Spelter—
John Davol & Sons.
Wm. S. Fearing.
Hendricks Bros.
Matthiessen & Hegeler Zinc Co.

Spice Cans, Dredge — See *Cans, Dredge, Spice.*

Spiders—
New York Stamping Co.

Spike Machinery—
National Machinery Co.
Totten & Hogg Iron & Steel Foundry Co.

Spikes, Dock, Wharf, &c.—
Allentown Rolling Mills.
Crescent Works.
Pennsylvania Bolt & Nut Co.
Pierson & Co.
J. H. Sternbergh & Son.
Tudor Iron Works.

Spikes, Railroad—
Central Iron & Steel Co.
Tudor Iron Works.

Spindles, Lathe—
Frankford Steel Co.

Split Pulleys, Wood—See *Pulleys, Wood, Split.*

Splitters, Packing House—
Nichols Bros.

Spinning Lathes—See *Lathes, Spinning.*

Spoke Extractors, Pointers, Shaves, Trimmers—See *Extractors, Pointers, Shaves, Trimmers.*

Spoke Header and Bender, Bicycle—
Waterbury Farrel Foundry & Machine Co.

Spoke Tenon Machines—
Silver Mfg. Co.
E. C. Stearns & Co.

Spoke Threaders, Bicycle — See *Threaders, Bicycle Spoke.*

Spoke Wire, Bicycle—See *Wire, Bicycle Spoke.*

Spokes, Bicycle—
Excelsior Needle Co.
Wire Goods Co.

Sponge Baskets—See *Baskets, Sponge.*

Spooled Wire—See *Wire, Spooled.*

Spooling Machines—
Fairmount Machine Co.

Spoons and Forks, Iron—
Acme Shear Co.
Sidney Shepard & Co.
Wallace Bros.

Spoons and Forks, *Silver and Silver Plated*—
Oneida Community.
Wm. Rogers Mfg. Co.
Upson & Hart Co.
Wallace Bros.

Sporting Goods, Jobbers—See *Jobbers, Hardware, Cutlery, Tools, Sporting Goods, &c.*

Spraying Pumps—See *Pumps, Spraying.*

Spreaders, Shot—
R. Heinisch's Sons Co.

Spring Balances, Brass, Bar Clips, Hinges, Oilers, Punches, Steel—
See *Balances, Brass, Clips. Hinges, Oilers, Punches, Steel.*

Spring Coiling Machines—
Garvin Machine Co.

Spring Steel, Watch—See *Steel, Watch Spring.*

Springs, Bicycle—
Tuck Mfg. Co.

Springs, Bird Cage—
Fred. J. Meyers Mfg. Co.
Ossawan Mills Co.
Charles Scott Spring Co.
Wire Goods Co.

Springs, Carriage, Wagon, &c.—
W. & E. T. Fitch Co.
Hansell Spring Co.
La Belle Steel Co.
Lee, Cowan & Bowen.
Wm. & Harvey Rowland.
Charles Scott Spring Co.
Singer, Nimick & Co.
F. W. Wurster & Co.

Springs, Check—
W. R. Ostrander & Co.

Springs, Clearer—
Wm. H. Haskell Co.

Springs, Clock—
Boston Gear Works.

Springs, Door—
Arcade Mfg. Co.
Caldwell Mfg. Co.
John Chatillon & Sons.
Chicago Spring Butt Co.
Norton Door Check & Spring Co.
Union Mfg. Co.
Van Wagoner & Williams Hardware Co.
Wire Goods Co.

Springs, Governor—
Sabin Machine Co.

Springs, Sash—
Hansell Spring Co.
Charles Scott Spring Co.

Springs, Steel—
Wallace Barnes.
Cambria Iron Co.
Clark & Cowles.
Crescent Steel Co.
Dunbar Bros.
Hansell Spring Co.
Jonas & Colver Continental Steel Works.
New England Specialty Co.
Wm. & Harvey Rowland.
Sabin Machine Co.
Charles Scott Spring Co.
Tuck Mfg. Co.
S. & C. Wardlow.

Springs, Tailboard—
Dodge, Haley & Co.

Springs, Typewriter—
Tuck Mfg. Co.

Springs, Window—
Stanley Works.

Springs, Wire—
Wallace Barnes.
John Chatillon & Sons.
Crescent Steel Co.
Dunbar Bros.
Hansell Spring Co.
Miller & Van Winkle.
Morgan Spring Co.
Charles Scott Spring Co.
Sabin Machine Co.
Tuck Mfg. Co.
Washburn & Moen Mfg. Co.
Wire Goods Co.

Sprinklers, Lawn—
Deming Co.
Enterprise Mfg. Co.
Humphryes Mfg. Co.
King & Knight.
McNab & Harlin Mfg. Co.
Fred. J. Meyers Mfg. Co.
H. F. Neumeyer Mfg. Co.
Pleuger & Henger Mfg. Co.

THE IRON AGE INDEX.

Sprocket Wheels — See *Wheels, Sprocket.*

Square Attachments—
Tower & Lyon.

Square Levels—See *Levels, Bit and Square.*

Square and Gauge Combined—See *Gauge and Square, Combined.*

Square and Hexagon Nuts—See *Nuts, Square and Hexagon.*

Squares, Iron and Steel—
Peck, Stow & Wilcox Co.
Russell & Erwin Mfg. Co.

Squares, Machinists'—
Athol Machine Co.
Henry Disston & Sons.
Hoggson & Pettis Mfg. Co.
L. S. Starrett Co.
J. Stevens Arms & Tool Co.

Squares, Pocket—
Bemis & Call Hardware & Tool Co.

Squares, T—
Henry Disston & Sons.

Squares, Try and Miter—
Athol Machine Co.
Henry Disston & Sons.
Stanley Rule & Level Co.

Squaring Instruments—See *Instruments, Leveling and Squaring.*

Squeezers, Lemon—
Erie Specialty Co.
Edward S. Hotchkiss.
Logan & Strobridge Iron Co.
John Sommer's Son.
A. C. Williams.

Squeezers, Puddle Ball—
Lloyd Booth Co.
A. Garrison Foundry Co.
Leechburg Foundry & Machine Co.
Totten & Hogg Iron & Steel Foundry Co.

Squeezing Machines, Can—
E. W. Bliss Co.

Stable Fixtures—
E. T. Barnum.
Champion Iron Co.
Columbus Wire & Iron Works.
Edward Darby & Sons.
Ellis & Helfenberger.
Estey Wire Works Co.
Gilbert & Bennett Mfg. Co.
Howard & Morse.
Ludlow-Saylor Wire Co.
Fred. J. Meyers Mfg. Co.
Scheeler's Sons.
E. C. Stearns & Co.
Stewart Iron Works.
Stowell Mfg. & Foundry Co.
W. S. Tyler Wire Works Co.

Stacks, Steel—See *Chimneys, Steel.*

Stackers, Hay—
Dain Mfg. Co.

Stair Treads, Brass—See *Plates, Brass Step.*

Stair Treads, Rubber—See *Treads, Stair Rubber.*

Stairs, Iron and Steel—
E. T. Barnum.
Champion Iron Co.
Fred J. Meyers Mfg. Co.
Stewart Iron Works.

Stake Chains — See *Chains, Picket, Stake, &c.*

Stake Holders, Wagon—See *Holders, Stake, Wagon.*

Stakes, Tinners'—
Peck, Stow & Wilcox Co.

Stamp Holders, Rubber—See *Holders, Rubber Stamp.*

Stamped or Milled Turned Metal Work to Order—See *Metal Work, Milled, Turned or Stamped to Order.*

Stamping Dies—See *Dies, Stamping.*

Stamping, Sheet Metal—
The Oliver P. Clay Co.
Hero Stamping Works.

Stamps, Rubber—
Geo. M. Ness, Jr.

Stamps and Dies, Steel—
Hoggson & Pettis Mfg. Co.
Geo. M. Ness, Jr.

Stanchions, Hand Rope—
W. & J. Tiebout.

Stand Trucks—See *Trucks, Barrel and Stand.*

Stands, Bicycle—
Boston & Lockport Block Co.
Bridgeport Gun Implement Co.
Logan & Strobridge Iron Co.
F. E. Myers & Bro.
H. K. Porter.
E. C. Stearns & Co.

Stands, Blower—
Peck, Stow & Wilcox Co.

Stands, Coffee Pot—
Logan & Strobridge Iron Co.
Peck, Stow & Wilcox Co.
Stover Mfg. Co.

Stands, Coffee Pot, Wire—See *Household Articles, Wire.*

Stands, Display, Garment—
Fred. J. Meyers Mfg. Co.

Stands, Flower Pot—
E. T. Barnum.
Columbus Wire & Iron Works.
Edward Darby & Sons.
Estey Wire Works Co.
Gilbert & Bennett Mfg. Co.
Howard & Morse.
Fred. J. Meyers Mfg. Co.
Scheeler's Sons.
Wright & Colton Wire Cloth Co.

Stands, Ironing, Folding—
G. A. Milbradt & Co.

Stands, Sad Iron—
Colebrookdale Iron Co.
Logan & Strobridge Iron Co.
Peck, Stow & Wilcox Co.
Pleuger & Henger Mfg. Co.
Stover Mfg. Co.

Stands, Umbrella—
E. T. Barnum.
Estey Wire Works Co.
Gilbert & Bennett Mfg. Co.
Logan & Strobridge Iron Co.
Peck, Stow & Wilcox Co.
Russell & Erwin Mfg. Co.

Stands, Wash—
Fred. J. Meyers Mfg. Co.

Stands and Lasts, Shoe—
Enterprise Mfg. Co.
Root Bros. Co.
See also *Lasts and Stands, Shoe.*

Standards and Sockets, Canopy Top—
E. D. Clapp Mfg. Co.

Staple Drivers—See *Drivers, Staple.*

Staple Machinery, Fence—
Stover Novelty Works.

Staples—See *Wrought Iron Goods.*

Staples, Wire—
Cobb & Drew.
Consolidated Steel & Wire Co.
Dillon-Griswold Wire Co.
I. L. Ellwood Mfg. Co.
Gilbert & Bennett Mfg. Co.
Indiana Wire Fence Co.
Pittsburgh Wire Co.
Quincy Hardware Mfg. Co.
Salem Wire Nail Co.
Geo. W. Stanley Co.
E. H. Titchener & Co.
Wire Goods Co.
Wright & Colton Wire Cloth Co.

Staples and Loops, Furniture—
Quincy Hardware Mfg. Co.

Starters, Bung—
Boston & Lockport Block Co.
Union Hardware Co.

THE IRON AGE INDEX.

Stationers' Hardware (*Inkstands, Clips, &c.*)—
Bradley & Hubbard Mfg. Co.
Peck, Stow & Wilcox Co.

Stave Knives—See *Knives, Machine.*

Stay Bolt Iron—See *Iron, Rivet and Stay Bolt.*

Stay Bolts, Rollers—See *Bolts, Rollers.*

Stays, Roller—
Lane Bros.
McKinney Mfg. Co.
Ney Mfg. Co.
Peck, Stow & Wilcox Co.
Reading Hardware Co.
Stowell Mfg. & Foundry Co.

Steak Pounders—See *Pounders, Steak.*

Steam Accumulators—See *Accumulators, Steam.*

Steamboats—
Merrill-Stevens Engineering Co.

Steam Boiler Inspection—
Hartford Steam Boiler Inspection & Inursance Co.

Steam Boilers, Engines, Fittings, Gauges, Hammers, Locomotives, Pumps, Radiators, Separators, Shovels, Traps, Valves, Whistles
—See *Boilers, Engines, Fittings, Gauges, Hammers, Locomotives, Pumps, Radiators, Separators, Shovels, Traps, Valves, Whistles.*

Steam Engine Governors, Indicators—See *Governors, Indicators.*

Steam Fitters' Supplies—
Chas. Millar & Son.

Steamship Outfits—
W. H. Thomas & Co.

Steel Balls, Bars, Belt Lacing, Billets, Bottles, Castings, Ceiling and Siding, Chimneys, Clamps, Cylinders, Flanges, Grapples, Ladders, Lamps, Mats, Pipe, Plates,

Rails, Rivets, Roofing, Sheets, Skelp, Spring, Squares, Stairs, Triangles, Wire—See *Balls, Bars, Belt Lacing, Billets. Bottles, Castings, Ceiling and Siding, Chimneys, Clamps, Cylinders, Flanges, Grapples, Ladders, Lamps, Mats, Pipe, Plates, Rails, Rivets, Roofing, Sheets, Skelp, Springs, Squares, Stairs, Triangles, Wire.*

Steel Brokers and Merchants—See *Iron and Steel Brokers and Merchants.*

Steel, Chrome—
Chrome Steel Works.

Steel, Clock Spring—
Hermann Boker & Co.
S. & C. Wardlow.
R. H. Wolff & Co.

Steel, Cold Rolled Sheet, Hot Rolled Sheet—See *Sheet Steel.*

Steel, Cold Rolled—
Hermann Boker & Co.
Wm. Jessop & Sons.
Geo. Johnson.
Singer, Nimick & Co.
S. & C. Wardlow.
Wilmot & Hobbs Mfg. Co.
R. H. Wolff & Co.

Steel, Corset—
R. H. Wolff & Co.

Steel, Crucible Cast—
Abbott, Wheelock & Co.
Hermann Boker & Co.
Crescent Steel Co.
Denman & Davis.
Francis Hobson, Seaman & Co.
Wm. Jessop & Sons.
B. M. Jones & Co.
La Belle Steel Co.
Singer, Nimick & Co.
S. & C. Wardlow.

Steel, Cutlery—
La Belle Steel Co.
Wm. & Harvey Rowland.
Singer, Nimick & Co.

Steel, *Double Shear—*
  S. & C. Wardlow.
Steel Goods Racks—See *Racks, Steel Goods.*
Steel Machinery—
  Crescent Steel Co.
  Ogden & Wallace.
  Singer, Nimick & Co.
Steel, *Mushet's Special—*
  B. M. Jones & Co.
Steel, *Nickel—*
  Bethlehem Iron Co.
Steel, *Plow—*
  Cambria Iron Co.
  Wm. & Harvey Rowland.
  Singer, Nimick & Co.
Steel, *Rock Drill—*
  Crescent Steel Co.
  Singer, Nimick & Co.
Steel Rolls, Hardened, Forged—See *Rolls, Hardened, Forged Steel.*
Steel, *Saw—*
  Hermann Boker & Co.
  Jonas & Colver Continental Steel Works.
  Singer, Nimick & Co.
  S. & C. Wardlow.
  R. H. Wolff & Co.
Steel, *Self Hardening—*
  Wm. Jessop & Sons.
Steel, *Shovel—*
  Wm. & Harvey Rowland.
Steel, *Skate—*
  La Belle Steel Co.
Steel, Swedish—See *Iron and Steel, Swedish.*
Steel, *Tire—*
  Singer, Nimick & Co.
Steel, *Tool—*
  Abbott, Wheelock & Co.
  Hermann Boker & Co.
  Crescent Steel Co.
  Denman & Davis.

Francis Hobson, Seaman & Co.
Wm. Jessop & Sons.
B. M. Jones & Co.
Pittsburg Tool Steel Co.
Singer, Nimick & Co.
S. & C. Wardlow.
Steel, *Watch Spring—*
  R. H. Wolff & Co.
Steel Wire Brushes—See *Brushes, Steel Wire.*
Steel Wire, Cast—See *Wire, Cast Steel.*
Steels, *Butcher, &c.—*
  John Chatillon & Sons.
  Goodell Co.
  C. & A. Hoffman.
  Nichols Bros.
  Nicholson File Co.
  John Wilson.
Steels, *Buffer and Scraper—*
  Tuck Mfg. Co.
Steelyards—
  Bemis & Call Hardware & Tool Co.
  Peck, Stow & Wilcox Co.
Steering Gears, *Steam—*
  Pawling & Harnischfeger.
Stems, Valve—See *Valve Stems.*
Stencils—
  Hoggson & Pettis Mfg. Co.
  S. G. Monce.
  Geo. M. Ness, Jr.
Step Ladders—See *Ladders, Step.*
Step Ladder Joints—See *Joints, Step Ladder.*
Step Plates, Brass—See *Plates, Brass Step.*
Steps, *Pantry—*
  Hill Dryer Co.
Steps, *Telegraph Pole—*
  J. H. Sternbergh & Son.
Steps, *Wagon—*
  Butts & Ordway.

Stew Pans, Sectional—See *Pans, Sectional Stew.*

Sticks, &c., Mop—See *Mop Sticks, &c.*

Stiffeners, Heel—
Stowell Mfg. & Foundry Co.

Stitching Machines, Wire—See *Wire Stitching Machines.*

Stirrups, Machine—
Wm. H. Haskell Co.

Stirrups, Timber—
American Bolt Co.
Port Chester Bolt & Nut Co.
Steward & Romaine Mfg. Co.

Stock Scales, Tanks—See *Scales, Tanks.*

Stock Waterers—
Stover Mfg. Co.

Stocks, Taps and Dies—
Armstrong Mfg. Co.
Ashcroft Mfg. Co.
C. H. Besly & Co.
Butterfield & Co.
S. W. Card Mfg. Co.
J. M. Carpenter Tap & Die Co.
Curtis & Curtis.
Humphryes Mfg. Co.
J. M. King & Co.
Morse Twist Drill & Machine Co.
Oster Mfg. Co.
Pratt & Whitney Co.
E. F. Reece Co.
D. Saunders' Sons.
Standard Tool Co.
Wells Bros. & Co.
Wiley & Russell Mfg. Co.

Stokers, Mechanical—
Babcock & Wilcox Co.
Alfred Box & Co.
Wm. Sellers & Co.

Stone Molding Machines, Planers, Saws, Wire—See *Molding Machines, Planers, Saws, Wire.*

Stones, Axe—
Cleveland Stone Co.
Pike Mfg. Co.

Stones, Emery—
Pike Mfg. Co.
Norton Emery Wheel Co.

Stones, Oil and Water—
Norton Emery Wheel Co.
Pike Mfg. Co.
Tanite Co.

Stones, Scythe—
Cleveland Stone Co.
Pike Mfg. Co.

Stoners, Cherry—
Enterprise Mfg. Co.
Goodell Co.

Stools, Camp—
Hill Dryer Co.
Stanley Works.

Stools, Store—See *Store Stools.*

Stops, Door—
Norwalk Lock Co.
Reading Hardware Co.
Weedsport Drill Co.

Storage, Pig Iron—
American Pig Iron Storage Warrant Co.

Store Door Shutter Screws—See *Screws, Shutter, Store Door.*

Store Fixture Brackets, Ladders, Trucks—See *Brackets, Ladders, Trucks.*

Store Fixtures, Wire—
Fred. J. Meyers Mfg. Co.
W. S. Tyler Wire Works Co.

Store Stools—
Fred. J. Meyers Mfg. Co.

Stove Blanks—
Matthiessen & Hegeler Zinc Co.

Stove Bolts, Brushes, Carriers, Lid Lifters, Linings, Pokers, Polishing, Putty, Repair Kits, Rods, Shovels, Trimmings, Trucks—See *Bolts Brushes, Carriers, Lifters, Linings, Pokers, Putty, Repair Kits, Rods, Shovels, Trimmings, Trucks.*

Stove Pipe Registers and Ceiling Plates — See *Registers and Ceiling Plates, Stove Pipe.*

Stoves, Cook—
Southern Queen Mfg. Co.

Stoves, Enameling Oven—
Lincoln & Co.

Stoves, Fire Brick—
Huntington & Wyatt.
Julian Kennedy.
G. W. McClure & Son.

Stoves, Heating—
Southern Queen Mfg. Co.

Stoves, Oil Lamp—
Plume & Atwood Mfg. Co.
Schneider & Trenkamp Co.
Taylor & Boggis Foundry Co.

Stoves and Ranges, Gas, Gasoline and Oil—
Schneider & Trenkamp Co.

Straight Edges—
Pratt & Whitney Co.
See also *Edges, Straight.*

Straightening Machines, Shaft—
See *Shaft Straightening Machinery.*

Straightening Rolls — See *Rolls, Straightening.*

Straightening and Cutting Machines, Wire—
John Adt & Son.
Belden Machine Co.
Stover Novelty Works.

Straightening Machinery, Plate—
Automatic Machine Co.
Bement, Miles & Co.
Hartford Machine Screw Co.
Hilles & Jones Co.
Philadelphia Machine Tool Co.
Pittsburgh Mfg. Co.
Wm. Sellers & Co.
Waterbury Farrel Foundry & Machine Co.

Strainers—See *Kitchen Articles, Wire.*

Strainers, Conductor Pipe—
American Steel Roofing Co.
Berger Bros.
Edward Darby & Sons.
Estey Wire Works Co.
Gilbert & Bennett Mfg. Co.
Fred. J. Meyers Mfg. Co.
Wright & Colton Wire Cloth Co.

Strainers, Tea and Coffee Pot, Wire—See *Household Articles, Wire.*

Stringers, Ham—
Nichols Bros.

Strap Protectors, Seals—See *Protectors, Seals.*

Strap and Eye Hinges—See *Hinges, Screw Hook or Strap and Eye.*

Strap and T Hinges—See *Hinges, Strap and T.*

Strap and T Hinges, Corrugated—
See *Hinges, Strap and T, Corrugated.*

Strapping and Buffing Machines—
See *Buffing and Polishing Machines.*

Straps, Blanket—
Covert's Saddlery Works.

Straps, Box—
Cary Mfg. Co.
Quincy Hardware Mfg. Co.

Straps, Curtain—
Covert's Saddlery Works.
McKinnon Dash & Hardware Co.

Straps, Hame—
Covert's Saddlery Works.

Straps, Sleigh Bell—
Bevin Bros. Mfg. Co.

Straw Knives—See *Knives, Hay and Straw.*

Street Lamps, Scrapers—See *Lamps, Scrapers.*

Stretchers, Box Strap—
Cary Mfg. Co.

Stretchers, Carpet—
Knapp & Cowles Mfg. Co.
Peck, Stow & Wilcox Co.
Seymour Smith & Son.

Stretchers, Fence and Wire—
Arcade Mfg. Co.
W. C. Heller & Co.
Holmes & Ward Bros.
Ludlow-Saylor Wire Co.
Ney Mfg. Co.

Stretchers, Saw—
Geo. H. Bishop & Co.
See also *Rods, Saw.*

Stretchers, Shoe—
Knapp & Cowles Mfg. Co.

Stretchers, Trouser—
Covert Mfg. Co.

Structural Material—
Ætna-Standard Iron & Steel Co.
Allentown Rolling Mills.
Berlin Iron Bridge Co.
Alphonse Bouchet.
Cambria Iron Co.
Barclay W. Cotton & Co.
C. B. Houston & Co.
Passaic Rolling Mills Co.
Phœnix Iron Co.
Pottsville Iron & Steel Co.
A. & P. Roberts Co.
Jos. T. Ryerson & Son.
Shiffler Bridge Co.
Wm. H. Wallace & Co.
A. R. Whitney & Co.

Stubs and Plates, *Store Shutter—*
Peck, Stow & Wilcox Co.
Reading Hardware Co.

Stud Bolts, Chains—See *Bolts, Chains.*

Studs, *Brass and Iron—*
Blake & Johnson.
Cincinnati Screw & Tap Co.
Hartford Machine Screw Co.
W. H. Haskell Co.
New Britain Hardware Mfg. Co.

Stuffers, Sausage—
Enterprise Mfg. Co.
National Specialty Mfg. Co.

Peck, Stow & Wilcox Co.
Silver Mfg. Co.

Stump Joints— See *Joints, Stump.*

Suction Faucets—See *Faucets, Suction.*

Sugar Augers, Cars—See *Augers, Car.*

Sugar Machinery—
Geo. V. Cresson Co.

Sulphuric Acid—See *Acid, Sulphuric.*

Summer Front and Grate Frames—
See *Grate Frames and Summer Fronts.*

Supplies, Foundry, Mill, Steam Fitters', Water Works, Well—See *Foundry, Mill, Steam Fitters', Water Works, Well.*

Supplies, Grinders' and Polishers' —See *Grinders' and Polishers' Supplies.*

Supporters, Belt—
Chapman Mfg. Co.

Supports, *Counter—*
E. T. Barnum.
Logan & Strobridge Iron Co.
Fred. J. Meyers Mfg. Co.

Supports, Porch—
Logan & Strobridge Iron Co.
Pleuger & Henger Mfg. Co.
Reading Hardware Co.
A. C. Williams.

Supports, *Shelf—*
Reading Hardware Co.

Surface, Surface Depth Gauges—
See *Gauges.*

Surface Grinders—See *Grinders, Surface.*

Suspended Scales—See *Scales, Suspended.*

Suspension Drills—See *Drills, Suspension.*

Swage Blocks—See *Blocks, Swage.*

Swages—
Henry Disston & Sons.
National Saw Co.
Simonds Mfg. Co.

Swaging Machines—
Excelsior Needle Co.
Waterbury Farrel Foundry & Machine Co.

Swedish Iron and Steel—See *Iron and Steel, Swedish.*

Sweeping Brushes—See *Brushes, Whitewash, Horse, &c.*

Swings, Barrel—
Lansing Wheelbarrow Co.

Swings, Child's—
Imperial Bit & Snap Co.

Swings, Lawn—
Fairfield Lawn Swing Co.

Switchboards—
Westinghouse Electric & Mfg. Co.

Switches and Frogs, *Railroad*—
Thos. Carlin's Sons.
Trenton Iron Co.

Swivels, *Chain*—
Bradlee & Co.
Garland Chain Co.

Swivels, Halter, Harness, &c.—See *Snaps and Swivels, Halter, Harness, &c.*

Swivels, *Pipe*—
Pennsylvania Bolt & Nut Co.

Swivels, *Rope*—
W. & J. Tiebout.

T Squares—See *Squares, T.*

T and Strap Hinges—See *Hinges, Strap and T.*

Table Cutlery—See *Cutlery, Table.*

Table Lamps—See *Lamps, Table, Banquet, Hanging, Piano, &c.*

Tables, Automatic Spacing — See *Spacing Tables, Automatic.*

Tables, Ironing—
Hill Dryer Co.

Tables, Locomotive Transfer—See *Transfer Tables, Locomotive.*

Tables, Onyx—
Edward Miller & Co.

Tables, Saw—
Dupont Mfg. Co.
Kimball Bros. & Sprague.

Tachometers—See *Indicators, Speed.*

Tack Claws, Hammers, Pullers—
See *Claws, Hammers, Pullers.*

Tack Machinery—
Kimball Bros. & Sprague.
W. A. Sweetser.

Tackle Blocks—See *Blocks, Tackle.*

Tackle Block Sheaves—See *Sheaves, Tackle Block.*

Tackle or Awning Pulleys—See *Pulleys, Tackle or Awning.*

Tacks, *Brads, Finishing Nails, &c.*—
Clendenin Bros.
Cobb & Drew.
William N. Merriam.
Milwaukee Tack Co.
Russell & Erwin Mfg. Co.
Shelton Co.
Taunton Wire Nail Co.
Tower Mfg Co.
Wire Goods Co.

Tacks, *Double pointed*—
Cobb & Drew.
Geo. W. Stanley Co.
E. H. Titchener & Co.
Wire Goods Co.
Wright & Colton Wire Cloth Co.

Tacks, *Trimmers'*—
Shelton Co.
Tower Mfg. Co.

Tacks, *Upholsterers' and Gimp*—
Cobb & Drew.
Milwaukee Tack Co.
Shelton Co.
Tower Mfg Co.

THE IRON AGE INDEX.

Tacks and Nails, Zinc—
  Clendenin Bros.
  Cobb & Drew.
Tacks and Nails, Copper—
  Clendenin Bros.
  Cobb & Drew.
  U. T. Hungerford.
  William N. Merriam.
  Shelton Co.
Tacks and Nails, Shoe—
  Clendenin Bros.
  Cobb & Drew.
  Milwaukee Tack Co.
  Shelton Co.
Tag Fasteners—See Fasteners, Tag.
Tags, Brass—
  Norwalk Lock Co.
  Waterbury Brass Co.
Tailboard Springs—See Springs, Tailboard.
Tallow Pots—See Pots, Tallow.
Tank Governors, Pumps, Towers—
  See Governors, Pumps, Towers.
Tanks, Gas, Air, Soda, &c.—
  Avery Stamping Co.
Tanks, Oil—
  Sidney Shepard & Co.
Tanks, Stock and Wind Mill—
  Mast, Foos & Co.
  Wm. B. Pollock & Co.
  Stover Mfg. Co.
  R. W. Whitehurst & Co.
Tannery Machinery—
  Geo. V. Cresson Co.
Tap Bolts, Drills, Holders, Wrenches—See Bolts, Drills, Holders, Wrenches.
Tape Measures—See Measures, Tape.
Taper Augers, Pins—See Augers, Pins.
Tapping Attachments, Automatic—
  Gould & Eberhardt.
Tapping Machines—
  Garvin Machine Co.
  Harvey Hubbell.
  E. J. Manville Machine Co.
  Pratt & Whitney Co.

  D. Saunders' Sons.
  Woodward & Rogers.
Tapping Machines, Nut—
  Acme Machinery Co.
  Howard Iron Works.
  National Machinery Co.
  Wells Bros. & Co.
Tapping Machines—See Drilling and Tapping Machines.
Tapping and Reaming Machines, Portable—
  Chicago Flexible Shaft Co.
  Stow Mfg. Co.
Taps and Dies—See Stocks, Taps and Dies.
Taps and Drills—
  Butterfield & Co.
  Cleveland Twist Drill Co.
  Port Chester Bolt & Nut Co.
Taps and Reamers, Pipe—
  D. Saunders' Sons.
Tea Bells, Kettles—See Bells, Kettles.
Tees—See Angles and Tees.
Teeth, Cider Mill—
  Shelton Co.
Teeth, Harrow—
  Cambria Iron Co.
  Tudor Iron Works.
Teeth, Rake—
  La Belle Steel Co.
Teeth, Threshing Machine—
  Rhode Island Tool Co.
Telegraph and Telephone Goods—
  W. R. Ostrander & Co.
Telephone Bells—See Bells, Telephone.
Telephone and Telegraph Goods—
  See Telegraph and Telephone Goods.
Telephones—
  Rawson Electric Co.
Temperature Recording Instruments—See Recording Instruments, Temperature.

Tennis Belts—See *Belts, Bicycle, Tennis, &c.*

Tennis Soling Rubber—
New York Belting & Packing Co

Tenon Machines, Spoke—See *Spoke Tenon Machines.*

Tenoning Machines—
W. F. & John Barnes Co.

Ten Pins and Balls—
Boston & Lockport Block Co.
See also *Balls, Ten Pin.*

Tension Carriages—
Link-Belt Engineering Co.

Terne Plate—See *Plate, Tin and Terne.*

Test Pumps, Boiler — See *Pumps, Boiler Test.*

Tester, Center—
L. S. Starrett Co.

Tester, Flour—
E. C. Atkins & Co.

Testing Machines, Iron—See *Iron Testing Machines.*

Testing Machines, Metal—
Wm. Sellers & Co.

Testing Machines, Oil—
Pratt & Whitney Co.

Testing Machines, Torsion—
Pratt & Whitney Co.

Testing Scales, Grain—See *Scales, Grain Testing.*

Tests, Drop—
Whiting Foundry Equipment Co.

Tethers, Animal—
Athol Machine Co.

Thermometers, Recording—
The Bristol Co.

Thermometers, Silver Plated—
The Wm. Rogers Mfg. Co.

Thermostats—
D'Este & Seeley Co.
W. R. Ostrander & Co.

Thimble Skeins and Boxes—See *Skeins, Thimble, and Boxes.*

Thimbles, Rope—
Covert Mfg. Co.

Thimbles and Hooks—See *Hooks and Thimbles.*

Threaders, Bicycle Spoke—
Detrick & Harvey Machine Co.
Waterbury Farrel Foundry & Machine Co.

Threaders, Bolt—
Acme Machinery Co.
Automatic Machine Co.
National Machinery Co.

Threading Tools—See *Tools, Threading.*

Threading and Cutting Machines, Pipe—See *Cutting and Threading Machines, Pipe.*

Threshing Machine Teeth — See *Teeth, Threshing Machine.*

Thumb Knobs and Plates — See *Knobs, Thumb and Plates.*

Thumb Nuts, Screws — See *Nuts, Screws.*

Thumb Nut and Screw Blanks—See *Blanks.*

Ticket Hooks, Punches—See *Hooks, Punches.*

Tie Plates, Railroad—See *Plates, Railroad Tie.*

Tie Rods—See *Rods, Tie.*

Ties, Bale—
W. J. Adam.
American Wire Co.
Dillon-Griswold Wire Co.
Malin & Co.
A. R. Whitney & Co.

Ties, Cattle—
Bridgeport Chain Co.
Covert Mfg. Co.
Covert's Saddlery Works.
Garland Chain Co.
Oneida Community.

Tighteners, Belt—See *Belt Tighteners.*

Tiling or Ditching Shovels—See *Shovels, Tiling or Ditching.*

Tiling, Rubber—
New York Belting & Packing Co.

Timber Dogs, Scribes, Stirrups—See *Dogs, Scribes, Stirrups.*

Time Checks—See *Checks, Time.*

Tincture Presses—See *Presses, Tincture.*

Tin—
American Metal Co.
John Davol & Sons.
Wm. S. Fearing.
Hendricks Bros.

Tin Boxes—See *Boxes, Tin.*

Tin Pails—See *Pails, Tin.*

Tin, Phosphor—
Halk & Neumann.

Tin Plate—See *Plate, Tin and Terne.*

Tin Plate Bars—See *Bars, Tin Plate.*

Tin Plate Machinery—
Lloyd Booth Co.
Frank-Kneeland Machine Co.
Leechburg Foundry & Machine Co.
R. Poole & Son Co.
Robinson-Rea Mfg. Co.
Totten & Hogg Iron & Steel Foundry Co.

Tinners' Rules, Shears, Snips, Stakes——See *Rules, Shears, Snips, Stakes.*

Tinners' Trimmings—
Arcade Mfg. Co.
Berger Bros.
Logan & Strobridge Iron Co.
Peck, Stow & Wilcox Co.
Pleuger & Henger Mfg. Co.
Sidney Shepard & Co.
Stowell Mfg. & Foundry Co.

Tinners' Tools and Machines—
Peck, Stow & Wilcox Co.

Tinners' and Plumbers' Furnaces—See *Furnaces, Plumbers' and Tinners'.*

Tinning—
Avery Stamping Co.
Logan & Strobridge Iron Co.
William N. Merriam.
Sidney Shepard & Co.
Turner & Seymour Mfg. Co.

Tins, Pie and Cake—
Sidney Shepard & Co.

Tinware—
Sidney Shepard & Co.

Tips and Fenders, Rubber—
H. O. Canfield.
New York Belting & Packing Co.

Tips, Pole—
Covert's Saddlery Works.

Tire Benders, Bolts—See *Benders, Bolts.*

Tire Drills, Markers, Shrinkers, Steel, Upsetters—See *Drills, Markers, Shrinkers, Steel, Upsetters.*

Tire Repair Outfits and Supplies—
Morgan & Wright.

Tires, Bicycle—
Morgan & Wright.
New York Belting & Packing Co.

Tires, Railroad—
Latrobe Steel Co.
Railway Supply Co.
Wm. H. Wallace & Co.

Tires, Wagon—
Old Dominion Iron & Nail Works Co.

Toasters—
Fred. J. Meyers Mfg. Co.
Schneider & Trenkamp Co.
See also *Kitchen Articles, Wire.*

Tobacco Boxes, Aluminum—See *Boxes, Tobacco. Aluminum.*

THE IRON AGE INDEX.

Tobacco Cutters, Hooks, Knives, Shaves—See *Cutters, Hooks, Knives, Shaves.*

Toe Calks, Clips—See *Calks, Clips.*

Toilet Clippers—See *Clippers, Horse and Toilet.*

Tongs—See *Shovels, Tongs, Pokers, Fire Sets, &c.*

Tongs, Blacksmiths'—
Heller Bros.
E. C. Stearns & Co.

Tongs, Carbon—
Billings & Spencer Co.

Tongs, Coal—
Logan & Strobridge Iron Co.
Peck, Stow & Wilcox Co.
Reading Hardware Co.

Tongs, Ice—
Knapp & Cowles Mfg. Co.
Palmer Hardware Mfg. Co.
W. T. Wood & Co.

Tongs, Pipe—
Ashcroft Mfg. Co.
Jarecki Mfg. Co.
D. Saunders' Sons.

Tongs, Pipe Hanger—
Berger Bros.

Tongs, Rivet—
Weedsport Drill Co.

Tongs, Roofing—
Peck, Stow & Wilcox Co.

Tool Chests, Grinders, Holders—
See *Chests, Grinders, Holders.*

Tool Handles, Detachable—See *Handles, Detachable, Tool.*

Tool Sets—See *Sets, Screw Driver and Tool.*

Tool Sets, Garden—See *Sets, Garden Tool.*

Tool Sets, Hollow Handle—See *Sets, Tool, Hollow Handle.*

Tool Steel—See *Steel, Tool.*

Tool Makers' Clamps—See *Clamps, Tool Makers'.*

Tools, Automatic Boring—
Millers Falls Co.

Tools, Boiler Makers', Butcher, Carving, Car Shop, Coopers', Ditching, Slaters', Tinners'—See *Boiler Makers', Butcher, Carving, Car Shop, Coopers', Ditching, Slaters', Tinners'.*

Tools, Compressed Air—See *Compressed Air Tools.*

Tools, Parting—
Tuck Mfg. Co.

Tools, Pneumatic—
Clayton Air Compressor Works.

Tools, Saw—
E. C. Atkins & Co.
Henry Disston & Sons.
National Saw Co.

Tools, Ship Carpenters'—
L. & I. J. White Co.

Tools, Thread Cutting Lathe—
Billings & Spencer Co.

Tools, Threading—
J. Stevens Arms & Tool Co.

Tools, Well—See *Well Supplies and Tools.*

Tools, Wood Turners'—
Buck Bros.

Top Braces and Rails—See *Braces and Rails, Top.*

Top Prop Blocks—See *Blocks, Top Prop.*

Torches, Gasoline and Oil—
Bridgeport Brass Co.
Schneider & Trenkamp Co.

Torsion Testing Machines—See *Testing Machines, Torsion.*

Tote Boxes—See *Boxes, Tote.*

THE IRON AGE INDEX.

Towel Holders, Rollers—See *Holders, Rollers*.

Towers, Cooling—See *Cooling Towers*.

Towers, Tank—
Stover Mfg. Co.

Toy Bells—
N. N. Hill Brass Co.

Toy Barrows—
Canton Cycle Mfg. Co.

Toy Braces—
Mason & Parker.

Toy Carpet Sweepers—
Canton Cycle Mfg. Co.

Toy Carts and Wagons—
Canton Cycle Mfg. Co.

Toy Chisels—
New England Specialty Co.

Toy Motors, Electric—See *Motors, Electric Toy*.

Toy Plane Irons—
New England Specialty Co.

Toy Sad Irons—
A. C. Williams.

Toy Saving Banks—
Reading Hardware Co.

Trace Buckles, Chains—See *Buckles, Chains*.

Tracing Wheels—See *Wheels, Tracing*.

Track Bolts, Chisels, Gauges—See *Bolts, Chisels, Gauges*.

Track, Overhead Carrying—
Coburn Trolley Track Mfg. Co.
F. E. Myers & Bros.
J. E. Porter Co.

Trammel Points—See *Points, Trammel*.

Trammels—
Stanley Rule & Level Co.
L. S. Starrett Co.
T. F. Welch Mfg. Co.

Tramways, Overhead—
Ed. Harrington, Son & Co.
Reading Crane & Hoist Works.

Tramways, Wire Rope—
Lidgerwood Mfg. Co.
Trenton Iron Co.

Transfer Tables, Locomotive—
Wm. Sellers & Co.

Transformers, Electric—
Westinghouse Electric & Mfg. Co

Transmission Machinery, Electric Power—
Eddy Electric Mfg. Co.
General Electric Co.
Westinghouse Electric & Mfg. Co.

Transmission Machinery, Power—
See *Power Transmission Machinery*.

Transmission, Rope—See *Rope Transmission*.

Transmission Sheaves, Power—See *Sheaves, Power Transmission*.

Transits—
C. F. Richardson & Son.
L. S. Starrett Co.

Transom Catches, Centers, Lifters
—See *Catches, Centers, Lifters*.

Transplanters—
Iowa Farming Tool Co.

Trap Door Hinges—See *Hinges, Trap Door*.

Trap Wrenches—See *Wrenches, Trap*.

Traps, Fish—
Fred. J. Meyers Mfg. Co.

Traps, Fly—
Estey Wire Works.
Fred. J. Meyers Mfg. Co.

Traps, Game—
Edward S. Hotchkiss.
Oneida Community.
Peck, Stow & Wilcox Co.

Traps, Mole—
Enterprise Mfg. Co.

Traps, *Rat and Mouse—*
  Edward Darby & Sons.
  Edward S. Hotchkiss.
  Knapp & Cowles Mfg. Co.
  Fred. J. Meyers Mfg. Co.
  Smith & Egge Mfg. Co.
  Wire Goods Co.
Traps, *Sewer—*
  Barnes Mfg. Co.
Traps, *Steam—*
  Ashcroft Mfg. Co.
  D'Este & Seeley Co.
  Jenkins Bros.
  Kelly & Jones Co.
Travelers, *Boom and Deck—*
  W. & J. Tiebout.
Traveling Cranes, *Hand, Power—*
  See *Cranes.*
Trays, *Soap—*
  Logan & Strobridge Iron Co.
Trays, *Wire Paper—*
  Wire Goods Co.
Treads, *Stair, Rubber—*
  New York Belting & Packing Co.
Tree Guards, Labels, Scrapers— See *Guards, Labels, Scrapers.*
Trellises, *Wire—*
  E. T. Barnum.
  Columbus Wire & Iron Works.
  Howard & Morse.
  Ludlow-Saylor Wire Co.
  Fred. J. Meyers Mfg. Co.
  Scheeler's Sons.
  W. S. Tyler Wire Works Co.
Triangles, *Steel—*
  Henry Disston & Sons.
Tricycles, *Children's Horse—*
  Canton Cycle Mfg. Co.
Triers, *Butter and Cheese—*
  Peck, Stow & Wilcox Co.
Trimmers, *Bolt Head—*
  National Machinery Co.

Trimmers, *Lamp—*
  Acme Shear Co.
  Bridgeport Brass Co.
Trimmers, *Photograph—*
  S. G. Monce.
Trimmers, *Spoke—*
  Millers Falls Co.
Trimmers' Tacks— See *Tacks, Trimmers'.*
Trimming Presses— See *Presses, Trimming.*
Trimmings, *Car, Brass—*
  Pleuger & Henger Mfg. Co.
Trimmings, *Shaft Leather—*
  McKinnon Dash & Hardware Co.
Trimmings, *Stove—*
  Logan & Strobridge Iron Co.
  Troy Nickel Works.
Trimmings, Tinners'— See *Tinners' Trimmings.*
Triple Punches— See *Punches, Triple.*
Trolley Carriages, Insulators— See *Carriages, Insulators.*
Trolley Materials, *Electrical—*
  H. W. Johns Mfg. Co.
Troughs, *Cattle—*
  Avery Stamping Co.
Trouser Guards, Stretchers— See *Guards, Stretchers.*
Trowels, *Brick, Plastering, &c.—*
  E. C. Atkins & Co.
  Geo. H. Bishop & Co.
  Henry Disston & Sons.
  National Saw Co.
Trowels, *Garden—*
  Avery Stamping Co.
  Knapp & Cowles Mfg. Co.
  New York Stamping Co.
  Peck, Stow & Wilcox Co.
Truck Casters, Wheels— See *Casters, Wheels.*

Truck Wheel Covers, Rubber—See Covers, Truck Wheel, Rubber.

Trucks, Basket—
Lansing Wheelbarrow Co.

Trucks, Barrel—
- Boston & Lockport Block Co.
Kilbourne & Jacobs Mfg. Co.
Lansing Wheelbarrow Co.
McKinney Mfg. Co.
Syracuse Chilled Plow Co.

Trucks, Barrel and Stand—
Enterprise Mfg. Co.

Trucks, Foundry—
Lansing Wheelbarrow Co.
Variety Machine Co.
Whiting Foundry Equipment Co.

Trucks, Lumber and Saw Mill—
E. C. Atkins & Co.
Kilbourne & Jacobs Mfg. Co.
Lansing Wheelbarrow Co.

Trucks, Store, Warehouse, &c.—
Boston & Lockport Block Co.
Buffalo Scale Co.
Kilbourne & Jacobs Mfg. Co.
Lansing Wheelbarrow Co.
McKinney Mfg. Co.
Sidney Steel Scraper Co.
Syracuse Chilled Plow Co.
R. W. Whitehurst & Co.
Wire Goods Co.

Trucks, Stove—
Arcade Mfg. Co.
Barnes Mfg. Co.
Kilbourne & Jacobs Mfg. Co.
Lansing Wheelbarrow Co.

Trunk Carriers, Hinges, Locks—
See Carriers, Hinges, Locks.

Truss Rods—See Rods, Roof, &c.

Try Squares—See Squares, Try.

Tub Ears, Handles—See Ears, Handles.

Tube Cutters, Holders — See Cutters, Holders.

Tube Expanders, Pointing Machines, Saws, Welding Furnaces
—See Expanders, Furnaces, Pointing Machines, Saws.

Tubes, Boiler—
National Tube Works Co.
Jos. T. Ryerson & Son.
Wm. H. Wallace & Co.
A. R. Whitney & Co.

Tubes, Grain Drill—
New York Belting & Packing Co.

Tubes, Speaking—
Berger Bros.
W. R. Ostrander & Co.

Tubing, Aluminum—
Pittsburgh Reduction Co.

Tubing, Bicycle—
John S. Leng's Son & Co.
Pope Tube Co.
Shelby Steel Tube Co.
Wilmot & Hobbs Mfg. Co.

Tubing, Brass and Copper—
Ansonia Brass & Copper Co.
Bridgeport Brass Co.
Clendenin Bros.
Eastwood Wire Mfg. Co.
Wm. S. Fearing.
Randolph & Clowes.
Scovill Mfg. Co.
Waterbury Brass Co.
Wilmot & Hobbs Mfg. Co.

Tubing, Bronze—
Scovill Mfg. Co.

Tubing, German Silver—
Scovill Mfg. Co.

Tubing, Rubber—
H. O. Canfield.
New York Belting & Packing Co.

Tubing, Silver—
Randolph & Clowes.

Tubing, Well—
W. & B. Douglas.
Kelly & Jones Co.
National Tube Works Co.
Riverside Iron Works.

THE IRON AGE INDEX.

Tubing, Zinc—
Bridgeport Brass Co.
Scovill Mfg. Co.
Waterbury Brass Co.

Tubs, Bath—See *Bathtubs.*

Tubs, Crockery, Laundry—
Humphryes Mfg. Co.

Tubular Well Tools, &c.—See *Well Supplies and Tools.*

Tufting Machines—
C. E. Coe.

Tumbling Barrels—See *Barrels, Tumbling.*

Tumbling Mills—
Byram & Co.
Whiting Foundry Equipment Co.

Turnbuckles—
American Bolt Co.
Berger Bros.
Central Iron & Steel Co.
Cleveland City Forge & Iron Co.
W. H. Haskell & Co.
Merrill Bros.
Pennsylvania Bolt & Nut Co.
Port Chester Bolt & Nut Co.
Rhode Island Tool Co.
J. H. Sternbergh & Son.
W. & J. Tiebout.

Turbine Water Wheels—See *Water Wheels.*

Turf Edgers—See *Edgers, Turf.*

Turning and Boring Mills — See *Mills, Boring and Turning.*

Turning and Felloe Webs—See *Webs, Turning, Felloe, &c.*

Turns, Cupboard—
Peck, Stow & Wilcox Co.
Reading Hardware Co.
Russell & Erwin Mfg. Co.

Turned Metal Work to Order—
Hartford Machine Screw Co.

Turners, Cake—
Knapp & Cowles Mfg. Co.
Upson & Hart Co.

Turn Tables, Bridge and Railroad—
Berlin Iron Bridge Co.
Thos. Carlin's Sons.
Link-Belt Engineering Co.
Wm. Sellers & Co.
Trenton Iron Co.
Whiting Foundry Equipment Co.

Turret Drills, Lathes—See *Drills, Lathes.*

Tuyere Irons—See *Irons, Tuyere.*

Tuyeres, Bronze—
Phosphor-Bronze Smelting Co.

Twine Boxes, Holders—See *Boxes, Holders.*

Twist Drill Grinding Machines—See *Drill Grinding Machines, Twist.*

Twist Drills—See *Drills, Twist.*

Type Setting Machines—
R. H. Brown & Co.

Typewriter Springs — See *Springs, Typewriter.*

Umbrella Stands—See *Stands, Umbrella.*

Union Scales—See *Scales, Union.*

Unions, Forged—
J. H. Williams & Co.

Universal Grinders—See *Grinders, Universal.*

Unmounted Grindstones—See *Grindstones, Unmounted.*

Upholsterers' Regulators—See *Regulators, Upholsterers'.*

Upholsterers' and Saddlery Hammers—See *Hammers, Saddlery and Upholsterers'.*

Upholstery, Hardware—
Turner & Seymour Mfg. Co.

Upholstery and Curtain Fixtures—See *Curtain and Upholstery Fixtures.*

Upright Pulleys—See *Pulleys, Upright.*

Upsetters, Tire—
Butts & Ordway.
Fulton Iron & Engine Works.

THE IRON AGE INDEX.

Vacuum and Compression Pumps—
See *Pumps, Compression and Vacuum.*

Vacuum and Steam Gauges—See *Gauges, Steam and Vacuum.*

Valve Discs, Rod Packing — See *Discs, Packing.*

Valve Stems—
Finished Steel Co.

Valve Wheels, Steam—See *Wheels, Steam Valve.*

Valves, Ammonia—
Chapman Valve Mfg. Co.

Valves, Check—
Lunkenheimer Co.
McNab & Harlin Mfg. Co.

Valves, Pump—See *Well Supplies and Tools.*

Valves, Reducing—
D'Este & Seeley Co.
Kelly & Jones Co.

Valves, Rubber—
Boston Belting Co.
New York Belting & Packing Co.

Valves, Safety—
Consolidated Safety Valve Co.
Lunkenheimer Co.
McNab & Harlin Mfg. Co.

Valves, Water, Gas and Steam—
Chapman Valve Mfg. Co.
Eastwood Wire Mfg. Co.
Jarecki Mfg. Co.
Jenkins Bros.
Kelly & Jones Co.
Lunkenheimer Co.
McNab & Harlin Mfg. Co.
Watson-Stillman Co.
R. D. Wood & Co.

Valves, Water Relief—
Consolidated Safety Valve Co.
McNab & Harlin Mfg. Co.

Vanes, Weather—See *Iron, Ornamental.*

Varnish Cans—See *Cans, Paint and Varnish.*

Varnishing Machines—
Chambers Bros. Co.

Vases, Coal—
Sidney Shepard & Co.

Vases, Lawn—
E. T. Barnum.
Champion Iron Co.
Ellis & Halfenbarger.
Ludlow-Saylor Wire Co.
F. J. Meyers Mfg. Co.
Stewart Iron Works.

Vault Lights—
Brown Bros. Mfg. Co.

Vegetable Boilers, Wire—See *Kitchen Articles, Wire.*

Vegetable Canner—See *Canner, Fruit and Vegetable.*

Vegetable Slicers—See *Slicers.*

Vegetable and Meat Cutters — See *Cutters, Meat and Vegetable.*

Ventilator Caps, Cord—See *Caps, Cord.*

Ventilating and Heating Apparatus—See *Heating and Ventilating Apparatus.*

Ventilators—See *Registers and Ventilators.*

Ventilators, Car—
Q & C Co.

Ventilators, Flue—
Stowell Mfg. & Foundry Co.

Ventilators and Chimney Caps—
Garry Iron Roofing Co.
Osborn Mfg. Co.
Wiley & Russell Mfg. Co.

Vise Clamps, Jaws — See *Clamps, Jaws.*

Vise Jaw Caps—
Newark Machine Tool Works.
Prentiss Vise Co.

Vise and Anvil—See *Anvil and Vise.*

Vises, Drill and Anvil—
  Millers Falls Co.

Vises, Bicycle—
  Lewis Tool Co.

Vises, Cabinet—
  Wyman & Gordon.

Vises, Hand—
  Athol Machine Co.
  Billings & Spencer Co.
  Goodell Bros. Co.
  Logan & Strobridge Iron Co.
  Millers Falls Co.

Vises, Horseshoers'—
  P. F. Burke.
  Butts & Ordway.
  Wiley & Russell Mfg. Co.

Vises, Parallel—
  Athol Machine Co.
  Barbour, Stockwell & Co.
  Bignall & Keeler Mfg. Co.
  Howard Iron Works.
  Lewis Tool Co.
  Millers Falls Co.
  Prentiss Vise Co.
  E. C. Stearns & Co.
  W. C. Toles & Co.
  Van Wagoner & Williams Hardware Co.
  Weedsport Drill Co.

Vises, Pipe—
  Armstrong Mfg. Co.
  Bignall & Keeler Mfg. Co.
  Butterfield & Co.
  Humphryes Mfg. Co.
  Jarecki Mfg. Co.
  Lewis Tool Co.
  Prentiss Vise Co.
  D. Saunders' Sons.

Vises, Saw—
  E. C. Stearns & Co.
  Seneca Falls Mfg. Co.

Vises, Solid Box—
  Eagle Anvil Works.
  Van Wagoner & Williams Hardware Co.

Voltmeters, Recording—
  The Bristol Co.

Wads, Gun—
  Peters Cartridge Co.
  Union Metallic Cartridge Co.

Waffle Irons—See *Irons, Waffle.*

Wagon Axles, Chains, Jacks, Springs, Steps, Tires—See *Axles, Chains, Jacks, Springs, Steps, Tires.*

Wagon Lock Shoes—See *Shoes, Wagon Lock.*

Wagon Spring Bumpers—See *Bumpers, Wagon Spring.*

Wagons, Children's Express—
  Canton Cycle Mfg. Co.

Wagons, Cycle—
  Canton Cycle Mfg. Co.

Wagons, Dump—
  Kilbourne & Jacobs Mfg. Co.

Wagons, Toy—See *Toy Carts and Wagons.*

Waiters, Dumb—
  F. S. Hutchinson Co.
  Storm Mfg. Co.

Wall Scrapers—See *Scrapers, Wall.*

Walk Scrapers—See *Scrapers, Walk and Street.*

Wardrobe Hooks—See *Hooks, Coat, Hat, &c.*

Ware, Aluminum—
  Sidney Shepard & Co.

Ware, Copper—
  Sidney Shepard & Co.

Ware, Hollow, Nickel Silver—
  Wm. Rogers Mfg. Co.

Ware, Hollow, Silver and Silver Plated—
  Wm. Rogers Mfg. Co.
  Upson & Hart Co.
  Wallace Bros.

Ware, Hollow, Steel—
Avery Stamping Co.
Cleveland Stamping & Tool Co.

Ware, Sheet Iron—
Sidney Shepard & Co.

Warehouse Trucks—See *Trucks,Store, Warehouse, &c.*

Wash Benches, Stands--See *Benches, Stands.*

Washboard Blanks—
Matthiessen & Hegeler Zinc Co.

Washboard Knives—See *Knives, Machine.*

Washer Cutters—See *Cutters, Washer.*

Washer Machines—
National Machinery Co.

Washers, Axle—
Steimer & Moore Mfg. Co.

Washers, Cast—
American Bolt Co.
Pennsylvania Bolt & Nut Co.
Pleuger & Henger Mfg. Co.
Port Chester Bolt & Nut Co.
Stover Mfg. Co.

Washers, Floor—See *Plates and Washers, Floor.*

Washers, Prop Block—
McKinnon Dash & Hardware Co.

Washers, Wrought—
American Bolt Co.
Avery Stamping Co.
Wm. H. Haskell Co.
McKinney Mfg. Co.
William N. Merriam.
Milton Mfg. Co.
Nut & Washer Mfg. Co.
Pennsylvania Bolt & Nut Co.
Port Chester Bolt & Nut Co.
Rhode Island Tool Co.
Shelton Co.
Stanley Works.
J. H. Sternbergh & Son.

Washers and Discs, *Rubber*—
H. O. Canfield.
New York Belting & Packing Co.

Washers and Street Hydrants—See *Hydrants and Street Washers.*

Washing Machinery, Coal--See *Coal Washing Machinery.*

Waste, *Cotton*—
Railway Supply Co.

Waste Baskets, Cans –See *Baskets, Cans.*

Watchmen's Clocks — See *Clocks, Watchmen's.*

Watch Spring Steel—See *Steel, Watch Spring.*

Water Closet Hinges — See *Hinges, Water Closet,*

Water Coolers, Filters, Gauges, Meters, Motors, Stones, Valves—
See *Coolers, Filters, Gauges, Meters, Motors, Stones, Valves.*

Water Pipe, Riveted--See *Pipe, Riveted Water.*

Water Purifiers, Feed--See *Purifiers, Feed Water.*

Water Wheels—
Jas. Leffel & Co.
R. Poole & Son Co.
R. D. Wood & Co.

Water Works Castings, Pumps
—See *Castings, Pumps.*

Water Works Supplies—
W. & B. Douglas.
Pleuger & Henger Mfg. Co.

Waterers, *Stock* –See *Stock Waterers.*

Watt Meters, Recording--See *Meters, Recording, Watt.*

Wax Melting Cups—See *Cups, Wax Melting.*

Weaners, *Calf*—
Carroll Muzzle Co.

THE IRON AGE INDEX.

Web Girts, Halters—See *Girts, Halters*.

Webs, *Turning, Felloe, &c.*—
Henry Disston & Sons.
Millers Falls Co.
National Saw Co.
Simonds Mfg. Co.

Wedges—
Van Wagoner & Williams Hardware Co.

Weeders, *Garden*—
Iowa Farming Tool Co.

Weights, *Hitching*—
Covert Mfg. Co.
Imperial Bit & Snap Co.
Pleuger & Henger Mfg. Co.

Weights, *Sash*—
E. E. Brown & Co.
Pleuger & Henger Mfg. Co.
Reading Hardware Co.

Welding Hooks—See *Hooks, Welding*.

Welding Furnaces, Tube—See *Furnaces, Tube Welding*.

Welding Dies—See *Dies, Welding*.

Well Chains, Curbs, Pumps, Tubing, Wheels—See *Chains, Curbs, Pumps, Tubing, Wheels*.

Well Supplies and Tools (*Points, Cylinders, Valves, Tubular Well Tools, &c.*)—
Barnes Mfg. Co.
Deming Co.
W. & B. Douglas.
Stanley G. Flagg & Co.
Jarecki Mfg. Co.
Lambert Gas & Gasoline Engine Co.
Mast, Foos & Co.
F. E. Myers & Bro.
Olmstead & Co.

Wharf Spikes — See *Spikes, Dock, Wharf, &c.*

Wheelbarrows—See *Barrows, Wheel*.

Wheel Boring Machines, *Car*—See *Boring Machines, Car Wheel*.

Wheel Dressers, *Emery*—See *Dressers, Emery Wheel*.

Wheel Presses, Hydraulic — See *Presses, Hydraulic Wheel*.

Wheels—See *Axles and Wheels*.

Wheels, *Barrow*—
Lansing Wheelbarrow Co.
Sidney Steel Scraper Co.

Wheels, *Car*—
Henry Levis & Co.
Pierson & Co.

Wheels, *Chilled Car*—See *Chilled Car Wheels*.

Wheels, *Dental*—
Pike Mfg. Co.

Wheels, *Emery*—
American Emery Wheel Works.
Diamond Machine Co.
Hampden Corundum Wheel Co.
New York Belting & Packing Co.
Northampton Emery Wheel Co.
Norton Emery Wheel Co.
Springfield Mfg. Co.
Sterling Emery Wheel Mfg. Co.
Tanite Co.
Vitrified Wheel Co.

Wheels, *Fifth*—
E. D. Clapp Mfg. Co.
Richard Eccles.
Scranton Forging Co.

Wheels, *Iron, Flanged*—
Lansing Wheelbarrow Co.

Wheels, *Measuring, Tire*—
Wiley & Russell Mfg. Co.

Wheels, *Polishing*—
Builders' Iron Foundry.
Compress Wheel Co.
Diamond Machine Co.
Northampton Emery Wheel Co.
Norton Emery Wheel Co.
Springfield Mfg. Co.
Sterling Emery Wheel Mfg. Co.
Zucker & Levett & Loeb Co.

Wheels, *Rubber Tired*—
Lansing Wheelbarrow Co.

Wheels, Sprocket—
Boston Gear Works.
Link-Belt Engineering Co.
Roberts Mfg. Co.
Superior Machine Co.
T. F. Welch Mfg. Co.

Wheels, Tracing—
Billings & Spencer Co.

Wheels, Truck—
Lansing Wheelbarrow Co.
R. W. Whitehurst & Co.

Wheels, Steam Valve—
Troy Nickel Works.

Wheels, Water—See *Water Wheels.*

Wheels, Well—
Arnold Metal Wheel Co.
Peck, Stow & Wilcox Co.
Pleuger & Henger Mfg. Co.
Reading Hardware Co.

Whip Sockets—See *Sockets, Whip.*

Whips and Whip Lashes—
Steimer & Moore Mfg. Co.

Whisk Brooms, &c.—See *Brooms, Whisk, &c.*

Whistles, Steam—
Ashcroft Mfg. Co.
Eastwood Wire Mfg. Co.
Lunkenheimer Co.
McNab & Harlin Mfg. Co.

White Brass—See *Brass, White.*

White Lead Machinery—
Geo. V. Cresson Co.
R. Poole & Son Co.

White Metal—
Pope's Island Mfg. Corporation.

Whitewash Brushes—See *Brushes, Whitewash, Horse, &c.*

Wickets, Railing—See *Iron, Ornamental.*

Winches—
Moore Mfg. Co.

Wind Mills—See *Mills, Wind.*

Wind Mill Pumps, Regulators, Tanks—See *Pumps, Regulators, Tanks.*

Winding Machines, Bobbin—See *Bobbin Winding Machines.*

Winding Machines—
Fairmount Machine Co.

Windlasses—
Thos. Carlin's Sons.

Window Brushes, Catches, Pulls, Screens, Springs—See *Brushes, Catches, Pulls, Screens, Springs.*

Window Screen Corner Brackets—See *Brackets, Window Screen Corner.*

Window Spring Bolts—See *Bolts, Window Spring.*

Window Stop Adjusters—See *Adjusters, Window Stop.*

Window Ventilating Bolts — See *Bolts, Window Ventilating.*

Window Screen Frames—See *Frames, Door and Window Screen.*

Wire, Aluminum—
Pitttsburgh Reduction Co.
Scovill Mfg. Co.

Wire, Baling—
Dillon-Griswold Wire Co.

Wire, Barb—
Cambria Iron Co.
Consolidated Steel & Wire Co.
Dillon-Griswold Wire Co.
I. L. Ellwood Mfg. Co.
Indiana Wire Fence Co.
Ludlow-Saylor Wire Co.
Quincy Hardware Mfg. Co.
Washburn & Moen Mfg. Co.

Wire, Bicycle Spoke—
R. H. Wolff & Co.

Wire, Brass and Copper—
Ansonia Brass & Copper Co.
Bridgeport Brass Co.
Clendenin Bros.
Wm. S. Fearing.

Hendricks Bros.
U. T. Hungerford.
Plume & Atwood Mfg. Co.
Scovill Mfg. Co.
Washburn & Moen Mfg. Co.
Waterbury Brass Co.

Wire, *Brass Pinion*—
Boston Gear Works.

Wire, *Cast Steel*—
Rudolf Giese.
New Haven Wire Mfg. Co.

Wire Cloth—See *Cloth*.

Wire Cloth Floors, Holders—See *Floors, Holders*.

Wire Chisels, Coilers, Cutters, Dies, Gauges, Lathing, Looms, Mats, Nails, Netting, Pointers, Reeds, Rods, Rope, Shears, Signs, Springs, Staples, Stretchers, Trellises—See *Chisels, Coilers, Cutters, Dies, Gauges, Lathing, Looms, Mats, Nails, Netting, Pointers, Reels, Rods, Rope, Shears, Signs, Springs, Staples, Stretchers, Trellises.*

Wire Cutting Machines—See *Cutting Machines, Wire.*

Wire Draw Benches—See *Benches, Wire Draw.*

Wire Drawing Machinery—See *Drawing Machinery, Wire.*

Wire Forming Machines—See *Forming Machines, Wire.*

Wire, *German Silver*—
Scovill Mfg. Co.
Waterbury Brass Co.

Wire, *Gold Bronze*—
Pope's Island Mfg. Corporation.

Wire Goods, *Bright*—
M. S. Brooks & Sons.
E. Jenckes Mfg. Co.
Ossawan Mills Co.
Turner & Seymour Mfg. Co.
Wire Goods Co.

Wire Goods, *Mill*—
M. S. Brooks & Sons.
E. Jenckes Mfg. Co.
Wire Goods Co.

Wire Goods, *Mill*—See *Mill Wire Goods.*

Wire, *Iron and Steel, Market, Fence, Stone, &c.*—
American Wire Co.
Consolidated Steel & Wire Co.
I. L. Ellwood Mfg. Co.
Igoe Bros.
William N. Merriam.
New Castle Wire Nail Co.
New Haven Wire Mfg. Co.
Norristown Wire Co.
Pittsburgh Wire Co.
Geo. W. Prentiss & Co.
Salem Wire Nail Co.
Stewart Wire Co.
Trenton Iron Co.
Washburn & Moen Mfg. Co.
R. H. Wolff & Co.

Wire Kitchen Articles—See *Kitchen Articles, Wire.*

Wire Mill Plants—
Morgan Construction Co.

Wire, *Music*—
Rudolf Giese.
Trenton Iron Co.
R. H. Wolff & Co.

Wire Nail Machines—See *Nail Machines, Wire.*

Wire, *Needle*—
Abbott, Wheelock & Co.
Hermann Boker & Co.
Francis Hobson, Seaman & Co.
R. H. Wolff & Co.

Wire, *Picture*—
Turner & Seymour Mfg. Co.
See also *Cord, Wire, Picture.*

Wire Pointing Machines—See *Pointing Machines, Wire.*

THE IRON AGE INDEX.

Wire Ring Machines—See *Ring Machines, Wire.*

Wire Rod Reels—See *Reels, Wire Rod.*

Wire Rope Fittings, Tramways—See *Fittings, Tramways.*

Wire, Special—
New Haven Wire Mfg. Co.
Pittsburgh Wire Co.
Geo. W. Prentiss & Co.

Wire, Spooled—
American Wire Co.
Ansonia Brass & Copper Co.
Malin & Co.
Ossawan Mills Co.
Washburn & Moen Mfg. Co.
Wire Goods Co.
Wright & Colton Wire Cloth Co.

Wire Stitching Machines—
R. H. Brown & Co.

Wire Specialties—
Kevorkian Co.

Wire Straightening and Cutting Machines — See *Straightening and Cutting Machines, Wire.*

Wire Trays, Paper—See *Trays, Wire, Paper.*

Wire Cables, Electric—
General Electric Co.
Washburn & Moen Mfg. Co.

Wire, Electric—See *Wire, Brass and Copper.*

Wires, Pointed—
American Screw Co.

Wood Engraving — See *Engraving, Photo and Wood.*

Wood Forks, Measures, Planes, Saws, Screws—See *Forks. Measures, Planes, Saws, Screws.*

Wood Turners' Tools—See *Tools, Wood Turners'.*

Wooden Mallets, Scoops, Shovels—See *Mallets, Scoops, Shovels.*

Wooden Specialties—
John Sommer's Son.

Woods, Electric—See *Electric Woods.*

Wrench Attachments, Pipe—
Prentiss Vise Co.

Wrenches, Bicycle and Pocket—
Billings & Spencer Co.
Bridgeport Gun Implement Co.
Chapman Mfg. Co.
Knapp & Cowles Mfg. Co.
Morgan & Wright.
Peck, Stow & Wilcox Co.
Tower & Lyon.
J. H. Williams & Co.

Wrenches, Bolt—
Butts & Ordway.

Wrenches, Carriage—
Goodell Co.

Wrenches, Drop Forged—
Billings & Spencer Co.
Rhode Island Tool Co.
J. H. Williams & Co.

Wrenches, Nipple—
Bevin Bros. Mfg. Co.

Wrenches, Pipe—
Armstrong Mfg. Co.
Belden Machine Co.
Bemis & Call Hardware & Tool Co.
Billings & Spencer Co.
Tower & Lyon.
J. H. Williams & Co.
Wire Goods Co.

Wrenches, Screw (Mechanics', Agricultural, &c.)—
Bemis & Call Hardware & Tool Co.
Billings & Spencer Co.
Coes Wrench Co.
Edward S. Hotchkiss.
Wm. G. Le Count.
Moore Mfg. Co.
Peck, Stow & Wilcox Co.
Smith & Egge Mfg. Co.

Wrenches, Tap and Reamer—
Armstrong Mfg. Co.
Billings & Spencer Co.
Butterfield & Co.
S. W. Card Mfg. Co.
J. M. Carpenter Tap & Die Co.

Morse Twist Drill & Machine Co.
Wells Bros. & Co.
Wiley & Russell Mfg. Co.

Wrenches, *Trap—*
Oneida Community.

Wringers, *Clothes—*
North Bros. Mfg. Co.

Wrought Iron Casing—See *Casing, Wrought Iron.*

Wrought Iron Goods, Hooks, Staples, &c.—
McKinney Mfg. Co.
Ney Mfg. Co.
Stanley Works.
W. & J. Tiebout.
Wire Goods Co.

Wrought Iron Pipe — See *Pipe, Wrought Iron.*

Wrought Steel Butts—See *Butts, Wrought Steel.*

Wrought Steel Sinks—See *Sinks, Wrought Steel.*

Wrought Washers — See *Washers, Wrought.*

Yacht Hardware—
W. & J. Tiebout.

Yokes, *Neck—*
Imperial Bit & Snap Co.

Yokes, *Ox—*
Iowa Farming Tool Co.

Zinc Battery Plates—See *Battery Plates, Rolled Zinc.*

Zinc, *Sheet—*
Matthiessen & Hegeler Zinc Co.

Zinc Tacks, Tubing—See *Tacks, Tubing.*

Zinc for Leclanche Batteries—
Matthiessen & Hegeler Zinc Co.

www.ingramcontent.com/pod-product-compliance
Lightning Source LLC
Chambersburg PA
CBHW030350170426
43202CB00010B/1325